THE CONSTRUCTION OF
LIFE AND DEATH

Born in Australia in 1930, Dorothy Rowe worked as a teacher and as a child psychologist before coming to England where she obtained her PhD at Sheffield University. From 1972 until 1986 she was head of the North Lincolnshire Department of Clinical Psychology. She is now engaged in writing, lecturing and private practice. Her research and therapy are concerned with the questions of how we create meaning and how we communicate.

Her other books are *The Experience of Depression* (1978) reissued as *Choosing Not Losing* (1988), *Depression: the Way Out of Your Prison* (1983), *Living with the Bomb: Can We Live without Enemies?* (1985), *Beyond Fear* (1987) and *The Successful Self* (1989).

The Construction of
Life and Death

DOROTHY ROWE

FONTANA/Collins

First published by John Wiley & Sons in 1982

This edition first published in 1989 by Fontana Paperbacks
8 Grafton Street, London W1X 3LA

Copyright © by Dorothy Rowe 1982, 1989

Printed and bound in Great Britain by
William Collins Sons & Co. Ltd, Glasgow

To Edward

ACKNOWLEDGEMENTS

Robert Conquest and Chatto and Windus, London, to quote his poem *1944 and after*.

James Carse and John Wiley and Sons, New York, to quote from *Death and Existence*.

Arthur Koestler, Hutchinson, London, and Hamish Hamilton/Collins, London, to quote from *Dialogue with Death* and *Arrow in the Blue*.

E. A. Robinson and the Religious Experience Research Unit, Oxford, to quote from *The Original Vision* and *Living the Questions*.

Don Taylor to quote from *In Hiding*.

The author's literary estate, Hamish Hamilton, London, and Editions Gallimard, Paris, to quote from *Words* by Jean-Paul Sartre.

U. A. Fanthorpe and Peterloo Poets for permission to quote from her *Inside*.

CONTENTS

PREFACE TO THE FIRST EDITION

Some twelve years ago I began working on a project to see whether that ubiquitous and terrible mental illness, depression, could be understood in terms of Personal Construct Theory. By the time I was ready to write a book about my work I could no longer refer to depression as an illness, and so I called my book *The Experience of Depression*. I had begun by talking to people – all patients at a psychiatric clinic – about their attitudes to their immediate reality, their ideas about themselves, their family, their environment, but as I pursued the interlocking relationships of a person's constructs, I found that we soon left discussions of immediate reality and instead we talked about the issues of life and death, that is, about the purpose of life, the supposed existence and nature of God, the possibility of annihilation or life after death, guilt, sin, punishment and reward, expiation and propitiation, fear and courage, forgiveness and revenge, anger and acceptance, jealousy and sharing, hate and love. The issues that these depressed people and I discussed were those that have exercised the minds of philosophers and theologians for thousands of years, and the solutions that my clients had espoused had led them inevitably to the prison of depression.

Our core constructs are our metaphysical beliefs, the axes on which our individual worlds turn. We all have metaphysical beliefs. The belief that reality is what I see and that life ends in death is just as metaphysical as the belief in an immanent and transcendant God and heavenly choir. Discussions about metaphysical beliefs are not easy. Psychiatric patients are quickly trained by doctors and nurses to answer questions about their sex life, but questions about their religious beliefs make patients afraid that they are going to be declared mad or to be pressured into a religious conversion (or a non-religious conversion) and declared sane. Many of my clients, I found, had profound and valued religious beliefs, and this caused me some embarrassment, since despite (or perhaps because of) a traditional Christian upbringing, I have never been able to believe in a personal God and an afterlife. I was, in this respect, a traditional psychologist. Gordon Allport, writing in 1951 about his famous predecessor at Harvard, said, 'During the last fifty years religion and sex seem to have reversed their positions. Writing in the Victorian age, William James could bring himself to devote barely two pages to the role of sex in human life, which he labelled euphemistically the "instinct of love". Yet no taboos held him back from directing the torrent of his genius into the "*Varieties of Religious Experience*". On religion he spoke freely and with unexcelled brilliance. Today, by contrast, psychologists write with the frankness of Freud or Kinsey on the sexual passions of mankind, but blush and grow silent when the religious passions come into view.'

Such a change over the past eighty years is not surprising. Since a person can hold any number of beliefs, both rational and metaphysical, and never carry out any action which indicates the holding of such beliefs, behaviourists have no access to a person's system of beliefs (except, as often happens now, by sidling out of the behaviourist system of beliefs). Freud set the psychoanalytic attitude to religion in 1907 when he wrote, 'One might venture to regard obsessional neurosis as a pathological counterpart of the formation of a religion, and to describe that neurosis as an individual religiosity and religion as a universal obsessional neurosis', and in that psychoanalytic tradition of having your cake and eating it, Freud wrote in 1927, 'Devout believers are safeguarded in a high degree against the risk of certain neurotic illnesses; their acceptance of the universal neurosis spares them the task of constructing a personal one.' Thus both the psychiatrists who espoused Freud and the psychiatrists who saw mental illness as the necessary outcome of pathological disturbance of the metabolism could ignore the metaphysical beliefs of their patients except where such beliefs were taken as evidence of delusions, pathological guilt, or merely neurosis. The only reference to religious belief in Slater and Roth's basic text *Clinical Psychiatry* is indexed as 'neurotic search for'. This refers to the statement that: 'Jung is probably right in holding that some neurotic subjects seeking help are really groping for *some system of religious belief* which will provide them with a source of strength and render their lives meaningful.

These probably include the individual whose problems were in former times dealt with by the priest, the confessor or the head of the family; the hesitant, the guilt-ridden, the excessively timid, those lacking clear convictions with which to face life.'

Jung, who trained as a psychiatrist and a psychoanalyst, diverged from both points of view. 'It would seem,' he wrote, 'to be more in accord with the collective psyche of humanity to regard death as the fulfilment of life's meaning and as its goal in the truest sense, instead of a mere meaningless cessation. Anyone who cherishes a rationalistic opinion on this score has isolated himself psychologically and stands opposed to his own basic nature. This last sentence contains a fundamental truth about all neuroses, for all nervous disorders consist primarily in an alienation from one's instincts, a splitting off of consciousness from certain facts of the psyche. Hence rationalist opinions come expectedly close to neurotic symptoms.'

So, to hold metaphysical beliefs which might be called religious is to be considered neurotic by Freudians and sane by Jungians. It seems, then, that the populations of Britain and the United States can be regarded as largely neurotic or largely sane. According to Argyle and Beit-Hallahmi, 'between 1945 and 1965 about 80 per cent of the British population said they believed in God' and that 'about 45 per cent of the British population believed in an afterlife', while in the United States between 1944 and 1968 the percentage of the adult population replying 'Yes' to the question 'Do you personally believe in God?' ranged from 94 to 98 per cent, and between 1936 and 1968 the percentage of adults replying 'Yes' to the question 'Do you believe there is life after death?' ranged from 64 to 76. When they looked at studies of the possession of religious beliefs by members of specific professions, Argyle and Beit-Hallahmi found that medical students who wished to work in psychiatry were more likely to declare no religious affiliation than medical students wishing to enter other specialities, while studies of the religious beliefs of psychologists reveal that 'Psychologists, who show a number of unconventional attitudes, are also generally low on measures of religiosity.'

Psychologists and psychiatrists apart, religious beliefs do seem to be important to many people. Every known culture, past and present, has developed at least one religion. Through the diligence of the anthropologists 'we now know much more about the religious feelings of Polynesians, North American Indians and various tribes of Africa than we do about our fellow members of Western civilization', wrote Alister Hardy, the zoologist who founded the Religious Experience Research Unit at Oxford. To right this balance, Hardy and his colleagues set out to discover what proportion of the British population report 'a deep awareness of a benevolent non-physical power which appears to be partly or wholly beyond, and far greater than, the individual self'. Their extensive studies to date show that at least 50 per cent of the population do make such a report.

Thus it seems that psychologists and psychiatrists have allowed their own metaphysical beliefs to blind them to important aspects of the phenomena which they, as scientists, are studying. No single book can right the balance, but here, in the following pages, I shall try to show that if we want to understand why a person behaves as he does, then we should seek to discover how that person sees the purpose of life and the nature of death.

In pursuit of this I have talked with clients, colleagues, and friends, and for their patience and tolerance I offer my greatest thanks and gratitude.

Eagle, Lincolnshire
April, 1981

DOROTHY ROWE

PREFACE TO THE SECOND EDITION

I have made a few small changes to the original text, most of which I wrote in the summer of 1980. Many of the ideas contained in this book I have explored and expanded in different ways in the books I have written in later years. Unfortunately, in the 'rational' and 'scientific' worlds of psychiatrists and psychologists little has changed. Death and the hopes, wishes and fears that death creates in us are still ignored. However, ignoring a truth does not make it any the less true. The meaning that we give to death determines how we live our lives.

Sheffield   DOROTHY ROWE
May, 1989

EPIGRAPH

1944 AND AFTER

Pinned down in the little valley – in its way
A trap, or would be if they had the strength.
Not very dangerous, with a little care.
Still, a long day
Pressed into hollows in the rocky, bare
Untrenchable soil, without food or drink
Or anything much to think
About; damp, coldish, shiny air . . .
Until, near dusk, at length
A few guns, manhandled across the bridgeless
Black ravine, suppress
The enemy strong-points, in a thundering glare.

Later, lost love pinned him down for years
But the relief came up at last – again
Covered the breakthrough to the warm, wide plain.

Life itself, some say, is just such waiting
Hemmed in a closed cirque of one's one creating
As cramped decade after decade runs
Towards the dusk.
                              – But where are the guns?

ROBERT CONQUEST

'Hemmed in a closed cirque of one's own creating'

We each live in our own individual prison. Freedom consists of choosing, consciously, the prison in which we live, and making our prison large and variable, with flexible walls, a spacious house with wide doors and windows open to heaven and earth. Unfortunately, so many of us reject freedom, for freedom means insecurity, openness to the unknown. Instead, we build our prison as an impregnable fortress, enclosing a meagre, empty space, and shutting out the myriad possibilities of heaven and earth. Moreover, we regard our fortress not as something we have chosen, but as an absolute and immutable fact of reality. Trapped and helpless, we cannot be happy.

I work as a psychologist and people who are in difficulties come and talk with me. Sometimes I put our conversations on tape, and it is these conversations that are in this book. Or rather, selections from them. No one other than me would want to listen to them in their entirety, with their gossip, dull anecdotes, repetitions, and platitudinous pleasantries. But they contain opinions, ideas, beliefs, themes – all threads that wind through the conversations and mesh into a tight and vital pattern. It is this pattern which forms the structure of the individual world in which each of us lives. This structure is the spectacles through which we see reality. Or, as the Talmud says, 'We do not see things as they are. We see them as we are.' Or as Epictatus said, 'It is not things in themselves which trouble us, but our opinions of things.'

Tony was a man of strong opinions. The first time he came to see me, he harangued me for two hours. He was a tall man, heavily built. The cut of his hair and his sweater and jeans matched the leftish views he was expounding with more passion than reason. His most trenchant attacks were made on the monstrous regiment of women who besieged him – his wife, mother, aunts, colleagues, acquaintances, women in general. Only his daughters were exempt. I felt sorry for his wife. I began to feel sorry for myself. So, having said very little all this time, I intervened to remark that perhaps he found it necessary to put on a show of bluster and anger so that I would not see how hurt and vulnerable he was inside. He sank down like a balloon deflating. He said I was right. I had earlier explained to him that our meeting was not a beginning of a series of meetings, since I was about to depart to Australia for two months. Now I said to him that if he wished, he could get in touch with me when I returned. He said he would do this, and so on my first day back he telephoned me for an appointment.

He came to see me each week and we talked for two hours. He talked at length, but more quietly and with less aggression. He explained this change in terms of what I was like.

'I wanted to stay with you right from the first session because something deep inside me tells me that I can't frighten you off. You see my aggressiveness as questions, rather than getting at you.'

I thought that all I did was to follow my rule that there is no point in arguing with a person until you know what it is that he is saying. With Tony it took me some eight weeks to find out.

We spent a lot of time talking about art, chiefly music since Tony was a musician, and about relationships. He said, 'I would like to find for myself some niche in life, not in society, in life. I'd like to carve out something and say in that I can reside and have my comfort and my being . . . the whole point about a guitar is a love affair. You hold it tenderly, gently – it's such a demanding bugger. It gives an incredible amount, but only if you get it right.'

I asked him why art was important to him.

'Because without it man has no reason to live.'

'So what you are saying, without art you have no reason to live.'

'Right.'

'What would happen to you if you suddenly found yourself in a world where there was no art?'

'I'd find the most convenient and most painless way of committing suicide. Wouldn't you?'

Later he said, 'The thing that interests me is relationships. Relationships with people primarily. Relationship with music, because music isn't a passive thing. It is an action and a reaction. . . .'

But while he called a close relationship 'the most important thing' he also called it 'the most difficult thing'. 'There's got to be a positiveness in a relationship to combat the absurdities that we all produce in our lives – the patterns we produce. I find people's patterns in daily living very hard to come to terms with. My wife says, "Why do you go on about it so? Why don't you let it alone?" I say, "Well, look, we're supposed to have a relationship, and you're the only wife I've got." '

When we spoke of love Tony said that he was always 'desperate for it, with the effect that when I found someone who responded actively and genuinely, I mean, there was nothing that would touch that!' His metaphor for his need for love was hunger. 'A deep relationship is my meat and drink . . . the reason I have a relationship, usually quite hectic, it's because you're ravenous, you're really hungry and you come across somebody and the chemistry works, and it's not often and, Jesus, you're hungry.'

'Do you see the lack of relationships as starvation?' I asked.

'Definitely, I mean, it would be fairer with rationing, at least you would be sure of your weekly ration – in a sense you feel you're living through a drought – there's no rain, nothing comes in to brighten your life.'

The way Tony defined relationships made for very great difficulties.

One day Tony arrived in high dudgeon about a friend who had promised him something and had 'failed to deliver'. I asked him why it was important to keep a promise.

'Promises should be kept because it exposes you, you have put yourself in a position where you are at risk. If you promise somebody something, you are actually laying yourself on the line. You diminish yourself by not carrying out the promise. A lot of people tell me I am too hard, but what alternatives have I got?'

'Why is it important to keep promises?'

3

'Because you are what you are by virtue of whether you keep them or not. You're laying your own self, you're laying your own integrity, you're laying your own being on the line.'

'You're demonstrating your own integrity?'

'Yes – and concern and love. What are you going to do? Throw all these things away?'

'What you're saying is that when a person breaks a promise to you you feel that that's a sign of a loss of integrity in that person, and that that person is showing you less love.'

'That's right. In the end it's those sort of human gestures that somehow determine the relationship. If somebody I don't care about promises me something and doesn't deliver, I'm not too worried, but if somebody I care about does that, I get worried.'

'Does the fact that your friend did not keep his promise suggest to you that he does not care about you as much as he says, or you had hoped?'

'Well, caring about me is only part of it. Caring full stop is the biggest part.'

'I always think "caring" is a transitive verb.'

'I don't think so. I see caring as a conceptual thing, that is a caring person. A phrase "a caring person" is a quality of that person.'

'Am I understanding you to say now that your friend projects himself as a caring person, yet where you're concerned, he does something which suggests a lack of caring? The implication in this is either when he projects himself as a caring person it's phoney, or if he is a caring person the caring does not extend to you.'

'No, it's not that. The caring includes me, but I'm not the most important thing about it. All he's done is tell me that he cares when he wants to care, as opposed to being a caring person.'

'So it's something he switches on and off.'

'That's right.'

'And there's no security in that.'

'Exactly. There's no security in it. I find no security anywhere. Very few people give me security.'

Tony went on to describe me as 'a caring person'. This confounded me. I could not see how I could have a quality of caring which existed in me, even if I lived in a vacuum. I know

4

that my eyes have a quality, blue, which remain the same no matter what I see out of them, but caring, for me, is an experience, something I do and feel, and it always relates to something outside of myself. In the language which Tony and I thought we shared were many traps for the unwary.

One day Tony remarked, 'Really, I'm not scared of living.'

'What are you scared of?' I asked.

'People who don't live.'

'Why do they scare you?'

'Because the whole thing's an act. You never get down to anything. You see, I rather expect that close relationships are short term. I don't see how fires that can burn so intensely can keep going for so long. I see long relationships in terms of stroking. I don't see meaningful relationships in terms of stroking. I see them as heights and depths. Jesus, I don't want to travel, hovering above the ground about six inches. I want to be right up there or right down there. I don't want to be down there, but I know if you go up there, you've got to be down there some of the time. In this life you do not experience one thing unless you experience the opposite.'

He subscribed to the Spanish proverb: 'Take what you like, says God, and pay for it.'

'I've never got away with anything in my life,' he said. In relationships nothing ever happened by chance. He would often say, 'For every action there's a reaction.'

Nevertheless, no matter what price he had to pay for close, meaningful relationship, he still believed that 'any relationship benefits from the start from one thing going for it and that's newness. The newness will carry it for a certain length of time, and it is the precise thing that leads on to other people, because you're after new experiences. That phrase from Hesse in *Narcissus and Goldmund*, "Can there be true love without true love's dangers?" That "dangers" could be translated into newness. By true love's dangers it meant that Goldmund was always finding a new girl, and he was somebody who didn't find a lasting relationship. I find I don't need any of that in terms of my daughters – newness isn't a constant in that sort of bond. But I think in sexual love it is a fact. It seems to be for me. But society condemns that out of hand. I'm probably talking about what

5

people have been finding since time began – newness of relationship is nothing new to the artist. I look around and I find it's evident – the new day, seasons of the year, every springtime – in a sense we know what we're going to expect, but so we do when we go into relationships. Certain things one knows are going to be there, but it's the discovery of them, the actual testing of them that is the attraction, isn't it? I think artists are sometimes brave enough to say this.'

'If you see goodness of relationships as relating to the newness of relationships, then you're going to get into difficulties in long-term relationships, aren't you?'

'Yes. It's more that business of confirmation. Perhaps it's that one is never enough. You need more to confirm.'

'You need relationships to confirm something about yourself?'

'Yes.'

'What?'

'That I'm still capable of them, for a start.'

'And so this is a kind of testing yourself out every time.'

'Yes, yes. I think it's the love factor. If anybody goes out of their way to show that they love me, I'm theirs.'

'What you're saying is that you want to confirm that you're still lovable.'

'Yes. Someone once told me that she'd never known anyone as generous with themselves as I was. And I find people tight, bloody tight.'

Tony often criticized his wife for not giving him the kind of relationship he craved. 'She does not care for the depth because of the hurt and the real living that has to go on because of that relationship. Me, I want it all.' I thought that most women would be reserved with a man who would declare, 'I don't think relationships last. It's one of the beautiful things about relationships that they're fleeting things. Like the butterfly, they can only exist for a length of time . . . The day I stop hurting someone I'll be dead. That must be the nature of life. I don't see relationships as being forever, with a person like me, anyway. I think the depth of a relationship is its own self-destruct mechanism. You're sort of living life as if each day is the last. For most women I have no attraction whatsoever. But for a few women I have a very great attraction.'

6

'What is it in you that they find attractive?'

'That I can deliver. When they look at me and they see what I'm promising and offering, I can make their dreams come true. I can actually deliver – but I can't deliver for ever.'

'Why not?'

'Because I don't think it's something that can be delivered for ever. It's an exhausting thing. It has the seeds of its own destruction in it. There's always a sense that I deplete stocks more quickly than I can build them up again.'

'You see your part of the relationship self-destructing because you run out of supplies. But if you find somebody else there could suddenly be a new source of supplies because this person is feeding you.'

'Yes, that's right.'

'So you find another source of supplies which again will run out and then you've got to find somebody else.'

'Yes. That's absolutely right.'

'That's a fairly exhausting way to live one's life.'

He laughed ruefully and said, 'You shouldn't mock the afflicted.'

The way Tony used the words 'close relationship' often rang in my ears like an empty cliche, so I pushed him to say what 'close relationships' meant to him. This was difficult for him to do, since relationships are something we feel rather than define. He spoke of 'concepts, notions of love, of what a relationship intrinsically was. It's being something to someone and someone being something to you. A relationship is not a negation of the self. It seems to me to be a more positive thing and to include a "we". There's still an "I", there's still a "you", but now there's a "we" – which is something which is a really important condition. What goes to make a "we" I'm not sure. It is the fact that you find you relate in terms of ideas, in terms of priorities, in terms of virtues, if you like. The continuation of the relationship is the acceptance of both selves.'

I commented, 'Then a relationship being a "we", what you've been saying all along, in essence, is that in your present life you don't belong to any relationship where you can say "we".'

'That's right. Hence I say I'm starving. My wife tells me she doesn't want that kind of relationship. And then she says "I love

7

you". My God, I don't know what's going on. I can't go to my wife and just hold her. I suspect that's all I want. The rest, the perks, other things, if you feel the same way as the other person you can discard them. In the end you know what the fundamental is. It's that holding someone close – and everybody that I want to hold close doesn't want to be held close.'

So a close relationship was loving, holding, sharing – and doomed. It reminded me of *Tristan and Isolde* or *La Traviata*, but I dared not say so. Tony tried to despise Romantic music. He talked of the beauty of Bach's music which 'has a beauty all of its own and it's really uncluttered by the sentimentalism of Romantic music. It's put in a confined space and within that space Bach makes things work and he doesn't have to say "Look, I'm free" because in the end you've nothing at all. It's terror, freedom.' But such freedom had its charms. He despised sentimentality, but for Tchaikovsky's *Pathetique*, 'I despise it but I still choke up. Indulgence and sentimentality really get me and I suspect I'm both. I still need my Tchaikovsky. I suppose I link that with women and I always feel that women are horribly sentimental, indulgent creatures.' But women were powerful. 'I see the world as being a woman's world, not a man's world. Men are far superior in terms of integrity.'

These words of his are but a faint echo of his tirade of abuse against women which often made him sound like the male chauvinist Aunt Sally that the less discriminating members of the Women's Movement like to demolish. Occasionally I commented that he sounded like a naive male chauvinist but forebore to point out the tautology of 'naive' and 'male chauvinist' since I gathered from his discourse that he divided the human race into men, women, and special people, and that I had earned a place in the last group.

In our second meeting, when we were trying to decide whether our discussions should have some particular aim, he said, 'It's a question of knocking out stupid or wrong choices or wrong questions. I think if you're on a journey from A to B you never actually get to B. You simply rule out all the hundreds of paths that will take you to places like the sewerage canal. I don't think it matters if you get to B. What matters is that you've tried to get there – whether you've been through the experience.' He returned to this point some weeks later. 'I don't care about results, objectives. What I want to know is, has the bloke done the journey, has he travelled the road?'

'Why is it important to go on that journey?' I asked.

'Because without it you don't know what another person is feeling. You don't know the processes that are involved. You've no concept of compassion, of inquiry, of the finenesses of intellect. You've none of these things. You're only half a person. One of the innate factors of man is surely the inquiring nature of man into himself. Which is what art is all about. It seems to me that there isn't anything more important than finding out the nature of what you are. We bring very little into the world. The need to survive is innate, but surviving can be achieved at the expense of real living. The inquiry after a god does seem to be one of the fundamentals that man has brought into the world. You can put a lot down to fear and ignorance, but you can't put all of it down to fear, superstition, and ignorance.'

Special people were, for Tony, the people who questioned life, who had set out 'on the journey'. He saw himself as a special person, and this was very important for him because, as he said, 'Ordinary people aren't remembered.' Being remembered was very important.

One day I asked him, 'How do you envisage your death?'

He sighed. 'I've no idea. One thing I fear is the same death as my father, of a tumour. Once it had been diagnosed, I had to wait three months, watching him die. I hope very much I don't die like that. Like Roger McGough, "Let me die a young man's death." I'd rather go out in a blaze of something. But I'm not brave. I don't really fancy being thrown out in the middle of a road from the seat of a motor bike. Death doesn't bother me but dying does. I don't want to become less than what I was – like my father. I travelled every day to that hospital. His condition was getting worse, and I'd keep making myself relive him as he was, a vital sort of person – very distinguished looking, attractive to women, a compassionate man, made a lot of mistakes. Really a very nice human being, and I would not allow this paralyzed half of a face with a drooping lip – it has impinged on my memory, but I try very hard to stop it stopping me remembering him as I really knew him. Christ, that must be false, that last three months must be false in the sense that they hid the man and what he was. Three months must be weighed against sixty years.'

'How old will you be when you die?'

'Sixty. And I'd prefer it that way. So I've never worried about pensions, you see.'

'What do you feel will happen to you after you die?'

'Nothing.'

'You see death as the end?'

He sighed, 'Yes, in the ashes to ashes and dust to dust sense. One returns to the atoms and particles that one came from.'

I asked, 'How do you see yourself being remembered?'

He was silent. Then he put his hand to his face and cried. 'I don't know,' he said, and a little while later he went on, 'Strangely, I find it somehow gratifying that it can move me to tears, real tears. There's so much hate down below. Can't seem to do anything about myself, and yet, I estrange myself, isolate myself, that's the sort of person I am and I don't think I can help doing it. I don't mean to talk in hopeless terms, but it's part of me. Trouble is, I can't cope with the result. Can't cope with the isolation – I can cope with it at a given moment, but when I'm on my own, there are times – I suspect that's no way to try and learn the guitar.' He lit a cigarette and said, 'I went to the clinic last week. He's a nice guy, that bloke.'

'Dr White?'

'Yes. He's a bloody nice guy. One of life's gentlemen, strange and eccentric, but really nice. He gave me all the time in the world and he said, "You know, I can't do very much for you", and I thought, you've given me an hour of your time. What better service could I have?'

'It sounds like what you are saying is that I don't expect people will remember me because I was a loving person.'

'Something like that. They see me as an awkward bastard.'

'And you don't see people remembering you as a great artist.'

'It's a shame. I think actually I could be passably good. I think I've got the capabilities. I think I could, it's possible, if not probable, for me to give a performance of integrity of music that needs that sort of interpretation – for someone to say, "That guy really understood what Bach was about." When you're trying to

10

make this achievement on the one thing that you think will save your life, and then it starts sinking, you know, and then you're left – the last time I had a guitar lesson it was dreadful, couldn't do a thing. I have this problem about doing anything in performance in a solo role. If I'm accompanying, no problems. When it's for myself, I can't do it. I sit there like an idiot.'

He described how, when a publisher had expressed interest in some of his songs, he told the publisher that few people would want to buy them, and the publisher went away. 'So,' said Tony, 'Out of the jaws of success I snatched failure.'

He told me about a story he was writing. 'When it's legible I'll let you read it. You'll be bored out of your mind.'

'You're telling me I won't enjoy reading what you're writing. That way you're stopping me from telling you I don't like it.'

'That's right. But do you know what I fear most? That someone will say "That's very good", and then put it away in a drawer for twenty years.'

'Why do you fear that?'

'Because it denies me. I don't really mind people saying "Bloody awful". But to be ignored I find terrifying.' He did, however, 'actually want all these stupid people's approval'.

'And when you get it, you'll despise it.'

'That's right – absolutely bloody right.'

Tony talked a great deal about what he expected the other person in a relationship should give him, but he found my question as to what he brought to a relationship a difficult one to answer.

'I don't know, I bring whatever I am into a relationship. I really don't know what I am, I suspect. I'm capable of love. I'm capable of making love. Well, those for starters. I think I give it my best. I always thought in life that people never wanted my best. They never wanted what I could actually do. They never wanted peak performance.'

'What happens to you when you offer people something and they don't want it?'

'Frustrated – intense frustration, and depression I suspect. That's not a very good word, but when your bed becomes your best friend, that time when you suddenly realize you've got problems, bed's the best place. You don't have to think.'

11

'Have you always felt this about yourself, that people didn't want your best?'

'Yes.'

'So that if you put yourself in a situation where you're going to demonstrate the best of what you're capable, you're putting yourself in a situation where people are going to reject you.'

'Yes.'

'So in a situation where you're going to give a guitar solo your anticipatory image is not one of going out there, playing well, and having people applaud. It's going out there, playing well, and people putting their hands over their ears and walking out.'

'Or the other anticipatory image is that I'm going to collapse. Then my audience will shake their heads, avert their eyes and gently file out. They don't want to be associated with me. Sometimes I feel that there will be people willing me on, but I'll fail them. I'll collapse under the pressure.'

'Whatever you do, the audience is against you?'

'Yes. I do make it very hard for myself, don't I?'

'If you look at the images that successful artists or racing drivers have, it's that they're going to go out there and win.'

'That's right. I've never felt that on a musical instrument. The thing just sits there and laughs at you. I'm deferential to the music. Any piece I've played I'm honoured to have played it. One thing I can't stand is praise when I've done something wrong. I really want to scream at that. It's almost as if I insist that everyone is as aware as I am of what I'm trying to do. In that case, I'm always going to lose, aren't I?' Then Tony quoted from Gerard Manley Hopkins' poem *Soliloquy* which he had set for voice and guitar, 'Birds build but not I build – no, but strain, time's eunuch – O Thou Lord of life, send my roots rain.'

I commented, 'The way in which you construe the outcome of every situation you make sure you don't achieve anything. You don't even allow the possibility of achieving.'

'The truth is,' he sighed, 'that maybe I want to win in my way.'

'What would your way be?'

'Did you see a film called *A Touch of Class*? Well, the first time they made love, he was putting his tie on and he said, "How was

12

it?", and she said, "Okay", and he was really offended.' Tony laughed at this. 'He got more and more irate, and she said, "What did you want me to tell you, that the stars flew round heaven? It was okay", and he was really furious. I know it. If a woman, if she didn't, didn't dare, break up into little bits, I'd be very insulted.'

'So you want people to go absolutely over the moon about your music. Just saying "That was good" isn't enough.'

'No, it isn't. You can't just enjoy it for that minute. You've got to rave about it, otherwise you'll insult the performer.'

Thus it was that while Tony prided himself on being a thinker, he despised those relatives and colleagues who, he said, 'set me up as a guru'. Of course he despised them for they were not capable of seeing how great a thinker he was, or could be, but even more because they had not 'made the journey'. 'I feel I have to fight night and day, almost, to maintain a position I've reached, whereas people who haven't made the journey, by their very not having made the journey, will wipe you out – their inertia breeds apathy and ignorance. They offend my humanity.' He put this in a poem which he gave to me.

> YOU
> who deny me
> with ev'ry breath you breathe
> YOU
> who offer life itself
> and are barren
> YOU
> who gain power
> knowing nothing of wisdom
> YOU
> who court success
> compromising your own existence to succeed
> YOU are not my Peers – neither will I recognise you.
>
> YOU
> who force me to fight you
> or be overwhelmed by triviality

13

> YOU
> *who indulge your excesses*
> *call me extreme*
> YOU
> *who are dedicated to pain's exclusion*
> *profess tolerance*
> YOU
> *who revere mediocrity*
> *mock talent*
> *YOU are not my idols – neither will I serve you.*
>
> *YOU have driven me from your world*
> *because I dared to dream of things substantial*
> *and dared to speak of them.*
> *YOU used me as your Oracle*
> *and when the words revealed your weakness*
> *YOU destroyed me.*

'I'm not one for middle roads. You end up nowhere,' said Tony. At the end of one session I ventured the suggestion that there is something to be said for tolerance in human relationships. Tony went away and brooded on this and came back the next week ready to argue the point.

'I thought that intolerance was – ' he paused and took a deep breath, 'probably a very important facet of all this. I'm not sure that I'm willing to give it up that easy.'

'There are too many payoffs to being intolerant, to give it up,' I said.

'Mm.' He went on to talk about 'special' people and then said, 'I really don't know what to do with praise. So people don't know whether to praise me or to boo me. If they boo me they get a mouthful back. If they praise me I never accept it.'

'Once you said I could write what I liked about you so long as it was good, bad, but not indifferent. So, if people are tolerant to you that would come across to you that they are indifferent to you.'

'Yes, that's true.'

'How would you feel if you woke up one morning and found you were a tolerant person?'

14

'I'd know I was different immediately. I see tolerance as a sort of blunting process. I'm very loath to see it as a virtue. Because everything that is written about tolerance is actually evasion or patronization, neither of which I want to know anything about. So people who are described as tolerant are evading something.'

'If you become a tolerant person you'd be bland and you wouldn't be complaining, fighting against unacceptable behaviour?'

'There's a sort of missionary zeal underneath it all.'

'So when I say to you that if you were more tolerant towards other people you'd find life a lot easier, I'm in effect saying to you, "Become a lesser person, a worse person than you are and you'll find life easier." And, of course, that kind of message no one will accept.'

'If you said that to me I would have to say, "You're putting my soul at risk".'

'If I give you advice "Be tolerant", I'm actually giving you, in your frame of reference, the advice "Be a bad person".'

'Yes.'

'And to give you that advice is, for you, "Put your soul at risk". This isn't a piece of new, brilliant insight on my part. I've had this conversation with a lot of women who've been sitting where you are now and saying to me, "I'm worn out. I do all this housework", and I say, "Why not do less housework?", and as I'm saying that I'm advising them to become a bad person, because it puts their soul at risk not to keep their houses immaculately clean. It's just what we regard as – '

'You can make a parallel, can you?' He was offended.

'Yes. We each have our own list of virtues.'

'Because I despise, not despise, laugh at, the woman who does too much housework. So I'm not happy about the sense of your parallel.'

'All I'm saying is that different people choose different things to regard as paramount virtues as proof of their essential goodness. What would happen to you if you became a tolerant person?'

'I think it would be the end of me. I think my wife admires and loves me in whatever way she has of admiring and loving because I am what I am. I think she really likes an intolerant bastard. She would accuse me of selling out if I went along with every whim of hers.'

'So in a way she needs you to be nasty and you need to be nasty.'

'There is something of that in it.'

'That's the basis of a long marriage, isn't it?'

He was able to laugh at this, but later he said that if he were not intolerant then he would be 'wiped out' by those people he addressed in his poem.

Tony had been brought up 'a strict Baptist' but when he was twenty-five 'I found that the God I'd been used to praying to and corresponding with at varying intervals and levels of sincerity all of a sudden wasn't available to me.'

'How do you feel about God now?'

'My thoughts waver from the neutral which I rarely am to levels of "If you're there you're a bastard". I'm not really sure. There's that first line of Hopkins, "Thou art indeed just, Lord, if I contend with Thee". As soon as you start contending with a God, then He is what you say He is, because you've acknowledged him. I know what I am, but the reason I'm coming here is because I don't know how to cope with it, the results of it, all the time. I can cope with misfortune, perhaps, better than I can cope with the lack of motivation. Most days you get up and the guitar gives you meaning because the guitar starts talking to you, it puts an alternative proposition to you. If I'd have lived a thousand years ago I'd have built an altar in the shape of a guitar.'

'When you were twenty-five you gave up being a Baptist but you didn't give up being religious.'

'Yes, I am a religious person, but my God is a – all sorts of things. He's first of all "to thine own self be true". I don't know whether I kid myself, but I find I've developed some facility for measuring honesty, cutting past all the shit, and guff, and going straight there – which has earned me no kudos at all. But I can't put a title to my God. Having given up titles, I don't know whether I would like to lumber Him with one. I have a great fear of the Christian God – He must be a bastard, what a bloody sick joke, creating this world. There must be some gods up there, sitting around, and He's a baby god among the bigger

16

immortals, and the baby's been given the world to play with, stirring things round in the world, seeing what havoc can be caused. If there is a God, then this God is some sort of holy maniac, an evil maniac. Evil because He allows enough food to keep the dream going. It's the biggest con trick ever played.'

'The dream? The dream of what?'

'That you're getting somewhere. When I talk of evil, that goes back to my Billy Graham days. That bastard! I was really conned. I was one of those that walked forward. I really could shoot myself for doing that. It embarrasses my soul, not my person. How could I be so out of touch with myself?'

'You feel you've been conned by the Christian God?'

'Oh, yes, very definitely. Not just by the people who serve the Christian God.' He went on to berate St Paul for naming the unknown god of the Greeks 'Yahweh'. 'The Greeks had put labels on so many things and still they felt that it didn't matter how many gods they made, there was still something you can't put your finger on. And that is a very uncomfortable situation. The Greeks, because they had a lot of time to think, could actually stand and bear this discomfort, but man nowadays is so rushing round, is so materialistic, that in the end he can't weigh himself down. He's got to put labels on things.'

'How well can you stand the unknown God?'

'With difficulty, with great difficulty intellectually.'

'But how about emotionally?'

He sat very still for a moment and then said, 'Emotionally, I think, badly.'

'Not that you need to know. You need to be close.'

'That's right.'

'The hunger that you talk about, the hunger in relationships. You want to be close.'

'Yes. In the end you know what the fundamental thing is. It's holding someone close. And everybody I want to hold close doesn't want to be held close.' He shaped his arms around the empty air.

'You don't see God as wanting to be held close?'

He thought about this. 'I suppose not. But I've never given it any thought before. After all, a person, a Being capable of living the life of the universe, it would be difficult to get close to. We're

17

talking in terms of infinity. I don't know what infinity is, but it scares hell out of me. There's no way I can cope with thinking about an infinite God. One of the virtues of death is that it will end it. Death actually has a lot of things going for it. I'm not trying to be perverse, but I do find the thought of some people and infinity more than I can bear.'

'If you think in terms of wanting to hold the unknown God and then you think "Life ends in death", then you haven't left yourself a lot of time to know that God. Then if you say that life doesn't end in death you're still lumbered with all the people that irritate you.'

'They don't irritate me. They offend me, mortally offend me.'

'Yes, mortally offend. You've used that phrase before.'

'It's one of my mother's. I find that people to whom I apply that expression do just that. They offend me, the essential me.'

'If you suffer a mortal wound you die. What we've just worked out together is – you could conceive of your life going on after death, but people who mortally offend you would still be there, and their presence stops you from having a life after death. So they have mortally offended you, haven't they?'

'I've never looked at it in that way before. But the first line of the poem I wrote was the indicative thing in terms of humanity. "You who deny me with ev'ry breath you breathe." If people talk crap and are admired for it – to them I say, "By your very nature you're calling me some sort of lunatic. So bloody well shut up, commit suicide, but get out of my hair. I don't want to see you, I don't want to know you." I haven't thought beyond that. Maybe I have in the way you're describing. But consciously I haven't thought about it.'

Later he said, 'If there is a God, then we must be a reflection of His image. God must be evil as well as good.'

'If you see God as being at least as potentially evil as man, then you can't have any trust or security in Him.'

'No.'

'Where do you look for security?'

'In other human beings. So I'm inevitably tripping over.'

'Do you see any security in art?'

'Yes. But not in art alone. I've always seen art as an expression of a relationship rather than as a descriptive piece of something.

Art is about doing the same thing in a different way. I suppose the reason I've fallen back on the classical guitar is because the only creativity left to one is interpretation.'

Tony saw himself as a thinker and he wanted to share his thoughts with me, but even he found it difficult to reveal to me, and sometimes to himself, his basic beliefs, the structure which supported and surrounded him. We do not display our set of basic beliefs any more than we display our skeleton. Yet, just as our skeleton determines whether we spread our fine bones in the shape of a hand or a wing, whether we stand upright or pad along on all fours, so our beliefs determine whether we shall act upon the world with mastery, or soar freely and confidently through life, or stand upright against life's buffeting, or plod through life's weary ways. We do not state some of our beliefs, or even bring them to mind, since we regard them as totally obvious and axiomatic. We hide our beliefs from others to prevent them from laughing at our childish faiths, or belittling our deepest fears, or chiding our foolish optimism. Or simply not understanding what was being told.

If Tony could have stated his beliefs simply and directly, all he need have said was 'There is no afterlife and God is a child who uses the world for His sport. I must fight against the people who offend me otherwise I shall be destroyed. The meaning and purpose of life lies in art and in close relationships. Close relationships do not last. I shall always fail as an artist. When I die I shall be forgotten.'

He did not say that directly, but he did say. 'I sometimes think that the main problem is coming to terms with a world that I don't have any affinity with and being motivated with it. I really can't see why I should do anything rather than spend my life being depressed and commenting to all and sundry on it.'

2

The Foundations of the Cirque

I. Constructing Our Individual Worlds

When we, as small children first awake into self-consciousness, we look about us upon a world which we take to be already there. We look at our world, we touch it, taste it, hear it, explore it, and we consider, without questioning, that this is reality. What we do not know, and what we may never come to know, is that what we experience is what we construct, and what reality is is something which lies beyond our senses. We are the prisoners of our body. Our soul is held, as Marvell said:

> With bolts of bones, that fettered stands
> In feet; and manacled in hands.
> Here blinded with an eye; and there
> Deaf with the drumming of an ear.

Other animals are equally imprisoned. A bird can never know what it is to curve a hand around a shape or pinch a solid between finger and thumb, and a fish can never know what it is to soar upon a current of wind or hold a loved one close. But fish, swimming in a shoal, which turns and weaves as one, can signal in ways unknown to us, while birds can detect a magnetic field and bacteria swim towards magnetic north. A vast reality lies outside the range of the senses of each species, and each species, animal or insect, differs in the range of its senses. What each species knows of reality is what its senses allow it to construct.

'Construction' implies 'pattern', and as we look about us it is patterns that we differentiate out of what is possibly the totally connected chaos of reality. We experience our patterns as the meaning or understanding which makes our existence as a person possible. As Michael Oakeshott wrote: 'Understanding is not such that we either enjoy it or lack it altogether. To be human and to be aware is to encounter what is in some manner understood. Thus it may be said that understanding is an unsought condition; we inhabit a world of intelligibles.'

Our world is completely intelligible, completely meaningful. Parts of it may, at times, seem unpredictable, irrational, unintelligible, meaningless, but unintelligibility and meaninglessness are themselves meanings. We are encapsulated in a world of meaning, constructed through our senses and our talents to create form. Our cleverest of constructions, our most talent form, is language, that which marks us off from all other animals. Man is, as Herder said, 'ein Geschopf der Sprache', a language creature.

It is out of language that we create a past and a future, and the hopes and fantasies without which our lives would be meagre and brief. Through language, wrote George Steiner, 'I establish and preserve my experience of self by a stream of internalised address. I realise my unconscious, so far as dreams or sudden rifts of delirium permit, by listening for and amplifying "upward" shreds of discourse, of verbal static, from the dim and middle of the psyche. We do not speak *to ourselves* so much as *speak ourselves*. We provide our self-consciousness with its only and constantly renewed guarantee of particular survival by beaming a current of words inward. Even when we are outwardly mute, speech is active within, and our skull is like an echo chamber.'

We not only act, but we reflect upon our actions, and through such reflections we come to know ourselves. Through language we come to know others and they come to know us. Discourse is essential, since humans find silence, isolation, intolerably painful. But discourse implies a shared language, a shared way of patterning reality. Reality can be patterned in an infinite number of ways, but becoming a member of a group means learning to pattern reality in ways similar to those of the group. Becoming a qualified member of a profession means demonstrating proficiency in the preferred patterns of that group. Being born and learning to speak means, as Herder said, to 'swim in an inherited stream of images and words; we must accept these media on trust; we cannot create them', since 'language expresses the collective experience of the group'.

21

Wilhelm von Humboldt wrote 'Man lives with his objects chiefly – in fact, since his feeling and acting depends on his perceptions, one may say exclusively – as language presents them to him. By the same process whereby he spins language out of his own being, he ensnares himself in it; and each language draws a magic circle round the people to which it belongs, a circle from which there is no escape, save by stepping out of it into another.'

Humans have created many more languages than have been recorded, and each week, it is said, a language dies. Still, the evidence is that no two languages have ever patterned reality in the same way. Gauchos of the South American pampas had little use for plants but much for horses, so they had few words for plants and many for varieties of horse-hides, while Arabs, caring for camels and for plants, devised a great lexicon of words for varieties of camels and varieties of plants. Myer Mendelson records that the Tahitian language has no words for depression, grief, and the like, though it has more than forty words for various shades of anger, thus, perhaps, following the advice in *The Hitch Hiker's Guide to the Galaxy* that 'the best way not to be unhappy is not to have a word for it'.

English has the verbs 'to wash' and 'to eat' which can be used to cover a multitude of activities, but in certain North American Indian languages at least thirteen different verbal forms carefully distinguish different modes of washing and different modes of eating. The passing of time, the relative positions in space, the delineation of 'I' and 'Other', distinctions of gender made by certain languages, can often be grasped only with great difficulty by those brought up in a world of Indo-European languages. Even among these languages great differences appear. The ancient Greeks carefully distinguished nine different kinds of love: *philia*, friendship; *physike*, kindness among creatures of the same race; *xenike*, benevolence towards guests; *hetairike*, mutual attachment of friends; *erotike*, sexual desire; *agape*, disinterested affection; *storge*, tenderness; *eunoia*, goodwill; *charis*, love of gratitude. In English the load of unstated meanings that has been placed on the one word, 'love', has made it into one of the most inadequate and dangerous words in the English language – inadequate since it makes so few distinctions among feeling and dangerous since it can carry the connotations that

Christianity has given it, that *agape* is good but *erotike* is sinful.

Morality and language are indissoluble. A very depressed young woman told me once, 'I never forgive myself for anything. I feel I have been running up a shopping bill and I have got to pay for it all before I can go on. I don't know who I owe, but I do feel in debt.' Had we been speaking in German there would have been no need to interpret her experience of being in debt as one of feeling guilty, for the German word for debt is the word for guilt – *Schuld*. Similarly, no Dutch mother need berate her children for 'sinful waste', for in Dutch 'waste' is 'sin' – *zonde*.

Part of our 'inherited stream of images and words' concerns how the culture we are born into determines how we learn to structure time and space. Were we born into Elizabethan England we would have been presented with a universe firmly organized into what is called 'a Chain of Being'. Tillyard has described this as:

> . . . a chain stretched from the foot of God's throne to the meanest of inanimate objects. Every speck of creation was a link in the chain . . . (but man) was the nodal point, and his double nature, though the source of internal conflict, had the unique function of binding together *all* creation, of bridging the greatest cosmic chasm, that between matter and spirit . . . a kind of Clapham Junction where all tracks converge and cross.

While the Chain of Being may now seem to us no more than an elaborate fantasy, we have not abandoned the basic geometry of the chain, a line, a progression from one point to another. Dorothy Lee brought this out very clearly in her study of the Trobriand Islanders who:

> . . . at no time mention circles or rings or even rows when they refer to their villages. Any word which they use to refer to a village, such as *a* or *this*, is prefixed by the substantival element *kway* which means *bump* or *aggregate* of *bumps* . . . the Trobrianders do not describe their activity lineally; they do no dynamic relating of acts; they do not even use so innocuous a connective as *and* . . . where

valued activity is concerned, the Trobrianders do not act on an assumption of lineality at any level. There is organisation or rather coherence in their acts because Trobriand activity is patterned activity. One act within this pattern brings into existence a pre-ordained cluster of acts . . . When the Trobrianders set out on their great ceremonial kula expedition, they follow a pre-established order . . . The order derives meaning not from lineal sequence, but from correspondence with a present, experience meaningful pattern; that which has been ordained of old and is forever. To the Trobriander climax in history is abominable, a denial of all good, since it would imply not only the presence of change, but also that change increase the good; but to him value lies in sameness, in repeated pattern, in the incorporation of all time within the same point. What is good in life is exact identity with all past Trobriand experience, and all mythical experience.

Dorothy Lee pointed out that in our society:

. . . our evaluation of happiness and unhappiness is bound with this notion along an envisioned line leading to a desired end . . . failure is devastating in our culture, because it is not failure of the undertaking alone; it is the moving, becoming, lineally conceived self which has failed.

The non-linear concept of reality appears in the metaphysics of ancient China. Joseph Needham described how:

. . . in co-ordinative thinking conceptions are not subsumed under one another, but placed side by side in a *pattern*, and things influence one another not by acts of mechanical causation but by a kind of 'inductance' . . . The keyword in Chinese thought is *Order* and above all *Pattern* (Organism). The symbolic correlations or correspondence all formed part of one colossal pattern. Things behaved in particular ways not necessarily because of prior actions or impulsions of other things, but because their position in the ever-moving universe was such that they were endowed with intrinsic natures which made that behaviour inevitable for them. If they do not behave in those particular ways they would lose their relational positions in the whole (which made them what they were), and turn into something other than themselves. They were thus parts in existential dependence upon the whole world-organism. And they reacted upon one another not so much by mechanical impulsion or causation as a kind of mysterious resonance . . . It was a picture of an extremely and precisely ordered universe, in which things 'fitted' so exactly that you could not insert a hair between them. But it was a universe in which organisation came about, not because of fiats issued by a supreme law-giver which things must obey subject to sanction imposable by angels attendant; nor because of the physical clash of innumerable billiard balls in which the motion of one was the physical cause of the other. It was an ordered harmony of wills without an ordainer; it was like the spontaneous, yet ordered, in the sense of patterned movements, of dancers in a country dance of figures, none of whom are bound by law to do what they do, nor yet pushed by others, coming from behind, but co-operate in a voluntary harmony of wills . . . In such a system causality is reticular and hierarchically fluctuating, not particulate and singly catenarian [like a net and not like a chain].

Aristotle contended that the natural state of the physical world was one of rest, and if something moved then something was causing it to move. What has been called the greatest step in the history of science was when Buridan and his colleagues changed this image into the natural state of matter as one of constant impetus, constant momentum, uniform velocity. Nuclear physicists use an image of reality which is curiously like that of the ancient Eastern philosophies. Heisenberg described the world as 'a complicated tissue of events, in which connections of different kinds alternate or overlap or combine and thereby determine the texture of the whole'.

Scientific thought tries to construct models of the world as it is, unaffected by human hopes and fears. But, as historians of ideas have shown, the scientific ideas which gain currency at a particular time in a particular culture in some way reflect and relate to the current concerns, purposes, preoccupations of that culture. Notions of linear progress, of the separateness of men, animals, and plants, and of certain categories of men, have become less valid, less trustworthy, in a century where wars have shown civilized men producing a savagery unknown to primitive men, where man in despoiling his environment despoils himself, and where the commercial decisions of a small group of men can have repercussions in every market-place throughout the world. Our universe is, indeed, a complicated tissue of events.

Try as we may to keep our scientific thought unstained by human needs and wishes, we create for ourselves a world where inanimate objects carry the projection of our humanness. Light has no colour and water no wetness; colour and wetness are aspects of our relationship with the outside world. Edmund Carpenter recorded how he once remarked to an Eskimo friend that the wind was cold. His wise friend corrected him. 'How,' he asked, 'can the *wind* be cold? You're cold; you're unhappy. But the wind isn't cold or unhappy.' A salutary reminder, but one which we prefer to ignore since, by projecting ourselves onto our world, by creating metaphors that link human experience with the world, we humanize our world and change it from being an environment which ignores our existence to one which reacts and responds to us. The response need not be friendly. As Tillyard remarked, 'If mankind had to choose between a universe that ignored him and one that noticed him to do him harm, it might well choose the second.' And, indeed, many people do.

We use the patterns we construct like yarrow sticks, Tarot cards, and crystal balls, to predict the future. We form patterns like 'The sun rises in the east' and 'It is dangerous to trust people', and we use these patterns to predict where we should look to see the rising sun or how we should behave towards other people. Our patterns are more successful than the fortune-telling arts since we expect our patterns to prove true, and, expecting this, we usually find that they do. Edmund Carpenter once wrote. 'We say, "If I hadn't seen it with my own eyes, I wouldn't have believed it", but the phrase should be "If I

26

hadn't believed it with all my heart, I wouldn't have seen it"!'

We do not readily see our patterns as patterns, something we have made, and therefore insubstantial and liable to change, first, because we are so busy using them we do not have time to inspect them and, second, because we cannot cope with the insecurity such knowledge would bring to us. Many scientists, philosophers, and theologians alike have and do insist that there are fixed and immutable laws, regularities of nature, which form the unshakable framework on which all the events in the universe are hung. Unfortunately, scientists, philosophers, and theologians have never agreed on what these fixed and immutable laws are, and the proliferation of pronouncements about these laws serves only to confirm what Vico (and Herder after him) said, 'We live in a world we ourselves create.' Knowing that we create our own world makes us free to create an infinite number of worlds, and to live with such freedom requires great courage. Not all of us possess such courage.

Knowing that we create our own world has another very great disadvantage. It robs us of the superiority of knowing that we are in possession of The Truth and that other people are wrong. We may be prepared to admit that other people see things differently but we do not wish to agree that they have the right, by their very nature as people, to see things differently. On such an attitude is built all discord between people, between individuals, and between nations.

Communication within a group of people is possible because there are patterns which every member of the group uses. Communication is difficult – and sometimes impossible – because each person in that group arranges his patterns in a different network, with different connections among the patterns. Thus, when the BBC broadcast a programme on patchwork, there was no controversy on what the pattern 'patchwork' meant. What was controversial were the values that should be attached to 'patchwork'. In a letter to *The Guardian* Mette Marston wrote: 'What is it about patchwork that sends husbands reeling while their wives are jumping for joy? When I informed my husband of my desire to watch the BBC programme on patchwork, he just groaned and told me that in his mind patchwork is inexorably connected with filthy rags, worn jackets in bed, and the wind howling through broken window panes. The image in my mind, on the other hand, is one of perpetual spring, honest, bare-scrubbed wood and white-washed walls, milk in stone pitchers and the mild wind playing with lace curtains.'

All human beings are aware of an inner turmoil which becomes differentiated into patterns labelled 'I love', 'I am angry', 'I am frightened', and so on. But individuals differ in how they use these patterns to make judgements upon themselves and predictions about the outcome of using these patterns. One person may decide, 'If I show that I am angry everyone will turn against me and I shall feel that I am a bad person.' Another person may decide, 'I have every right to be angry, and if I show that I am then people will do what I want.' One person may be sure that in this life 'All you need is love', while another may be equally certain that to love someone fully is to risk the soul-destroying pain of being rejected. 'I have always,' said the heroine of Mary Gordon's *Final Payments*, 'preferred a sense of deprivation to a sense of loss.' (She was a Catholic and would have been taught that hell may not be a matter of fire and brimstone, but rather a permanent sense of loss.)

The network of patterns each individual creates is a closed system which curves back upon itself in such a way that metaphors like 'an individual's world' or 'a microcosm' are used to describe it. John Shotter wrote:

Such worlds are both *coercive* and *reflexive*, as well as being *incorrigible*. That is, a) they provide a world in terms of which persons who inhabit it *must* determine their actions, if they want to remain living, that is, acceptable persons within it. For example, the Azande of Africa [whose magical practices were described by Evans-Pritchard] *must* view the workings of what we would call their poison-oracle as a magical process . . . (They) *all* would account for it in terms of magic, sorcery, and witchcraft. Similarly, all Skinnerians *must* see the human world in terms of stimuli and responses, and *must* structure their explanations . . . in terms of discriminative

28

stimuli and schedules of reinforcement. Their world is *morally* coercive, in the sense that to remain living in it they must act as it requires. And b), in so determining their actions, there is no way in which their actions can lead to results *beyond* that reality; it is reflexive in the sense that, no matter what happens, it will be understood and dealt with in terms that the reality provides. Piaget called this the self-regulating property of structures. But further, c) even apparent refutations of the reality's basic beliefs will be re-worked, using elaborations of those beliefs, into actual verifications of them . . . for us too, as for the Azande, in daily life, there exist basic, irrefutable certainties (*certum*). People's basic beliefs, the pre-suppositions in terms of which they live their lives are thus *incorrigible* in the sense that there is no simple way they can, if wrong, be corrected.

In literature we say that a person in his coercive, reflexive, incorrigible world acts 'in character'. If a character in a novel or play acts 'out of character', he ceases to be believable. The predicament in which the character finds himself and the outcome of the predicament are determined by the way the character is, in a sense, a prisoner of his own microcosm. Maggie Tulliver could not turn to her own advantage an overlong boatride with the man she loved any more than she could step outside her century and, like a girl born a hundred years later, see nothing compromising in being alone with a male friend. Raskolnikov's microcosm turned on the axis of guilt and responsibility, and, as he found, to deny their existence was only to confirm them.

Our individual world, whose patterns are presented and experienced as actions, feelings, and images, as well as words, form systems which have an idiosyncratic logic which may be largely reasonable to their owners, but not necessarily reasonable to outside observers and certainly not meeting the canons of Aristotelian logic. After all, as Gödel showed, any logical system which has any richness cannot be guaranteed to be consistent. Our individual worlds are corrigible, in the sense that they assimilate and accommodate certain experiences to form new or modified patterns, but there are certain complexes of patterns in our worlds which define the dimensions of our worlds and which remain incorrigible. Such patterns concern how we construe reality and the nature of life. Our individual worlds turn on the axes of our individual metaphysics.

II. Individual Metaphysics

Metaphysics, 'the science of being as such', where 'science' means the study of 'first causes' or 'first principles', has had little popularity with psychologists and psychiatrists reared in the positivist tradition. In psychoanalysis, as Ernest Jones said, 'the religious life represents a dramatization on a cosmic plane of the emotions, fears and longings which arose in the child's relation to his parents'. Freud regarded religious beliefs as evidence of a neurosis, and many psychiatrists, while perhaps rejecting Freud's theories, agree with him in this. Some psychiatrists, perhaps themselves Sunday Christians, feel that a belief in God, along with respect for the Queen or loyalty to the American flag, is part of the make-up of a decent person, and most patients are decent people. Inquiry into such matters is not necessary. In taking a history, the psychiatrist will inquire about the patient's sexual habits, but not about his religious beliefs. If a patient volunteers information about his religious beliefs, perhaps his agony over his separation from his God, or his terror that at any moment the force of Evil will defeat the force of Good, such information is treated as evidence of a symptom of depression or of psychosis and not as a belief as valid as the metaphysical beliefs of the psychiatrist. The psychiatrist may regard himself as an atheist, but as a practising scientist he must have one basic metaphysical belief, one he shares with those who believe in magic, astrology, or the mysteries of the occult – the belief that every event has a cause and that these causes form a regular, repeatable pattern.

The belief in the regularity of nature is to scientists what the belief in *karma*, rebirth, is to Hindus, and neither belief is capable of proof – or disproof. Danto, in his *Mysticism and Morality*, wrote:

It is a striking fact that karma is almost never defended or attacked in Indian philosophy. It is taken for granted. One of the fundamental presuppositions of Indian reflection, karma is accepted as a fact of nature, like the ebb and flow of the tides or the wheeling of the planets, except it would be difficult to find a natural fact that plays so profound a presuppositional role. Perhaps the belief in the regularity of nature in Western science would be a functional analogue, in the sense that it is difficult to formulate conditions under which we would give it up even if we could give it up, since it is exactly this belief that defined the conditions under which beliefs are given up in science. To help give it up, though it would be factual, would be like giving science up, and there is no scientific way of doing that. Like the concept of the uniformity of nature, the theory of karma becomes so intimately co-implicated with a wide class of practices which are perhaps co-extensive with the way of life that has evolved in India over the millennia.

The belief in the regularity of nature has the corollary that such regularities, or at least some of them, are discoverable, and actions based on these two beliefs have created much of the world we live in today. A second corollary is that a truer account of the regularities can be given by someone who stands outside and separate from the occurrence of the regularity than by someone who is part of it. The idea that an observer can be separate from what he observes, neither contaminating nor contaminated by the object of his observation, and thus obtain a closer approximation to the truth, whatever that may be, is an idea which has dominated the theory and practice of psychiatry. Nuclear physicists may describe the relationship between the behaviour of the particle and the behaviour of the observer, psychologists like Rosenthal may demonstrate the effect of the behaviour of the experimenter on the behaviour of the subject, but the standard textbook *Clinical Psychiatry* by Slater and Roth carries the injunction to the practising psychiatrist: 'It is even more important to know what the facts are than what the patient makes of them.'

31

But just what is a fact is always a problem. George Brown and his colleagues have accumulated many thousands of 'facts' about women who get depressed and women who do not get depressed. Brown's studies have demonstrated significant correlations between certain 'life events' and the presence or absence of depression. Such life events include the early death of the subject's mother, low self-esteem, and the absence of a confiding relationship. Neither the level of self-esteem nor the participation in a confiding relationship can be known by anyone but the subject herself. She can report 'I don't think much of myself' or 'I have no one I can really talk to', and she can lie, but there is no one who can challenge her on this lie. Only she knows the truth of her level of self-esteem, her closeness to other people. The observer can know the fact of her mother's death, but what he cannot know until she tells him is what this death means to her. One woman may rest secure in the belief that one day she will join her mother in heaven and in the meanwhile her loving mother watches over her as a beneficent guardian angel. Another woman may still harbour the guilt of having, in some mysterious way, caused the death of her mother; or she may still be angry and resentful that it was her mother who died and not someone else's mother; or she may fear that the illness that took her mother lies in wait for her. The holding of such beliefs does not promote happiness.

The founder of behaviourism, Watson, had determined that he would do away with the study of what goes on inside a person and instead concentrate on behaviour which can be seen by an outside observer. He and his followers set about the study of the effect of reward and punishment on behaviour and made some remarkable discoveries, which were written about and discussed without reference to the fact that behaviourism is, in essence, a theory of meaning. Whether a stimulus is a reward or a punishment depends on the meaning that the recipient, not the experimenter, gives it. Rats cannot tell us why they press levers and obtain food, but people can, if they wish, tell us why they persist in behaviour which to the outside observer appears unrewarding or why they fail to take advantage of rewards which the observer sees as rosy. Suffering can be construed as bringing merit and immediate pleasure a necessary precursor of future pain. The wise behaviourist takes time to find out something of the meaning of his subject's world, and he develops methods which aim at changing the meaning that his subject imposes on his world.

To understand another person we need to know that person's wishes, intentions, fears, and hopes. We feel that another person understands us when that person shows that he acknowledges our wishes, intentions, fears, and hopes, and, in doing so, he understands the decisions, the choices that we make. We do not feel understood when the other person assumes that his construction of his world is superior to the way we construe ours, when we are told: 'You behave like that because you're just like your father/you have a mental illness/an unresolved oedipal conflict/a low IQ/an inherited predisposition/ are a member of a certain class/race/nationality/sex/age.' Of course, it is much easier to explain another person's behaviour in terms of these categories than to search out and to strive to understand the often labyrinthine reasoning a person may use to arrive at a decision. The processes by which we make a choice are little understood and little studied, since the question of choice raises the question of freedom which conflicts with the strict determinism on which so much of psychology is based. To say that a person is free to choose not only undermines the determinism of psychology as a science, but it also renders uncertain our day-to-day world. If I know that you are always going to behave like your father, or like a schizophrenic, or like the person you were yesterday, then I can predict your behaviour and feel safe. How often do we hear one person say of another in tones of praise and affection, 'He's always the same'!

No one is always the same. Each of us is changing, evolving continuously. Yet something in us remains the same. I often quote to my students my teacher, Jack Lyle, at Sydney University, who would remark, 'The older we get, the more like ourselves we become'. There seems to be part of us that is constantly reinforced, constantly strengthened, not by what happens to us, but by how we interpret what happens to us. When we look back over our lives, when we chance upon essays, notes, diaries, letters we wrote in our youth, we are often amazed at the length of time we have held certain ideas, attitudes, opinions, and when we meditate upon events early in our childhood we can often find the event that crystalized such an idea. Then we can see in the story of our lives the events which reinforced such ideas in the overdetermining manner that Freud described.

When we examine such ideas we see that they have become rules, expectations, predictions about life in general. Whatever we experience we interpret in terms of these general rules and predictions, even though other interpretations would be equally valid. When I was a small child I became convinced that my life would turn out well, and although I have had much evidence to lead me to expect the contrary, I still hold to this belief. A lot of good things have happened to me. However, I have met many people whose lives have contained no more troubles and difficulties than mine has, yet such people are convinced that their lives have and always will be filled with pain and misery. Of these people, those who hold, like me, that individual life ends with death and we must, therefore, make the most of our lives, such people are wracked by the pain and anger of despair, jealousy, frustration, and a sense of waste. If we construe death as the end, it is a good idea to construe our lives as satisfactory. If, however, we see death as a doorway to another life, then suffering in this life may serve to improve our life in the next. Thus it is advantageous to construe many events as the source of suffering.

Constructions like this, how we see the progress of our life, how we see death and its implications, form what the personal construct theorists call 'superordinate constructs', the general rules on which all other personal constructs depend. The metaphor here is of pyramidal ladder. The metaphor I prefer is that of these general rules, predictions about life and death, being the diameters on which the person's world turns. (Of course, any spatial metaphor is limited and necessarily inaccurate. Inner space has more dimensions than outer space and relates to Aristotelian logic much in the way that the space of the physicists relates to Euclidian space.)

Such superordinate constructs, dimensions, form what William James defined as a religious belief, 'the belief that there is an unseen order, and that our supreme good lies in harmoniously adjusting ourselves thereto'. 'Buzz' Aldrin, the second astronaut on the moon, in a BBC interview about 'his long journey from the moon down to earth', said, 'My views towards a higher power have matured. I feel that what I felt to be the hypocrisy of my early religious teachings has given way to a more cosmic religious feeling, as Einstein calls it – a greater awareness of the spiritual laws that are available for each human being to take advantage of as he sees fit in a world of free choice. Just as there are physical laws that govern material objects, I feel that there are spiritual laws that govern the behaviour, the relationships between human beings, and that we can be in tune with these and harmonious with these laws and accepting of them, or we can be in opposition. And if we are in opposition to them we are generally not very happy.'

Those of us who lack all belief in God and heaven and suchlike still need to believe there is a pattern to the world and that we should strive to live in harmony with that pattern. (We can say, 'I believe that life is about helping other people' or 'It doesn't matter how hard you try, things never turn out right. I may as well give up trying.') Bertrand Russell who saw religion as 'a disease born of fear and as a source of untold misery to the human race' considered that 'the good life consists of love guided by knowledge', a moral code as demanding as any devised by religion.

Each of us, atheistic or theistic, sees some pattern in the relationship of life and death. As Alister Hardy and his colleagues have shown, many people can report some experience which brought intimations of a reality beyond the mundane, and even those whose attention is always focused on the immediate present and who are not given to metaphysical speculation will say when asked, 'There must be some reason for all this.' 'A reason for all this' is found in each religion, and in the history of the human race there is not one culture that has failed to produce a religion. It was once thought that the pygmies of the Ituri forest were deficient in this regard, but, as Mary Douglas reported of the work of the anthropologist Colin Turnbull, 'So little ritual do (the pygmies) perform that their first ethnographers assumed that they had, to all intents and purposes, no religion, no culture even, of their own . . . They

perform no cult for the dead, they reject the Bantu idea of sin.
. . . Their religion is one of internal feeling, not of external sign.
The moods of the forest manifest the moods of the deity, and the
forest can be humoured by the same means as the pygmies', by
song and dance. Their religion is not concerned with their
correct orientation within cosmic transgression, nor rules of
purity; it is concerned with joy. It is a religion of faith, not
works.' (There are a number of religions that could be improved
by an infusion of joy.)

The reason that each of us has to arrive at an explanation of life
and death is that none of us can live our life solely within
the confines of events which have a rational and practical
explanation. The inexplicable intrudes on us with an urgency
and awesomeness that cannot be denied. The inexplicable
demands a metaphysical explanation. Malinowski in his study of
the Trobriand Islanders contrasted the methods they used in
fishing in the lagoon and fishing in the open sea beyond the
coral reefs. The islanders were skilled boat builders and
knowledgeable about wind and water and the ways of the fish.
Their predictions would lead them to regular catches made in the
safety of the lagoon, but fishing in the open sea was a much
more chancy business. The organization of lagoon fishing was
accompanied by as much religious ceremony as is used in the
daily organization of the London underground. But it was
fishing in the open sea that needed prayers and gifts for the
gods. A farmer nowadays may not begin his spring ploughing
with religious ritual, but if a series of flood, hail, and fire ravages
his crops, he may well come to feel that there is someone up
there who does not like him, or even that he must accept the
punishment for the sins he has committed. Depression may be
for the psychiatrist a chance metabolic aberration, but for many
depressed people it is a punishment for past sins. Hence it
should not be relinquished until the sin has been expiated.

The inexplicable that first intrudes upon us is not an
awareness of the grandeur and mystery of the universe, but the
self-consciousness of our own puniness and vulnerability. When
we as children first experienced our own individuality we learnt
of our inevitable death. 'Why am I?' we asked, 'Why must I die?'
To preserve our individuality we look for some magical power

beyond us which, while it may not preserve us, at least invests our life with some meaning and purpose. We are more than just some chance grains of matter blown about in the endless desert of the universe. 'We always rely on something that transcends us', wrote Ernest Becker in his book *The Denial of Death*, 'some system of ideas and powers in which we are embedded and which supports us. The power is not always obvious. It need not be overtly a god or openly stronger person, but it can be the power of an all-absorbing activity, a passion, a way of life, that like a comfortable web keeps a person buoyed up and ignorant of himself, of the fact that he does not rest on his own center. All of us are driven to be supported in a self-forgetful way, ignorant of what energies we really draw on, of the kind of lie we have fashioned in order to live securely and serenely.'

The transcendent power that each of us identifies need not be a God, a religion. The power may be seen to lie in the idea of permanent revolution, or in art for art's sake. Proust saw literature as providing the meaning and purpose of life. Janie Fricke's popular song *I Believe in You* is a hymn, not to Jesus Christ but to her lover. This song describes the transcendent power that many people in our culture place on romantic love. The passionate commitment that some people have to sport reveals not merely an enjoyment of exercise and competition but a belief in an ideal beyond the immediate and the real. Whatever transcendent power we see as supporting us, be it God, Allah, the Tao, the celestial influences, art, science, humanity, love, sport, we create a story, a myth, in which to incorporate this power. Myth-making, according to Ernst Cassirer, is one of the basic organs or tools by which we structure our world. Some of us know that our particular myth is no more than 'a comfortable web' that buoys us up in this formless chaos of reality. Some of us do not know this, and see, instead, our myth as absolute reality. But whether we see our myth as real or as a construction, we draw from our myth the rules by which we live our lives. We are, as Dr Johnson said, 'perpetually moralists'. We are always part of the myth that we have created.

III. Models of Human Beings

We are born into this world carrying with us a model-making kit, a kit capable of creating an infinite variety of models. One of the earliest models we make is of a reappearing object which we later come to call 'mother' or variants of that word. Then we develop another model which relates to the mother-model and to other objects. This is a person-model, as distinct from a dog-model or a chair-model or any of the other models we create with remarkable rapidity. As we get older we change our person-model as we draw conclusions from our experience of people. Our person-model becomes a very important part of our construction of our world, since we are constantly in the business of trying to make sense of what other people are doing.

It is often hard to understand why people behave as they do. If our car refuses to start we can peer at the engine, and, if we have a good enough model of a car in our head, the reason for the car's behaviour is there to be seen. But we cannot peer into other people's heads, and so we have to keep making up hypotheses about why people behave as they do. The source of our hypotheses is the model we have of a person. We say, 'She did that because she is so generous and forgiving' or 'He's a chip off the old block' or 'What can you expect of a person with an IQ of only ninety-six?'

Everyone has his own model of a person, and it would probably be safe to say that no two models are exactly alike. It would be very difficult to get universal agreement even on any aspects of the models, except, perhaps, that we would all agree that nobody is perfect. Everybody shows a mixture of good and bad behaviour. We are always quick to find the flaws in those people who appear to be approaching sainthood, and even the greatest villains of history are reputed to have shown some acts of kindness and affection. So, whatever model we make of a person, we have to explain this mixture of goodness and badness.

It is extremely rare for a person to display what we might call equal quantities of goodness and badness. From our personal vantage point our world divides into goodies and baddies. When we were small children we knew the nice teachers and the nasty

38

ones, who were our friends and who were our enemies. Only our parents presented us with a confusing mixture of good and bad, a necessary preparation for the confusions of right and wrong in adult life. Life is much simpler when the goodies and baddies are clearly defined. Those of us old enough to remember the Second World War can look back nostalgically to the days when the British Empire, the United States, and the USSR were good and Germany, Italy, and Japan were bad. Life was never to be as simple again.

That people never display equal and invariable amounts of goodness and badness leaves us with only two basic hypotheses. We can say that a person is born good but can be corrupted, or we can say that a person is born bad but can acquire goodness. If we use a model of essential goodness, if we see the baby coming into the world 'trailing clouds of glory', then we can deplore the effects of the world as the 'shades of the prison-house begin to close upon the growing boy', but we can hope that such essential goodness can be brought forth, led out, as our word 'education' implies by its derivation. If, on the other hand, we use a model of essential badness ('born in sin'), then we can see the effects of the world as increasing or controlling or eradicating this badness. Hope lies in expiation, redemption, and salvation.

Whichever model we use we reveal it in the kind of statements we make about our expectations of other people. Sir Melford Stevenson, a judge renowned for the severity of his judgements, said in a BBC interview 'I have no doubt that the softening of the penal system towards the young offender has done infinite harm. I know that "do-gooders" is a term of abuse, but they exist. They are dedicated people and they are very good people, and most of them start their work with the sincere conviction that they have a gift for work among boys and so they have, and mostly it works out quite well; but they also suffer from the illusion that a high proportion of people are capable of redemption and I don't think it is so.' By contrast, Arthur Scargill, the Yorkshire miners' leader, told his BBC interviewer, 'I'm a Christian and I've also got faith not only in my belief as a socialist but a tremendous belief in human beings, and I know that we can produce a society where man will not simply go to work and have a little leisure, but will release his latent talent and ability and begin to produce in the cultural sense all the things I know he's capable of: music, poetry, writing, sculpture, whole works of art that, at the moment, are literally lying dormant simply because we, as a society, are not able to tap it.' Arthur Scargill, like Abraham Maslow, believes in the possibility of the person 'actualizing his potential' and one's 'full Humanness'.

Whether we hold a model of the essential goodness or the essential badness of mankind we have to decide whether our model allows for improvement. Can a person become a better person – approach, and perhaps achieve, perfection? Can the human race, or certain sections of it, achieve progress? Not everyone answers 'yes' to these questions. 'Human nature never changes' is a commonplace, while many observers of history would support Talleyrand's 'Plus ça change, plus c'est la meme chose'. Gibbon saw the causes of the decline and fall of the Roman Empire as essentially human weakness and depravity. The rise and fall of great civilizations would continue, he believed, since human nature does not change. The ancient Greeks saw neither men nor gods as perfectable. The gods, as described by Homer and Hesiod, would deceive, steal, and commit adultery. Their intervention in the lives of men and women, for good and all, is the core of Greek tragedy. Capricious though the gods may be, there was one sin they would not forgive and that was hubris, spiritual pride, the seeking of self-sufficiency or perfect happiness. There are many people today who believe that to seek happiness is to invite disaster. There are others who believe, like Calvin, that their lives, their salvation or damnation, are predestined. Mary Gordon wrote of one of her characters: 'His belief in fate . . . was the morose faith of a primitive or a desert father: there was no need to act, actions would not change things and could conceivably harm the direct flow of the preordained.' A belief in 'the direct flow of the preordained' can lead to a person not seeking therapy or not being offered therapy.

If our model of a person allows for improvement we then have to decide whether this improvement can come about through the person's own efforts or through some outside agency. Institutions like psychiatry and the Christian Church are divided on this issue. Psychotherapy, whatever form it takes, is based on the idea of helping the patient to discover his own power to help himself, while in chemotherapy, electroconvulsive therapy, and psychosurgery the power to cure lies in the hands of the psychiatrists. The Christian is charged 'Be ye therefore perfect, even as your Father which is in heaven is perfect', but to achieve perfection we should 'Trust in the Lord with all thine heart: and lean not unto thine own understanding'. St Augustine argued that perfection could be achieved only by loving God with one's whole heart and soul, and since the Fall man has been incapable of doing this as his will is corrupted by original sin. The Christian, therefore, is dependent upon the grace of God. Pelagius argued against the idea of original sin and claimed that man could rely on his own efforts, with God's guidance, to achieve perfection. Pelagianism was condemned by the Council of Carthage in 417, and from then on it was Roman Catholic doctrine that men could not perfect themselves without special grace from God. The Protestant movement challenged the view that salvation lies in the external power of the grace of God. St Paul had written, 'If thou shalt confess with thy mouth the Lord Jesus, and shalt believe in thine heart that God hath raised him from the dead, thou shalt be saved', and so Luther argued for justification by faith and Wesley for acceptance of free grace. William James pointed out the similarity between the mind-cure movement (now called psychotherapy) and the Lutheran and Wesleyan movement. 'To the believer in moralism and works with his anxious query, "What shall I do to be saved?" Luther and Wesley replied, "You are saved now, if you would believe it." And the mind-curers come with precisely the same words of emancipation . . . "Give up the feeling of responsibility, let go your hold, resign the care of your destiny to higher powers, be genuinely indifferent as to what becomes of it all, and you will find not only that you gain a perfect inward relief, but often also, in addition, the particular goods you sincerely thought you were renouncing." This is salvation through self-despair, the dying to be truly born.' Relax and be successful, say the psychotherapists.

The idea of progress, a society's movement along a line of gradual improvement, is comparatively new in world history. 'There was nothing in the heritage of antiquity', wrote Sidney

Pollard, 'to support the idea of evolution and progress. Experience did not encourage the belief in an upward movement, while mythology rather suggested a decline from a golden age . . . In the world of the classical pagan, man's striving must be individual and internalized, he must solve the problem of living and dying for himself, rather than as a member of a growing, hopeful body of humanity. That society could be 'a growing, hopeful body of humanity' was generally an unthought idea until the seventeenth century when adventurous men could break out of the roles imposed by a now changing society and seize the chance to make their own fortunes. The waves of unrest in Europe sent adventurers to the New World and with them went the belief that man had within him the power of self-improvement and the hope that life was capable of infinite improvement. Such ideas were handed down from one generation of Americans to another, and now the differences in the American and the European models of man and society are reflected in the differences between American and European interpretation of the theories of psychoanalysis and existentialism. Freud saw man as essentially bad, and his life as a conflict between the demands of his id and the demands of society. Psychoanalysis could benefit man by turning uncomprehending neurosis into common unhappiness, but man and society were, in the end, doomed. Such pessimism is certainly not shared by all American psychoanalysts, while the great men of psychotherapy, Fromm, Rogers, Maslow, and May, have at the core of their theories a model of the self that is essentially good. Neither do American existentialists and phenomenologists share the resignation of their European counterparts. William Barrett told the story of how 'Sartre recounts a conversation he had with an American visiting this country. The American insisted that all international problems could be solved if men would just get together and be rational; Sartre disagreed and after a while discussion became impossible. "I believe in the existence of evil," says Sartre, "and he does not."' The American phenomenologist Peter Koestenbaum wrote, 'Evil can and should be totally eliminated from the world, because evil does not possess the solidity and permanence of good. Evil is not as entrenched in the structure of being as is good. The proper attitude, therefore, toward evil is to struggle for its total elimination.'

When we construct our model of a human being, intrinsically good or bad, perfectable or incorrigible, we distinguish it from other models and we create sub-groups within our model. Human beings, we can decide, are different from animals. Animals have no souls, or do not feel pain in the way we do (hence it does not matter what we do to them). We can ignore Darwin and, like Ian Paisley, cry, 'I believe that God created man; as the Book of Genesis said He created man. I object to teachers saying that we came from monkeys. Now I absolutely object to that!' We can see races other than our own as being less than human or filled with all manner of vices while we are virtuous. Or else we can claim that 'suffering is the badge of all our tribe'. Working-class patients, I find, see their West Indian or Pakistani neighbours as having an easy life, while my middle-class patients often claim that 'working-class people don't feel things the way we do'. The activities of the Women's Movement have brought into clear relief the different models men and women have of the sexes and what little understanding there is between the sexes. Nowadays we pay a lot of attention to children and develop models of childhood. By contrast, Philippe Aries tells us 'in medieval society the idea of childhood did not exist . . . Nobody thought, as we ordinarily think today, that every child already contained a man's personality. Too many of them died.'

When we construct our model of the person and draw its demarcation lines we do not simply draw a graph on the dimensions of good-bad and perfectability – incorrigibility. We are much more creative than that. We create an image, a metaphor. Sometimes we spell this image out; sometimes it is simply implicit in what we say and do. Psychologists usually make their metaphors clear. Man can be seen as a puppet on the strings of metabolic changes or of intrapsychic forces or of S–R connections. Such metaphors describe the person as passive, a necessary outcome of determining causes, and as such are metaphors which power-holders like psychologists and psychiatrists prefer to apply to other people rather than to themselves. Then there are the active metaphors, Kelly's 'man-the-scientist', Mead's 'the self', Shotter's 'the self-defining agent'. Such models are made by people who can cope with the ideas of indeterminacy and ambiguity.

My model is, of course, of a model-maker. While I admit that there is much evidence to the contrary, I believe that people are basically good. I like this belief since it gives me hope and stops me from being frightened of other people. Badness I see not as evil but as stupidity. (It should be remembered that a high IQ is not a contra-indication of stupidity.) However, in the long run it seems that the effects of stupidity are indistinguishable from the effects of evil.

I find that whenever I make a mistake, whenever I do something, or fail to do something, which makes me feel ashamed or guilty or angry with myself I chide myself with words like 'You fool, what a stupid thing to do.' The evil we perceive inside us can take many forms, and to understand another person we need to discover the metaphor by which the person knows himself. Peter, a client of mine much troubled by violent rages and abysmal despair, once said, 'If I could construct a model of me, inside it would be something in the form of a bucket which was full of broken glass which was being rattled about rather violently, and bits fly off and this is highly dangerous. And somehow that should be organized into something which has system and pattern and symmetry, but I'm not sure how to organize it and I'm not sure what the symmetry and pattern ought to be.'

IV. The Purpose of Life and the Nature of Death

Our model of the person, our model of ourselves, does not exist in isolation. Our model is always set in a landscape, the landscape of the world that we have constructed. A curious paradox of human life is that while we can actually live in the present, we give meaning to the present in terms of our past and our future. 'I am what I am,' we say, 'because of what has happened in the past, and I do what I do now because of what will happen in the future.' The causes of our actions lie in our

44

past and the intentions of our actions lie in our future. Thus the world we each construct encompasses not just the immediate present but also a past and a future.

We can find our past intriguing and often ponder on it, but it is our future that engages most of our attention. 'What have I got to do at work today?' we ask ourselves on waking. 'Where'll I go for my holidays this year?' we say, reading January's newspapers. We react with joy to something that engages our interest as a possible goal. The greatest misery is to be without a goal, to see no purpose in living. We create goals, make decisions like 'I must lose some weight/scrub the kitchen/visit Aunt Milly' even though we know that some activities are trivial and Aunt Milly does not like visitors. By setting such goals and working towards them we know that we are fulfilling some part of the purpose we have given to life. *We know that life must have a purpose because life is finite. If there was not death, if life was infinite, we would need no purpose. We could do this, and then that, and then some other thing. There would be no rush to get things done, no need to work in order to eat. We would not have to think about the future; we could live entirely in the present. But death exists, and it is death that fixes our attention on the future.*

Knowledge of death comes to us early in our lives. A child cannot avoid the question of death, since it is necessary to fear death in order to learn how to survive. Without the terror of death, Hume argued, mankind itself would not have survived. Sylvia Anthony, in her book *The Discovery of Death in Childhood and After*, showed how early in life the child encounters death and how he tries to deal with that knowledge, not just the knowledge that all things die but with the knowledge that 'I shall die'. Piaget considered that the child's encounter with death plays a special part in his intellectual development since it arouses the child's curiosity. Death needs a special explanation.

The specialness of the event of death is marked by the special acts that the survivors carry out, the 'funerary rites' as they are called. In all cultures it is a most shameful thing to throw dead bodies away as though they were rubbish or to treat them with disrespect. President Carter chided the Iranians for displaying as trophies the bodies of the American soldiers killed in their attempt to rescue the American hostages. The specialness of death was known even to the hominids, the Neanderthal men who carried out funerary rites, as did our early ancestors, the Cro-Magnon men who, for thousands of years, sprinkled red ochre on the bodies of their dead relatives as a symbol, perhaps, of eternal life.

Primitive men, so anthropologists tell us, believe neither in the inevitability of death nor in its finality. 'Death,' wrote Jacques Choron, 'is the result of the action or malign influence of an enemy in either human or spiritual form; one can be killed, or magic can induce a deadly sickness. But for these hostile acts, no one would ever die. The various myths about the origin of death found among the primitive bear out the conclusion that during the long prehistory of the race, death was not considered a necessary attribute of the human condition. Man was believed to have been created deathless. Death came into the world because of the mistake made by the messenger bearing the gift of deathlessness, who either garbled the message out of forgetfulness or malice or did not arrive on time.' The primitive blamed the gods for death; the Old Testament blames man. God warned Adam, 'But the tree of knowledge of good and evil, thou shalt not eat of it: for in the day thou eatest thereof thou shalt die.' But Adam ate the fruit of the tree of knowledge and so brought death into the world. St Paul taught that 'as by one man sin entered the world, and death by sin; and so death passed upon all men, for that all have sinned' and that the Christian message of hope is 'the wages of sin is death; but the gift of God is eternal life through Jesus Christ our Lord'. This, too, was the teaching of St Augustine and of Luther and Calvin, and thus is a basic assumption of both the Protestant and Catholic Churches.

However, whether death was brought by the gods or by man, for primitive and ancient peoples, life did not end in death but continued in some form or other. As Ernst Cassirer wrote, 'While of the level of thought, of metaphysics, the mind must seek proofs for the survival of the soul after death, the contrary relation prevails in the beginning of human culture. It is not immortality but mortality that must here be proved.' At our stage of culture we may think that the opposite obtains, that it is immortality, not mortality, that has to be proved. Yet even those of us who reject all beliefs in immortality have to agree with

46

Freud that the annihilation of one's own identity is unimaginable. We see the world going on without us, and in our imagination we experience ourselves as observing the world going on without us. Some people commit suicide so as to observe the remorse of their loved ones, while others, believing that death is the final end which will obliterate their suffering and release them from all duties, are tacitly aware that there must be something of oneself still existing to know the bliss of the end of pain. Simone de Beauvoir wrote of her death, 'I may try to come closer to it by fantasies, by imagining my corpse and the funeral ceremonies. I may meditate upon my absence; but it is still I who meditate.'

It is, indeed, difficult to conceive of one's own death. Many people would rather not contemplate the subject, preferring, as Pascal said, to 'run toward the precipice, after we have put something before our eyes in order not to see it'. Some people say that they never think of death; others like Freud, say they think of it every day. But thinking of it or not, we all know that death, that most uncertain certainty, lies in wait for us. Not knowing when our death will come gives urgency to the question of what we should do with our lives, but to answer this question we have to decide whether death is the end or whether it is a doorway to another life. Some of us are quite sure which it is, and some of us have doubts, but even the doubters can say on which of the two possibilities they would place their bets. Sometimes the choice is made through following the voice of authority; sometimes the choice follows personal preferences of life styles. Some people feel that 'there must be a reason for all this', 'life must go on somewhere else'. Other people long to join loved ones or are appalled at the thought of having to share eternity with 'all those dreadful people'. Some people cannot countenance the personal insult of their identity being wiped out while others long for the bliss of eternal rest. Whatever we imagine, if we are asked, 'Does life end in death?', we can all give an answer.

Early in life we ask ourselves this question, and when we have answered we know, albeit in a vague and confused way, the meaning and purpose of our life. The conclusions we come to do not necessarily fill us with joy, since not all of us can agree with

Socrates that: 'We may well hope that death is good, since it is either dreamless sleep or the migration of the soul from one world to another.' The meaning we give to death, our personal death, can fill us with satisfaction or with pain and terror.

If we see our life as ending in death then we interpret our life as, in the popular phrase, 'the real thing, not a rehearsal for something else'. If we are to live comfortably with ourselves and not be overwhelmed by bitterness and regret at the prospect of our death we have to devise a purpose to our lives which has a good chance of being fulfilled. We need to feel some success and satisfaction, to know that we have not wasted our lives. The question is, what success shall we seek?

For some people success means the acquisition of worldly goods. Of course some people find great pleasure in their possessions. They look with pride on their fine homes and take care to provide for their children things which they themselves never had. But such possessions have to be bought with hard work. One cannot take personal pride in inheriting money one has never earned, and so to see our lives as successful in terms of the acquisition of money, land, buildings, and objects, we have to work hard. In doing so we are in danger, as Seneca said, of spending 'life in making preparation for life'. Moreover, whatever we buy, we can always see something else that we could purchase, and we may envy those who possess the things we desire and cannot afford. Envious of others or not, we become the object of envy, and so we can find ourselves the prisoners of our success, locked away from predators. Suburban homes, like the homes of Paul Getty and the Los Angeles rich, can become lonely fortresses. And no matter how much we acquire, we are constantly reminded that 'you can't take it with you'.

We might, instead, decide to devote our lives to the pursuit of pleasure. But the pleasures of fine food and drink, beautiful clothes, unlimited sex, travel, and entertainment are expensive, and so the effort we spend in acquiring the money to buy our pleasures may rob us of the time and energy to enjoy them. We may eschew the expensive pleasures and instead resolve to lead a simple, non-working life. But eating is a necessary condition of life, and society has never treated well those who will not work (except, of course, those groups of people who have been able to persuade their neighbours that their mere existence is necessary to the stability of society. Today we are less ready to accept this idea, and so we are often assured that our Royal family works very hard).

A hedonistic life, however expertly managed, tends to pall, and the hedonist is left with a sense of failure. Some people, rather than risk failure to achieve their goals, affect to despise life, to agree with Sophocles that 'it is best of all never to have been born, and second-best – second by far – if one has made his appearance in this world, to go back again, as quickly as may be, thither he has come'. Not all pessimists commit suicide. They prefer instead to expect little of life and, while denying themselves the joy of anticipation, they protect themselves from the pain of disappointment. They merely become grey people in a grey world.

We may not believe in our continued existence after death but we may still believe with Samuel Butler that 'To die completely, a person must not only forget, but be forgotten, and he who is not forgotten is not dead.' How better to be remembered, and thus not to die, than through one's descendants. When Yahweh wished to bless Abraham He did not promise him personal immortality but rather: 'I will make of thee a great nation, and I will bless thee, and make thy name great.' Many cultures, like the Hindu and the pre-revolutionary Chinese, made the commemoration and veneration of ancestors the centre of their religious practices. Old age in our society is not honoured, but many people still see the creation and rearing of their children as the central core of their lives. This is not simply parental affection. Such parents can describe how they see their children as a thread which weaves them into the warp and woof of life, a thread without which the person would see himself as drifting aimlessly with no more significance than a puff of thistledown. This is the reason why some unmarried or childless people are so envious of those with children and why people stay in the kind of marriage which others would flee from in haste. Many children benefit from parents who see their salvation in their child, but equally many children suffer from parents who demand that the child be precisely what the parent wants him to

49

be. After all, if we are going to be remembered by our children we want them to be a credit to us.

Not relying on our children to remember us, we can aim to become famous, 'to leave,' as Samuel Beckett said, 'some stain upon the silence'. I had not realized how many people believed in the immortality of fame until my first book was published, and so many friends and acquaintances remarked on their pleasure, their envy even, that I had achieved a permanent niche in this vast and shifting universe. I could not share their view. When I consider the millions of books that have been written and will be written, it seems to me nothing but a foolish enterprise to swell their number by a minute one or two, and I would not bother were not writing an enjoyable enterprise for me. But many people do believe that the purpose of life is to create some memento, or to ensure that one's name is inscribed in the history books or even just a newspaper. For some people notoriety serves the same purpose as fame. Many criminals begin and continue their criminal activities, despite the best efforts of society to punish and to reform them, since to live unnoticed is to die. But people's memories are short, and even those dead whose stories are still told in the various historical forms that we enjoy must have been in life very different from the way in which they are remembered. We may look to fame to give us a purpose in life and to overcome our fear of death, but all the time we know, as Simone de Beauvoir said of personal fame, 'if you love life immortality is no consolation for death'.

Seeking personal fame is a selfish enterprise, and so many people seek to leave an imprint on the world through the good that they do for others. Those people who wished to leave the world a better place than they found it have been the ones who have turned at least our culture from a life which is 'nasty, brutish, and short' to one where concern and tolerance for others are seen as necessary strengths rather than foolish weaknesses. There is so much pain and suffering around us that to help to reduce these evils can make us feel that our life has been worth while, but if we see helping others as the sole reason for our existence we are bereft when life leaves us with no one we feel we can help. To survive, we may need to create suffering in order to relieve it. Such an attitude may be the mainspring of the actions of people like the 'interfering mother-in-law'. We can rejoice that good can come out of evil, that disasters like the Second World War meant that for the first time in history all English children were adequately fed, but the fact that good can come out of evil cannot in the end justify evil or recompense the sufferers of that evil. The minister conducting the mass burial in Manchester of the people killed in the 1980 plane crash at Las Palmas spoke of good coming out of evil, of these people's deaths leading to improvements in air safety. This may have brought comfort to onlookers but not to the mourners whose family life had been rent and destroyed. When my father left for France in 1916 he was told in a farewell speech by one of the town's dignitaries that there was nothing nobler a young man could do than to lay down his life for his country. This, my father later told me, was not an ambition that appealed to him, and he worked hard in France at keeping himself alive. Many of his companions were not as successful as he. The Australian war cemetery at Villers-Bretoneux consists of rows of tiny headstones and one large marble slab on which is carved 'They will be remembered forever'. This is a lie, a lie which is used to justify the evil of war.

If we hold life dear, expecting that it is all that we are going to have, we can try to make the most of it by prolonging it. We look after ourselves, we take care of other people, we support schemes to promote public health. Such efforts have certainly improved the quality of life and enabled people to live happier and fuller lives. But while more of us live longer, the upper limit of life expectation has not increased, and so eternal life on earth or even a race of Methuselahs are goals unlikely to be reached. That a great many of us currently alive should live to old age will be, so economists tell us, not a blessing but a disaster, since the country's economy will not be sufficient to support us adequately. For many people old age is as much to be feared as death, and so some people try to prolong not just life but youth. But there is no plastic surgery for an ageing mind and, as Somerset Maugham found, hormone injections do not ward off senility. The last desperate hope of those who want to live forever is cryonics, the freezing of the dead body in the hope that it can be unfrozen when, at some future date, a cure for the illness that caused the death has been found. When it comes to death, some people are prepared to believe anything, and on such credulity salesmen grow rich.

If we see life as ending in death we have then set ourselves the task of making something satisfactory out of our lives. Mere pleasure is fleeting and pessimism is boring. We may seek to continue our existence through the memories of others – those who read our tombstone or our books, who tell our story or recall our courage and good works. For many of us this is entirely satisfying and we do not ponder upon the possibility that the sun may grow cold and all memories fade away. But before the cooling of the sun we may wipe ourselves out with nuclear destruction, and then we shall all be well and truly forgotten, for there will be no one left to remember the world as it was. Such a thought is too dreadful for many people to contemplate. It is not surprising that more and more people are bringing reports of a life after death, and that people like Elizabeth Kubler-Ross, who started out writing about death as the great unknown that we must face with courage, no longer just praise courage in the face of uncertainty but seek to comfort us with the promise of eternal life.

The belief in a life after death, while it brings great comfort to many people, does not resolve all difficulties and remove all fear. Many of us ask with Hamlet, 'For in that sleep of death what dreams may come', and agree with Achilles that it is better to be a slave on earth than a king in the realm of phantoms. For immortality to be satisfactory it must be personal and pleasant. Thus we can conceive of heaven as a beautiful place where we shall be reunited with our loved ones, where the inequalities of the world are met with justice, and where 'God shall wipe away all tears from their eyes; and there shall be no more death, neither sorrow, nor crying, neither shall there be any more pain: for the former things have passed away.'

It would not be fair if heaven were to open to all comers, irrespective of the lives they have lived. So a belief in heaven necessitates a belief in some sort of judgement. 'In ancient Egypt' wrote Marina Warner, 'where it was believed that Osiris ruled in the judgement of the dead, and that each man at his death was brought before him and his heart weighed in the scales held by the god Anubis, Maat, goddess of truth and justice, or her ideogram, the feather, was placed in the scales' other pan, and if the dishes balanced Osiris spoke: "Let the deceased depart victorious. Let him go wherever he wishes to mingle freely with the gods and the spirits of the dead". If the man's heart were light in the balance, Ahemait, the "Devourer", part lion, part crocodile, swallowed him up'. The capricious Greek gods might wreak a tragic vengeance on those who offended them, while those the gods favoured were transported to the Elysian fields. The portals of Valhalla open only for warriors of outstanding courage, while for the Christian 'the dead, small and great, stand before God; and the books were opened; and yet another book was opened, which is the book of life; and the dead were judged out of those things which were written in the books according to their works . . . And whosoever was not found written in the book of life was cast into the lake of fire.' 'God,' said Billy Graham, 'is a God of judgement, a God of wrath.' A belief in heaven implies a belief not only in some kind of judgement but also in some kind of punishment. 'Hell,' wrote convent-educated Marina Warner, 'is burned into the brain of every Catholic child.' Jesus had warned the ungodly, 'Depart from me, ye cursed, into everlasting fire, prepared for the devil and his angels.' However kindly and forgiving our God may appear to us, as Arnold Toynbee said, 'The price of a human being's belief in the survival of his personality after his death is anxiety during his lifetime.'

St Paul had preached, 'Behold, I shew you a mystery; we shall not all sleep, but we shall be changed. In a moment, in the twinkling of an eye, at the last trump: for the trumpet shall sound, and the dead shall be raised incorruptible and we shall be changed.' The novelty of his message was that of bodily resurrection. His Greek listeners, with their knowledge of the Orphic mysteries and the metaphysics of the early philosophers and of Socrates and Plato, would have been quite familiar with the idea of the soul surviving the death of the body. Such a state of affairs is easy to imagine, and so it is not surprising that many people believe in the existence of bodiless spirits. The leading Cambridge philosopher at the turn of the century, J. M. E. McTaggart, argued that, 'The self's eternal existence, which appears as enduring throughout all time, implies pre-existence no less than post-existence. The self must have existed before the event appearing as the birth of its present body, and it will exist after what will appear as the death of this body. Now that which appears, *sub specie temporis*, as our present life is probably very short as compared with our life future and past. And this longer stretch of life is probably divided into many lives of which each is terminated by events that appear as births and deaths of different bodies. Even were the memory of each life beyond recall in each later one, this would not destroy the self's identity. Memory is not lost, it is dormant.'

Just how these spirits come into being and then function are questions which have provoked a variety of answers. In some cultures the spirits of the dead are treated with more concern and ceremony than are living people, since the spirits are seen as having the power to interfere in daily life and to intercede with the gods. Many Christians believe in ghosts, and many pray for the intercession of the Virgin Mary and the Saints. In some cultures the spirits of the dead are believed to be reincarnated, a grandfather returning to life in the body of his grandson. However, reincarnation need not be a family affair. The Hindu may hope, and indeed believe, that the members of his family are with him in each reincarnation, but essentially rebirth is seen, as Danto describes, as the re-embodiment of a self following its latest death. Such a re-embodiment is automatic and routine, and proceeds without a recording angel or a Judgement Day, when the soul must contemplate its sins. Rather, under the universal influence of *karma*, the life the believer gains at each birth is precisely and automatically determined by the choices he made in his previous life, but he can by right living affect his lives that are yet to come.

If the believer in *karma* and reincarnation sees his present life as successful then he can rejoice in the wisdom of the choices he made in an earlier life. Tony Benn, writing in *The Guardian* about his mother, Lady Stansgate, told the story of how she met the industrialist Henry Ford:

Mr Ford discoursed on the subject of his own personal authority with such a degree of emotional satisfaction that my mother felt sure it must be rooted in something more than an individualistic view of economics. Shooting a bow at a venture, she was moved to ask him if he believed in reincarnation. 'Yes, ma'am,' he replied his eyes lighting up, 'I do! I believe I've been on this earth millions and millions of times before!' And then he went on to imply that his position of wealth and power over others in the present derived from his achievements in earlier lives of his own. When my mother later asked his personal aide if Mr Ford was a student of eastern philosophy he replied with considerable emphasis: 'I have never known Mr Ford to be a student of anything but his own ideas.'

Not all believers in karma and reincarnation share Henry Ford's confidence. For those believers whose life goes badly, such misfortune can appear as punishment for misdeeds in a past life, and to refuse to accept such punishment is to ensure an even worse life after one's next death. The person who construes his depression as an expiation of sins in an earlier life will resist having his punishment taken away from him (as will the person who believes that the more he suffers in this world, the greater his bliss in heaven). Elizabeth, who was very much a recluse, told me: 'The bad days when I feel ill is when I feel that for some reason I've been harmful to others. Then I withdraw and feel ill and can't cope . . . Either in some past life or in this present life, either we are trying to atone for what we did or what we are doing now, and we are not aware of it . . . I can see reincarnation – I don't understand it – but I can see some life process where a being must return until it reaches a state of perfection, that one is learning lessons as one goes along – almost like the development of the foetus and so on – and just as one does not have the knowledge as a foetus, perhaps it's progress like that, and it's a circular thing. I can see that much more easily than I can see this gang waiting up there to receive me.' Elizabeth and her sister had been to a service at a Mormon church. 'We found it delightful that people could be so firm in their knowledge and have such faith that things were going to turn out all right. We gazed at each other in wonder as we said, "Why don't we believe like that?" and then we jokingly said, "We didn't get it right the first time. Obviously we're too thick, too stupid. Perhaps we have to keep coming back until someone actually hammers home the message that's trying to come across. And whether it's religious." I suppose the other thing that made us decide that it (reincarnation) had to go on was that it all seems to be such a waste. We could see why some people were born – they have a value – but if one looks at one's own life, it's valueless. There seems to be no point in having been born, if you're just going to die anyway, if you haven't accomplished anything whilst you're living. It's a waste of time and space, and so therefore we argue there must be something else – it's illogical that it should just end in death.'

A belief in reincarnation can be part of the belief that death, the final death, is a merging with the great Cosmic Whole. Hindus hope for *moksha*, release from karma, and Buddhists for the cessation of desire and entry into Nirvana. Buddha said:

> There is a condition wherein there is neither earth, nor water, nor fire, nor air, nor the sphere of infinite space, nor the sphere of infinite consciousness, nor the sphere of the void, nor the sphere of neither perception nor non-perception: where there is no 'this world' and no 'world beyond': where there is no moon and no sun. That condition do I call neither a coming nor a going nor a standing still nor a falling away nor a rising up: but it is without fixity, without mobility, without basis. THAT IS THE END OF WOE.

Preceded by one life or many, death can be seen as a merging with Nothingness, a kind of continued existence as an indistinguishable part of a great whole. The idea of Nothingness can be viewed in a number of ways. William Barrett wrote:

> Human moods and reactions to the encounter with Nothingness vary considerably from person to person and from culture to culture. The Chinese Taoists found the Great Void tranquilizing, peaceful, even joyful. For the Buddhists in India, the idea of Nothing evoked a mood of universal compassion for all creatures caught in the toils of an existence that is ultimately groundless. In the

traditional culture of Japan the idea of Nothingness pervades the exquisite modes of aesthetic feeling displayed in painting, architecture, and even ceremonial rituals of daily life. But Western man, up to his neck in things, objects, and the business of mastering them, recoils with anxiety from any possible encounter with Nothingness and labels talk of it as 'negative' – which is to say, morally reprehensible.

Not all Western men have rejected the idea of Nothingness. Bruno, and Spinoza especially, had much in common with Eastern thinkers, while the nineteenth century Romantic poets made much, perhaps too much, of death and nature. For Herman Hesse, 'To die is to go into the Collective Unconscious, to lose oneself in order to be transformed into form, pure form.' For myself, I share the attitude of the Sceptical Taoists who saw the continued existence of the individual soul as likely as the continued existence of the sharpness of a knife after the steel has crumbled. I believe that when I die all of me will blend into the cosmos. When I look at the trees and the grass, the flowers and the birds, rivers and mountains, animals and people, I find this belief most pleasant and satisfying. But no doubt Madame de Stael was right when she wrote in criticism of the Romantic poets: 'That the individual in us disappears, that the inner qualities which we possess, return to the Great Whole of eternal creation, this kind of immortality has a frightening similarity to death; because physical death is nothing else than the universal taking back from the individual the gifts which it lent to him.'

When one conceives of death as an imperceptible blending with the Great Void, or a rising on Judgement Day of a pristine version of oneself, or a return to earth in another shape, such beliefs imply a belief in some form of reality different from the one we ordinarily observe. Such a reality is the realm of magic, and no amount of science and progress will make us give up our fascination with magic. Indeed, Colin Wilson argues that the present resurgence of interest in the occult 'is a reaction against the worst absurdities of modern science, its insistence that the universe is meaningless and purposeless, that evolution is a matter of chance, that man must be judged purely as an animal –

worse still, as a bundle of mechanical reflexes'. Whether this increase of interest in magic in its many forms is a criticism of the scientific attitude or whether it is what it has always been, an attempt to increase our power over the universe, to predict our future and perhaps influence it, there is no doubt that many people believe in magic in some form or other – horoscopes, the Tarot, the I Ching, if not telepathy, telekinesis, ouija boards, and witchcraft. We are all in the business of prediction every minute of our working day ('If I finish writing this book, will anyone read it?', 'If I put on a sweater, shall I feel warmer?'). We can look to our immediate reality to guide our prediction ('The publishers must think so', 'I usually feel warmer when I put a sweater on') or we can infer that there are forces beyond immediate reality that influence the outcome of events ('My stars predict a good year', 'There's an evil spirit in this room, so I'll be cold no matter what I put on'). Such forces are usually construed as being either good or bad. That most popular writer on the occult, Dennis Wheatley, described how he construes these forces in a statement at the beginning of his book *The Devil and All His Works*:

> Existence as we know it is dominated by two Powers – Light and Darkness.
>
> With Light is coupled warmth; with Darkness, cold.
>
> All forms of life are dependent on Light for their growth and well-being.
>
> All progress is checked during Darkness; and when, as winter, its hours exceed those of Light, it brings about decay and death.
>
> Therefore, from time immemorial, Light has been associated with good, and Darkness with evil.
>
> During the course of the year, in any part of the world the total hours of Light and Darkness are the same.
>
> Hence the influence wielded by the two Powers on mankind is equal.

It is death that awakens us to a consciousness of evil. If we did not die, then starvation, disease, injuries, wars, pestilence, earthquakes, floods, fires, another person's anger would hold no terror for us. *Death creates the problem of evil.*

In constructing our life we have to decide just what evil is. 'There are people for whom evil means only a maladjustment with things' wrote William James, 'a wrong correspondence of one's life with the environment. Such evil as this is curable, in principle at least, upon the natural plane, for merely modifying the self or the things, or both at once, the two terms may be made to fit and all go merry as a marriage bell again. But there are others for whom evil is no mere relation of the subject to particular outer things, but something more radical and general, a wrongness or vice in his essential nature, which no rearrangement of the inner self can cure, and which requires a supernatural rememdy.' If we construct a model of the human being as essentially good, and see the universe as good, or neither good nor bad but simply there, then we can construe evil as 'a wrong correspondence of one's life with the environment' and so believe that we can, with intelligence and cooperation, solve all the world's problems, even, perhaps, the problem of death. We can agree with Herakleitos that 'all things are beautiful, good and right; men, on the other hand, deem some things right and others wrong'.

The ancient Greek philosophers were the first to examine in a rational and systematic way the question of the origin of evil. Socrates saw evil as the result of the lack of episteme, knowledge of how to seek virtue. The Cynics saw evil as the result of the pursuit of wealth and fame. Epictetus, the original personal construct theorist, remarked that 'It is not things in themselves which trouble us, but our opinions of things.' In forming our opinions we make choices, and choices, said Marcus Aurelius, which are based on ignorance and thus thwart the intentions of God lead to evil in an otherwise non-evil world.

The belief that evil is created by people and thus is curable by people is a belief held only by those of us who enjoy a certain sense of security. Those of us whose experience of life has led us to the conclusion that life is a chancy business where the bad often, and perhaps always, defeats the good, see evil as 'something more radical and general'. In his book *The Devil; Perceptions of Evil From Antiquity to Primitive Christianity*, Jeffrey Burton Russell describes evil as – 'meaningless, senseless destruction. Evil destroys and does not build; it rips and it does

59

not mend; it cuts and does not bind. It strives always and everywhere to annihilate, to turn to nothing. To take all being and render it nothing is the heart of evil. Or as Erich Fromm puts it, evil is "life turning against itself" or "attraction to what is dead, decaying, lifeless, and purely mechanical".' Russell goes on to point out: 'Whether one perceives the Devil as a supernatural being, or an uncontrollable force arising in the unconscious, or as an absolute aspect of human nature is less important than the essence of the perception, which is that we are threatened by alien and hostile powers. "Evil is terribly real for each and every individual," Jung said. "If you regard the principle of evil as a reality you can just as well call it the devil".' 'I sense the power of evil quite often,' said Billy Graham, 'Satan doesn't want me to read the Bible or to pray.' Billy Graham believes that 'Satan won't win because he's already been defeated at the Cross', but not everyone shares Billy Graham's optimism, that the forces of good will ultimately defeat the forces of evil. Many people whose lives are consumed by fear, no matter how secure their personal circumstances may be, interpret all the world's problems as evidence that the forces of good are at the point of being overwhelmed by the forces of evil.

In speaking of the forces of evil and the forces of good I have implied a separation of good and evil, a dualism which is certainly not reflected in all religions. Many of the world's religions have a god or a number of gods who demonstrate the interrelation of good and evil, or creation and destruction. In Hinduism the four-faced Brahma and the dancing Shiva create and destroy; Kali, the terrible devourer, is the eternal mother of the world. In ancient Greece the gods were manifestations of one great power and were themselves far from virtuous. They represented *moira*, the cosmic order which ruled men and nature. For mortals, to violate one's proper place in the scheme of things was to invite the punishment of Nemesis, the goddess of the sacred grove. The plays of Aeschylus and Sophocles are concerned with how the gods wreak their will upon humans.

The Greek philosophers took the question of evil out of the realm of mythology and subjected it to rigorous examinations, all of which served to illuminate but not resolve the problem that if our God is omnipotent he cannot be all good, and if he is all good he cannot be omnipotent. The monist religions opt for a god that is both good and bad and the dualist religions for two gods, one good and one bad. Zoroastrianism was a thoroughly dualist religion, with Ahura Mazda, the lord of goodness and light, and Angra Mainyu, the lord of evil and darkness, in constant conflict with one another. Judaism preserved the unity of Yahweh and made him thus an awesome figure: 'I am the Lord, and there is none else, there is no God beside me . . . I form the light, and create darkness; I make peace, and create evil; I the Lord do all these things.' Satan, Yahweh's contender, is an ambiguous figure in the Old Testament, but he, as the Devil, becomes Christ's adversary from whose power Christ came to save us. In the New Testament the Devil is not merely a force of evil. He takes on a human form to snare the unwary. 'Get thee hence, Satan,' Christ orders.

And so, when we come to construct our model of life and death, we can choose between a number of possibilities. We can see our life ending in death or proceeding to some afterlife in heaven or hell, or in a re-birth, or as a merging with the cosmic whole. We can see the universe as containing all that there is, or we can postulate a further reality represented by spirits, or forces of good and evil, or gods in human-like form who may reveal an awesome blend of good and evil or who may be entirely good or entirely bad and thus contend among themselves. Whatever choice we make, we shall find that it has both good and bad implications, but whatever choice we do make we shall also find that it provides us with a setting which matches, complements, our lives. We do not look at the bare bones of the possibilities that I have assembled here. Rather, we create a myth, a richly furbished and peopled stage which symbolizes our lives. Our myth builds our life and our life builds our myth. As Montesquieu once remarked, 'If triangles had a god, he would have three sides.'

When once I asked a very lonely, frightened, depressed young woman, Teresa, whether she believed in God she said, 'Something must have made the universe – everything comes from something. Something must have been there to make the planets, if not us.'

'What is this something?' I asked.

'Not human – something all over the planet, something more intelligent than us. They're like people, but not people. They're beings. They take an interest in us but they don't interfere. They watch what we do. No, they don't judge us. They're above that sort of thing. They are everywhere, sat watching. They look at us as a community, not as individuals.'

'Can we contact them?'

'No, I don't think so. They could contact us if they wanted to. If they contacted us we would not be as we are now. There'd be no more unhappiness. There'd be peace.'

'What part do these beings play in your life?'

'None.'

Teresa's description of these intelligent, superior beings reminded me of the Hindu gods or the Catholic saints and angels, but unlike these gods, saints, and angels, Teresa's beings were remote, uninvolved, like the Tirthankaras, the ideal beings of Jainism, who are beyond the reach of human prayers and offerings. Instead of making her world populous and busy her gods made it cold, empty, and lonely. I asked her about this.

'I see life as lonely,' she said, 'You're always on your own, you're always lonely. Some people don't see it like that but I think it applies to everyone . . . Life is not good or bad, it's just lonely. Occasionally you get close to people, but only for a short time, a very short time.'

When Teresa said 'Life is lonely' she was not saying 'Life is lonely for me but not for other people'. She was making an axiomatic statement about life which applied to all people at all times and places. When I suggested that life is not necessarily lonely she said that she could not see it that way, and neither she could, any more than she could see the sky as being down and the ground as being up. So when she felt close to her husband and child she knew that this closeness would end as surely as a ball thrown up in the air comes down. To think otherwise, to accept the possibility that life was not necessarily lonely, would involve too radical a change. To do that she would have to trust other people and let her gods come down to earth. She dared not contemplate such a change.

V. Belief

Whatever the beliefs about life and death that we choose to structure our world, such beliefs have a peculiar nature. They are different from the kinds of belief we have about such things as the relative merits of one kind of car over another or the usefulness of aspirin in the cure of headaches. There are some beliefs that we can check against experience and some beliefs that we can take only on trust. 'Whenever belief receives a great deal of reinforcement,' wrote Gordon Allport, 'so that it conforms with the beliefs of others, we are likely to call it knowledge. When belief is deprived of all these supports we call it delusion. In between these limits, where belief rests on probabilities, we call it faith.' Of course, one man's delusion is another man's faith, and faith has been maliciously defined as belief in something for which there is no evidence. The term 'faith' usually implies some voluntary decision to trust something or somebody. Metaphysical beliefs do not always have that voluntary aspect. Here I shall keep to the word 'belief', and distinguish 'metaphysical belief' from 'rational belief'. Another term for 'metaphysical belief' is 'overbelief' which the OED defines as 'Belief in more than is warranted by the evidence or in what can be verified'. William James remarked that 'the interesting and valuable things about a man are usually his over-beliefs'.

How do we distinguish our metaphysical beliefs from our rational beliefs?

The world is full of such a multitude of events that we would be quite overwhelmed had we not the capacity to simplify and categorize. 'All our life', wrote Gordon Allport 'is biased in the direction of obtaining simplified perceptions and categorical meanings. If we say that the intelligibles of religious people leap far ahead of verifiable evidence, we must never forget that the intelligibles of irreligious people do likewise. All our cognitive operations press towards coherence and unity. Whether we be theists or atheists we are prone to stereotype the world we live in.' Both metaphysical and rational beliefs simplify our perception of our world and cause us to trust beyond the evidence. We may hope that the sun will rise tomorrow, and put our faith in God or in the scientific rule that if something has happened often in the past there is a fair chance that it will continue to happen in the future. When we are attached to a theory, be it a religious faith or a scientific hypothesis, we not only carefully select the facts that fit our theory but we alter the facts to fit the theory. 'Nietzsche proclaims the will to power,' wrote Ernst Cassirer, 'Freud signalizes the sexual instinct, Marx enthrones the economic instinct. Each theory becomes a Procrustean bed on which empirical facts are stretched to fit a preconceived pattern.'

Rational beliefs are supposed to be consistent, but functioning systems of beliefs, rational or not, cannot be guaranteed to be consistent. Work in the natural sciences has the insecure basis of the probabilities of quantum mechanics, while in the social sciences the unresolved question of free will and determinism leads to many inconsistencies. Concerning this problem, a young sociologist remarked to me recently, 'I see myself as having a choice, but other people don't. Their lives are determined.'

The main differences between metaphysical and rational beliefs seem to be in their capability of proof and the ease with which they are given up. Rational beliefs are capable of proof, and when disproved can be relinquished. Metaphysical beliefs do not lend themselves to proof, not in this world at least, and, once held, are not easily relinquished. For many people the proving of their metaphysical beliefs is irrelevant. 'Faith,' said St Augustine, 'comes before understanding.' When rational arguments fail to convince, such as when an Afrikaner refuses to accept evidence of the intellectual ability of the Bantu, it is a metaphysical belief, not a rational belief, that is being defended. In his study of the nature of belief William James wrote:

> If we look on man's whole mental life as it exists, on the life of men that lies in them apart from their learning and science, and that they inwardly and privately follow, we have to confess that the part of it of which rationalism can give an account is relatively superficial. It is the part which has the *prestige* undoubtedly, for it has the loquacity, it can challenge you for proofs, and chop logic, and put you

down with words. But it will fail to convince or convert you all the same, if your dumb intuitions are opposed to its conclusions. If you have intuitions at all, they come from a deeper level of your nature than the loquacious level which rationalism inhabits. Your whole sub-conscious life, your impulses, your faiths, your needs, your divinations, have prepared the premises, of which your consciousness now feels the weight of the result, and something in you absolutely *knows* that the result must be truer than any logic-chopping rationalistic talk, however clever, that may contradict it . . . The truth is that in the metaphysical and religious sphere articulate reasons are cogent for us only when our inarticulate feelings of reality have already been impressed in favour of the same conclusion . . . Our impulsive belief is here always what sets up the original body of truth, and our articulately verbalised philosophy is but its showy translation into formulas. The unreasoned and immediate assurance is the deep thing in us, the reasoned argument is but a surface exhibition. Instinct leads, intelligence does but follow.

Sarah, the heroine of Graham Greene's novel, *The End of the Affair*, wrote to her lover:

I believe there's a God – I believe the whole bag of tricks, there's nothing I don't believe, they could subdivide the Trinity into a dozen parts and I'd believe. They could dig up records that proved Christ had been invented by Pilate and I'd believe just the same. I've caught belief like a disease. I've fallen into belief like I've fallen in love.

Metaphysical beliefs seem to be held with greater certainty than rational beliefs. Thouless, in 1935, and Brown, in 1962, asked their subjects to indicate on a seven-point scale their degree of agreement or disagreement with statements concerning certain religious and rational beliefs. Both researchers found that the religious items provoked more extreme judgements, with disbelief being as dogmatic as belief.

Theoretically, we have a choice about our metaphysical

beliefs, but in practice it seems not to be so, as we find when we try to change someone's metaphysical beliefs. If a client presents me with a proposition like 'I find it best never to trust anybody' then I can argue and demonstrate and perhaps convince him that some people in some circumstances are trustworthy and that life goes along better if we have a modicum of trust in one another. But when a client says that he sees the universe as the battleground of the forces of evil and the forces of good, and the evil forces are winning then there are no arguments, no demonstrations that will lead him to modify a belief that probably took root when he was a small child at the mercy of the moods and actions of the adults around him. 'One never possesses a metaphysical belief,' said Jung, 'but is possessed by it.' An attack on our metaphysical beliefs arouses us to anger in a way that an attack on our rational beliefs never does. Our metaphysical beliefs arise in us and are there, impervious to reason or to resolutions on our part to change them. We can no more voluntarily generate a change in our metaphysical beliefs than we can voluntarily generate love or hate. Practising believing impossible things, six times before breakfast as the White Queen recommended to Alice, simply does not work. No wonder Billy Graham said in frustration, 'I wish I could drive this into you like a nail – if only I had a pill I could give you to make you believe!' Tony and I had many arguments over tolerance. I see tolerance as a virtue. For him tolerance was apathy, and apathy leads to horrors like Nazi Germany. His angry intolerance kept him in constant strife, but for him to act any other way would be morally wrong.

'That's the position,' he said, 'If you ask me to abandon a moral, then a moral is something that you've come to the conclusion, that you've refined over a period of many years, and that is something that even if I wanted to chuck it away, how is my mind going to chuck it away? How is it going to do that? Look, Dorothy, I am not a fool. If something inside of me said, "This is absolutely ludicrous to hold on to that", I would and could chuck it away. It's the part of me that is very, very strong, so far as it does not even have to speak to me. It's sort of embedded to such a point that it does not have to justify its existence. Therefore it's very strong. What do I do about that? So long as that is there, there is no way that I'm going to throw it away. I mean, okay, I know I've been conditioned – up to here – I know I have. I've been in the bloody Baptist Church to the age of twenty-five, and you can't get a much better walloping than that. But I broke out of that. I became an agnostic and that was a very painful time in my life. For years I didn't have anybody to pray to, and I've been praying to people all my life, praying to God all my life, and no longer was He around, I couldn't do it. I had to face the possibility that there might not be a God. I don't think you realize how difficult that is. But intellectually it was a possibility and it had to be faced. I can't change, not because I wouldn't, but because I can't change, I can't move. I can see myself as more tolerant, more easy going, but I can see definite lines beyond which I can't go.'

Arthur Danto told the story of how one of the early missionaries to China, Father Matteo Ricci, a mathematician who corresponded with Galileo, offered the Chinese ministers the opportunity to learn about the methods and discoveries of European science. They considered this matter, and then refused, since, as they said, they had a form of life which worked quite well. Danto commented that we might find such a decision strange since we value scientific enquiry, but, if we think about it, we can see that we do not 'lightly surrender a system of beliefs that facilitates experience that renders it tractable and smooth'.

Our metaphysical beliefs do not always serve to render life tractable and smooth, but they do serve a purpose which no rational belief can fulfil. If we look at the world rationally, we see that it is a chancy, unpredictable place and that we are an insignificant speck amongst teeming millions on a planet which is itself an insignificant speck in a universe whose very vastness and nature are beyond human ken. Our metaphysical beliefs restore a sense of proportion with which we can live. Whether we believe in a God in whose hands the universe rests, or in science through whose powers the secrets of the universe are revealed, we can put ourselves in those hands or share those powers, and so give ourselves a measure of security. The idea that we are in some way related to a great power, be it God or science, is essential to our vanity, and vanity is essential to the survival of puny human beings in this world. Where vanity is concerned, it does not matter that our metaphysical beliefs have to encompass evil – that our gods are not always benevolent and science can do us harm – personal significance can be more important than happiness. Moreover, from our metaphysical beliefs we draw the rules by which we should live our lives, rules such as how we should pray or how we should assess evidence, and as we follow these rules we can feel that we have shown ourselves to be virtuous and in some way to have gained power over nature and over other people.

Beliefs, whether rational or metaphysical, are not merely ideas in our heads. They are actions. 'It would be inconsistent both to believe in God and not recognize an obligation to worship him,' wrote Ninian Smart, 'Thus the form of words "I believe in God" expresses a commitment of submission to God.' Hindus are not impelled to improve the lives of those less fortunate, as are humanists, since by the law of karma, all suffering and all rewards are deserved. Writing about the difficulties of a European living in India, Ruth Prawer Jhabvala said, 'Another approach to India's basic conditions is to accept them. This seems to be the approach favoured by most Indians. Perhaps it has something to do with their belief in reincarnation. If things are not to your liking in this life, there is always the chance that in your next life everything will be different. It appears to be a consoling thought for the rich and the poor. The rich man stuffing himself on pilao can do so with an easy conscience because he knows he had earned this privilege by his good conduct in previous lives; and the poor man can watch him with equanimity for he knows that next time round it may well be *he* who will be digging into that pilao while the other will be crouching outside with an empty stomach. However, this path of acceptance is not open to you if you don't have a belief in reincarnation ingrained into you.' (The belief in reincarnation may have something to do with the fact that Communism has never gained much of a following in India.)

'A belief is not a mere state of the mind or of the soul, an inert trait,' wrote Arthur Danto, 'When a man believes something, he is disposed, generally, to act in a certain way, or in certain ways. If I believe that my child is in danger, it is not merely a matter of giving an affirmative answer to the question whether I believe she is in danger. My entire mode of behaviour is implicated and all my relevant factual beliefs activated.' The danger we perceive may be that of the child drowning in the river into which she has fallen, or of the child, through wrong acts, losing her immortal soul, but either perception impels the loving parent into action. Or, more accurately, both sets of beliefs, rational and metaphysical, forming an intimate relationship, determine our actions. We may choose a particular car to buy because it has been shown to be more reliable than other makes of cars. If we are asked why reliability is important we may relate this to the necessity of being a reliable person, being trustworthy, and we may see trust between people and trust between ourselves and our God as the essence of our existence. In such a way our metaphysical beliefs link with our rational beliefs to determine our actions.

Of course we doubt our beliefs, our rational as well as our metaphysical beliefs. I often doubt that the vitamin B tablets I take do me all the good they are supposed to do. Doubt brings our beliefs to mind for inspection and for modification or reaffirmation. Doubt is part of belief, as is shown in the prayers 'Lord, I believe: help Thou my unbelief', and from the Rg-Veda, 'O faith, endow us with belief'. But even when we doubt, as William James said, 'Of some things we feel that we know that we are certain: we know, and we know that we know. There is something that gives a click inside us, a bell that strikes twelve, when the hands of our mental clock have swept the dial and meet over the meridian hour. The greatest empiricists among us are only empiricists on reflection; when left to their instincts, they dogmatize like infallible popes.' That arch-sceptic, Bertrand Russell, has commented, 'Every philosopher, in addition to the formal system which he offers the world, has another, much simpler, of which he may be quite unaware. If he is aware of it, he probably realizes that it won't do; he therefore conceals it, and sets forth something more sophisticated, which he believes because it is like his crude system, but which he asks others to accept because he thinks he has made it such as cannot be disproved. The sophistication comes in by way of refutation of refutations, but this alone will never give a positive result: it shows, at best, that a theory *may* be true, not that it *must* be. The positive result, however little the philosopher may realize it, is due to his imaginative preconceptions, or to what Santayana calls "animal faith".'

What causes us to 'dogmatize like infallible popes' from the basis of our 'animal faith' is what Peter called 'a loyalty factor'. As he said, 'If I am a Celt, then I've got to pay some sort of service to the rules I believe are Celtic rules, Celtic identity. Then I have got to subscribe to some of those superstitions, otherwise I lose contact with myself. I'd have nothing to hold on to.' It is not just people who cannot cope with life who have such loyalty to their metaphysical beliefs. Michael Dummett, Wykeham Professor of Logic at Oxford, was interviewed on television and was asked how difficult it was for him to reconcile his work with his Catholic faith. He said that the reconciliation presented no difficulties, but to explain how he did it was difficult. All he could say was that it was a matter of loyalty, for him, loyalty to the idea of the sacred.

And so we each construct our world, a world which turns on the axes of our metaphysical beliefs and which we must always strive to see as being firm and solid, since it is only the world which we construct that keeps at bay the formless chaos of reality.

3

Tragedy is a Granny Knot
in Heaven's Thread

None of the other psychologists in the hospital would see Siegfried. 'It's your job,' they said to me, 'you're in charge.' It was not that they were being unkind. They were embarrassed, the embarrassment we feel when someone whom we see as presenting himself as powerful and competent stumbles and falls. For Siegfried was a consultant psychiatrist, and in our narrow hospital world consultant psychiatrists should never become psychiatric patients. But, of course, they do.

There are different kinds of consultant psychiatrists. Some see themselves as scientists. These find university departments with small, well-equipped clinics, where the doctors wear white coats and speak a language not known to ordinary mortals. Some see themselves as psychotherapists. They speak modestly of their knowledge of medicine, wear undistinguished suits, and espouse a manner which may range from the friendly avuncular to the self-effacing. Some of this group may advance so far that they abandon suits for the simple clothes of current fashion, and desks and chairs for cushions and rugs, and have behind them the comfort of a private practice. But the fate of most psychiatrists lies not in the austere splendour of a university clinic nor in the impressive ambiguities of the therapy room. The fate of most psychiatrists lies in the large psychiatric hospital, known colloquially as 'the bin'.

Most of these hospitals, once called asylums, were built in the nineteenth century to house the 'pauper lunatics', and since such people were an offence to the eye the hospitals were built well outside the boundaries of the town. The towns grew, and now most of these hospitals are within the city bounds, but even though the great gates that once clanged shut and locked at sunset have been dismantled, the old asylum, despite a change of name, never became an ordinary part of the community. The local populace still fear to go there; it is still a shameful thing to be one of its patients, however briefly; and the staff that work there are thought to be at least a little odd. Every so often one of these hospitals is in the news – a report of a scandal, some alleged cruelty or negligence, and for a day or two the papers carry pictures of the blank walls, the narrow windows of this unfriendly edifice, and an editorial demanding reform. Every so often a sociologist or one of the multifarious band of psycho-therapists gains the attention of the media to expound his views on the sins and inadequacies of what is called 'traditional psychiatry', and once again the consultant psychiatrists of the psychiatric hospitals suffer public criticism. Not all criticism is made public. Various committees, investigating various matters, descend on the hospital. They deplore the buildings, they commend the diligence of the staff, but their questions imply the criticism which becomes quite plain in the report which follows. But when the newspapers have found some other eyecatching scandal, when the sociologist starts another book or the psychotherapist a new therapy, when the committee of inquiry has gathered its papers and departed, the consultant psychiatrist is left, still with the same collection of inhospitable wards, the same dementing old women, the bizarre, posturing old men, the frightened, the inadequate, the flotsam and jetsam of all the sorrows of this world, and it is his responsibility to look after them. Like Housman's mercenaries, 'What God abandoned, these defended' but, unlike Housman's mercenaries, he works, not just for pay, but out of an inarticulate love, or at least concern, for his patients. (Many such 'bins' have now closed and the patients have been put 'in the community', but the role and the relationships of the psychiatrist have not changed.)

Each consultant leads a team composed of junior doctors, nurses, a social worker or two, and perhaps a psychologist. The consultant may enjoy the satisfaction of leading a group of people who work together with enthusiasm and in harmony and he may share the camaraderie of a group of people who see themselves as belonging together, but the consultant, while defining his own role as the person with ultimate responsibility and authority, may define the roles of the other team members in ways which emphasize his separateness from them. Junior doctors, however able, must endure the discipline of the medical profession and be respectful to their seniors. Social workers cannot be entirely trusted since they have allegiances outside the team, while psychologists are dangerously idiosyncratic people who read books critical of psychiatry. The doctor may feel closest to the nurses, but in the hospital hierarchy nurses are inferior people who are capable of only limited responsibility. Of course, they are not as inferior as patients, but then patients are a race that must be kept apart. It was for my own safety that a nurse in a select clinic snatched a clean and shiny glass from my hand with the cry, 'You can't drink out of that. It's a patient's glass.'

There is always the possibility that the consultant may find himself a lonely leader. Support, then, can come from his colleagues. In a psychiatric hospital consultants may fight quite bitterly among themselves, but once they are attacked by someone who is not a psychiatrist they react like individual balls of mercury that suddenly roll together and form one globule which, while glinting metallically, quakes and quivers to itself. It is rare for one consultant to be expelled from the group, but when a consultant suspects that, behind a well-mannered facade, his colleagues are colluding to banish him he feels the chill of Siberia.

Support, too, can come from the consultant's family, but some families have paid a high price for his consultancy. During the children's school years, when even the happiest of marriages can feel a strain, he was a junior doctor, absorbed in examinations and the responsibilities of his work. So his children may have grown up as strangers to him, perhaps with problems of their own, and between him and his wife may be a gulf that seems to him to allow no bridge.

Thus it is that some consultants who have accepted the precepts and standards of their profession and have worked hard and responsibly find themselves increasingly alone. Some become exceedingly bitter or autocratic, some join the ranks of the great English eccentrics, some seek release in suicide or a slower death by alcohol. Siegfried was one of these. 'If I don't drink,' he said, 'I can't get to sleep.' And if one cannot sleep, one cannot work.

We talked a lot about work. One day I asked him why he had decided to become a psychiatrist.

'I'd rather wanted to do general medicine,' he said, 'But I didn't do a great deal of work as a student – I was the typical, average, brutal, licentious medical student. I loved charging round the rugby field on a Saturday afternoon and drinking lots of beer afterwards. I didn't get the house jobs, so I looked round for something I thought I'd quite like and in which I could get a consultant job, so it was psychiatry. I think, too, that I had my eyes set on being the boss of whatever I do. People become consultants because they want to be in command. Over the last week I've been giving some thought to that. Why does it matter so much?'

'Why do you want to be in charge?' I asked.

'Conceit again. I think I'm the most likely to get it right. That's a revolting thing to say.'

'I'm asking you for truthful things, not just what sounds nice. This is how you see yourself.'

'I can get people to work for me,' he admitted, 'and they accept my decisions. If I went straight back to work from here I'd be the same. I'd be the boss in my department. I don't know any other way of working.'

But boss or not, Siegfried did not enjoy his work. 'I was going to say there aren't many things that I can't tackle, but I can easily prove myself wrong. But I'm bored. Nothing exciting happens. I'd like to have something to take charge of, to get my teeth into. Boredom and tedium in day-to-day work. Most of which I know will come to nothing.'

'And so for a long time you've known you've been in a job that doesn't extend you, but if you say that to your friends, relatives, colleagues, then this will sound very conceited.'

'And they would say, rightly, "You're fifty-four, you've left it too late".'

Siegfried was not making an empty boast when he said that he found his work did not extend him. His drinking may have affected his liver, but his intellectual powers were unimpaired. The intelligence tests he did in hospital showed him to be of very superior intelligence. Rarely in his life had he been fully extended, and so he knew that 'if I were given a job to do

74

which would really take something out of me I'd come to life again'.

When we are children we discover within ourselves talents, powers, that we know are truly an essential part of ourselves and, being so, can become the source of the greatest meaning we can find in life. We feel impelled to explore our world through our powers, but most of us are stopped from doing this. Poverty, rigid education, the demands that we fill certain roles in society block us so that sometimes we have to forget the possibilities we once glimpsed, or, not forgetting, suffer punishment like the servant in the parable who buried his talent. When, so Jesus said, his lord discovered this, he commanded that the servant be cast 'into outer darkness: there shall be weeping and gnashing of teeth'. The gap between what we know we could have achieved and what we have achieved is usually filled with much weeping and gnashing of teeth.

When Siegfried said, 'I'm not the person I could have been,' I asked him what he would have liked to have been.

'Sounds childish – I'd like to have had command of my ship for longer – I was in command for only one week.'

The sea and ships meant a great deal to him, but he had chosen to work in a city many miles from the sea, and he saw no opportunity now of developing a life which related to the sea. Instead he worried about whether he should return to his old job. If he did not, 'Would I be the little boy who ran away? We all adopt our persona, don't we? I've adopted the wrong one.'

'It sounds like very early on you've given a rule to yourself, "Never run away from a dangerous situation. Always go towards it".'

'Yes. Childish pleasures, very childish in a way. I remember reading on my flimsy when I came out of the Service, "Reliable in action". I enjoyed that. Didn't matter. If I hadn't been, someone behind me would have made sure I was.'

'Why is it important not to run away?'

'That's an extremely difficult question, isn't it? Training to some extent. My formative ages were, I suppose, eighteen to twenty-five. The training I had was that you did what you were told and you did your job. No one said thank you if you did your job, but they said what the bloody hell if you didn't.'

'So it's important to do your job because if you don't people get angry with you, say "What the bloody hell".'

'Less now because by and large I could get away with murder if I wanted to, I could do as little as I care to.'

'So it's yourself that says "What the bloody hell".'

'These habits, they're ingrained.'

'But if you've got this kind of choice, of doing a job well or doing it badly, facing up to difficulties or not facing up to difficulties, what you're saying is that if you face up to difficulties, you're not getting any praise for it, but if you don't face up to difficulties, people get angry with you, and the people are the people inside yourself. What would happen if neither you nor other people thought well of you?'

'The bottle, I think.'

'But the bottle is an escape. What would happen to you?'

'Mm, the most awful things that can happen to anyone. The loss of respect of one's family, one's friends. A man I know, and tried to treat once, the managing director of quite a big firm, and he wasn't a big enough man for the job, and he's more or less in the gutter. That would frighten me.'

'So, amongst your friends who've given you all this advice, the ones who say, "Don't try so hard, take things easy, you set too high standards for yourself, you ought to relax more, you're getting older now, you can't expect to do what you've done in the past", all this kind of advice, while being said with the best of intentions, comes over to you as something extremely frightening because carrying it out would mean becoming the kind of person you've always dreaded being, because if you became that kind of person, you would be the kind of person who had no respect, completely lost.'

'Yes – but one has to be realistic. It didn't break my heart when I found I couldn't run round a rugby field any more.'

'What does break your heart?'

'I haven't achieved very much.'

But Siegfried had difficulty in acknowledging what he had achieved. As he said one day, 'It's going to take me a while to forgive myself, because I'm almost liking it in here. Several of my staff, junior doctors, nurses, have been here to see me. I think it's quite ridiculous. "Dr Maximillien has gone away because he was overworked and depressed." When I go back they'll have to take me as they find me.'

'How do you think they feel about you now?'

'Well, how does a man say this? They think I'm pretty good.'

'You feel they don't think any the less of you because you're in here.'

'No.'

'But you think less of yourself?'

'Yes – what a peculiar thing to say, "They think I'm pretty good".'

'That's not a peculiar thing to say. Why do you think it's peculiar?'

'Oh, the sort of thing one thinks, doesn't say.'

'Why not?'

'Our culture, I suppose. A man doesn't boast. "Think nothing of it, old boy".'

'Why is it important not to boast?'

'I don't know. I don't like to hear someone boasting. I think it's in bad taste. Breach of ordinary good manners.'

'From what you say it sounds like "If I say anything good about myself I'm boasting".'

'Mm, well, there's a reverse kind of boasting I enjoy enormously.'

'What, saying bad things about yourself?'

'In a sense. In my last year at school we had a remarkable science section in Sixth Form and one or two inspired masters. There were four of us and I'm the only one without a Ph.D., but I'm making more money than the others.' He laughed. 'That is a permissible form of boasting because I think there's some element of humour, and if humour comes into it, then almost anything can be justified, can't it?'

'We use humour to say something we don't dare say straight. But it sounds like you've got rules about never saying anything good about yourself. That there's something dangerous about saying something good about yourself.'

'Yes. Well, isn't it a fact saying something good about oneself, to be honest, you have to say some bad things too.'

'To balance up the picture?'

'Yes, and not becoming the most terrible bore.'

'If you only said good things about yourself you'd become a bore. What would people think of you?'

'Go back to being a little boy who has a good opinion of himself – prove he's as good as he thinks he is.'

'So, if you say good things about yourself, you're setting standards, competitions, that you don't have to live up to – '

'That you *do* have to live up to,' he corrected me.

So, to say something good about oneself was not to make a statement about some fact of life, but to create an area of doubt, of contest. Prove yourself, or for your sin of hubris the gods will strike you down. Feel guilty about not achieving and frightened when you do.

Siegfried saw his family as being very disappointed in him. 'I'm a miserable old devil most of the time. When I've drunk half a bottle of gin I go to sleep in an armchair. We don't talk much.'

'How much are you able to tell your children you love them?'

'Not much. I find that embarrassing.'

'If you're embarrassed about telling your children that you love them, then perhaps they're embarrassed about telling you.'

'Yes, yes, we're an undemonstrative family. It's inherited from generation to generation, isn't it?'

'It's learned. You can't claim genes for that.'

'Habit.' He put out his cigarette and said, 'I'm taking up a lot of your time.'

I went on to talk about how in some families people are prepared to show anger but not love. He responded with an anecdote which had nothing to do with what I had said and concluded his story with, 'Are we going to meet again?'

'You're wanting to stop now?'

'I think I'm taking up too much of your time.'

'There's no rush. You got anxious the moment we started talking about affection.'

'I don't think I was getting anxious talking about affection. I was, quite honestly, thinking of your time. I am frightened of affection. Over the course of many years I had a lot of girlfriends and got frightened off when they started getting affectionate. Rather a dirty trick, really. When I was quite a small child, and I had a fairly horrific childhood, I've always been rather

78

concerned about the possibility of being emotionally dependent on anyone.'

'What would happen if you became emotionally dependent on anyone?'

'On previous form, I'd tend to back out.'

'But what would happen if you didn't back out? What do you feel would happen if you became dependent on anyone?'

'I'd assume I'd get hurt.'

'The person would turn on you and be angry with you, or would the person go away, rejecting you?'

'Rejection, non-concern, letting one down, unreliable in crises. I think my brothers had the same experience to some extent. The three of us were closely knit. I suppose in a funny sort of way our parents might have been fond of us, but we got nothing from them except a lot of misery and a lot of fright. It's a hell of a long, involved story.'

'But the trouble is that when a child has had that kind of experience which leads him to draw the conclusion to make the rule, "Never love anybody completely and so save yourself from getting hurt", when a child makes up that rule in childhood, it can, at the time, be a sensible rule to make, but when you make up that rule and continue it for the rest of your life, then it becomes quite a bad rule. This is the problem. In childhood we learn a lot of rules which continue to be true throughout life, "Fire burns", "Don't run on busy roads", and then we learn other rules, or we see the necessity of other rules in relationships, and then when we get older, we don't always review these rules and see whether they still apply.'

'There's the simile or metaphor, if you get your hand burnt, put your hand in a handful of tar, but if you get hurt emotionally, there's nothing to slap on to that.'

'But you can build up your own little wall, defensive wall, against getting hurt again.'

'Well, it can be a fairly good wall.'

'As you get older you don't realize that loving and being loved is a reciprocal relationship, and if you don't let any love out, you don't let any love in. The less love you let in, the more you wither, grow cold at the centre.'

'That's when I get back to Beethoven, Mozart, Bach, and

Wagner. I just sit and listen to them. It's all very obvious, isn't it? But it doesn't help a great deal. The sad thought intrudes from time to time – "Does it all matter" – if I've cocked up my job, if I've failed in my capacity to make relationships.'

One day Siegfried asked me, 'Have you ever been in love?' and having ascertained that I knew what he was talking about, went on to say, 'I was in love once. It was a marvellous experience – a real killer, isn't it? But even on that first glorious occasion, there are still limits, aren't there? Making love to someone whom one loves – human contact, the emotion is really very beautiful. But there are still limits. It's always a sad business, isn't it?'

'You're looking to me for confirmation of all this – '

'Yes.'

'Some people have different experiences.'

'Not many.'

'Would you say that all love comes to an end?'

'This first sort of mad happiness comes to an end, and in all probability that particular love affair comes to an end. There are other things which are never quite the same which can be very pleasant – respect, affection, regard. Even things like ordinary good manners. All quite important. Not the same as love's young dream.

'No.'

'And I had the misfortune to be at sea when I got my Dear John letter too. Bad luck – bloody guardsman, the bastard.'

'And that was the only time you've been in love?'

'In that sense, yes. It was around that time of my life, I think, as far as one can, never to be very, very firmly committed to anyone again.'

'You decided never to be committed – '

'Yes. I think it was a fairly cold-blooded decision. It was reinforced a bit, one of my brothers was killed, and, not surprisingly, my parents took this pretty hard. At the time there was a lot of people dying, anyway, many of my friends, and just after the war my other brother went to New Zealand, not to be seen for many years again. My mother was terribly upset. We went down to see him off and I was puzzled by this, my mother's distress. If someone went back off leave, maybe one would see him again, maybe not. I remember that feeling very distinctly. Not a very healthy one. But a boy in his early twenties makes these sort of firm decisions, doesn't he?'

'You must have been meeting lots of other people you could have loved.'

'I met a lot of people. Made some very good friends. Most of them were male friends – apart from my wife. Most of us were ex-service people, and extremely good friends. If something went wrong, you could count on them.'

At our next meeting Siegfried said, 'I told you something last week that I've never told anyone before. I don't know why I bothered. About having been in love. It was quite ridiculous. I was eighteen and she was twenty-six. I was naive to the point of thinking that going to bed with a girl was as marvellous as it was improper. It's something that does stay with one. Pity I wasn't twenty-six. Would you like a cup of tea?'

Siegfried always referred to his wife in a way which reflected considerable fondness and respect, and I wondered how much he underestimated her affection for him. One day I said to him, 'I've got the impression from what you've said about your wife and children that you see them as not disliking you, but being disappointed in you. There's that sort of gap. When we feel that someone is disappointed in us, we don't feel that we can communicate with that person easily.'

'I think that went sour, and my wife thinks so too, when she had a puerperal depression with the first baby. I had difficulties, too, in that respect. Coming from being a carefree medical student, suddenly a married man with a small child. My wife got very depressed after the first baby. Dealing with someone who is depressed is jolly hard. And there was a chilliness over the years. I thought on a number of occasions of packing in my job and going back into the Services. When the kids were small they were gorgeous. I used to laugh a lot and play silly games at lunchtime with the children. But I got interested in playing hockey and squash and used to call at the hospital club most evenings and had a couple of pints on my way home. Used to rather hope that the children were in bed by the time I got home. It was rather chilly for a number of years'

'Did you feel that your wife had rejected you?'

'Yes. I felt her sole concern was for the kids. We never went anywhere. We didn't make many friends. This gives an unfair picture of my wife who is really a very nice person.'

'Yes. But this is what happens in a lot of marriages. Things fall apart after the baby's born.'

'At the moment my wife and I are fonder of one another than we have been for a long time. Perhaps with the kids being more independent and she's got a job.'

Siegfried talked a lot about his friends in the Services and in medical school, but now he said, 'My GP described me as a loner. This is not basically so. I have become so over the past few years. I quite like my fellow beings if I can talk to them.'

'But there's not many you can talk to?'

'No. I've a friend, a professor of physics, who's finding the same thing. He and I used to have some good conversations, but those times are past.'

'When a person gets into a position of power that person often finds the position very isolated. Do you find that?'

'On the whole, no, but I've been very lucky. My colleagues in the hospital are as intelligent as I am – perhaps even more so – and we talk to one another quite a lot. One or two of them share my interest in words and in ideas and know far more about music and art than I do. We all have a similar grotesque sense of humour. If I had been there on my own over the past years, then I would have cracked, but we can talk to one another. Being on one's own in a job like that would be awful.'

'What about the other members of your team – the nurses and so forth?'

'Jolly hard to size up, isn't it? I think they quite like us and they believe us to be competent. They know if something goes wrong we'll carry the can.'

'But there's nothing in those relationships which is over and above what is a good working relationship?'

'No, I'm not going to bed with any of them. We're friends in different sorts of ways. It is possible to be friends with someone whose decision you overrule. In fact that hardly ever happens because they know how we run things and what we like to do. We're set in our ways.'

'The kind of picture that has built up in my mind about your

82

life – where there's a well-defined pattern of relationships which are basically good relationships. There's no part in your pattern of relationships where you're under any threat or danger or feel yourself attacked, but they're relationships where you're at a bit of a distance.'

'Yes.'

'And sometimes the distance is created by the style of the relationship, like the relationships with your nursing staff, or – '

'This is in some ways a warmer one than the one at home, in some ways, I think.'

So Siegfried found his closest relationships within the hierarchical structure of the hospital. Siegfried remembered his years of war service as 'the happy times', and there are a lot of similarities between life in the Services and life – for a member of staff – in a big hospital. There is the clearly defined hierarchy which gives each person a specified amount of power and control and which limits the amount of responsibility each person has to take for his own life. In a psychiatric hospital there is the constant sense of battling with inadequate resources against huge forces which might recede but never vanish, which provoke sudden and often terrible crises, all in scenes revealing an amount of human pain and misery which is matched only by the utter ridiculousness and futility of human endeavour. The essential survival kit is a sense of humour, and the camaraderie, the gossip, the in-jokes can become more important than the danger and the pain.

To fit within a hierarchy with some measure of ease we have to be able to accept the basic tenets of that hierarchy. Never having been a member of the Armed Services, I had always thought that to be an officer was a fairly straightforward activity. However, Siegfried, who was still passionately interested in all things military, lent me several of the books he was reading on war history, and, from one, *The Face of Battle*, by John Keegan, I learnt that to be an army officer was to try to reconcile two disparate points of view, a reconciliation as difficult as the reconciliation of the two views which a doctor entering psychiatry has to try to achieve. John Keegan wrote:

The student officer . . . is simultaneously undergoing two

processes of education, each with a dissimilar object. The one . . . aims, if not to close his mind to unorthodox or difficult ideas, at least to stop it down to a fairly short focal length, to exclude from his field of vision everything that is irrelevant to his professional function and to define all that he ought to see in a highly formal manner . . . the other process of education the student officer undergoes is the normal 'academic' one, which aims to offer the student not a single but a variety of angles and vision; which asks him to adopt in his study of war the standpoint not only of an officer, but also of a private soldier, a non-combatant, a neutral observer, a casualty; or of a statesman, a civil servant, an industrialist, a diplomat, a relief worker, a professional pacifist – all valid, all documented points of view.

The student psychiatrist similarly undergoes two processes of education. One is the formal training of a scientist which is concerned with simplifying complex situations, looks for single causes, follows the laws of contradiction and identity, and is based on the assumption of an objective reality which consists of repeating and discoverable patterns. The patterns which concern the scientific psychiatrist are those of the chemical and physiological changes which underlie and explain human behaviour. At the same time the student psychiatrist has to develop 'not a single but a variety of angles of vision'. He must become proficient in those vague and variable disciplines of psychology and sociology; he must grasp the complex ideas contained in psychoanalytic and existential theory; he must learn to explain behaviour, not by looking for a single cause, but by describing a complex, interrelated, changing, and idiosyncratic pattern. These contrasting modes of thought are often simplified to the debate over the contribution of nature and nurture to behaviour, whether a person's 'illness' can be explained by his genetic inheritance or his family life. In practice, psychiatrists tend to favour one view over the other, and Siegfried certainly followed the traditions of British psychiatry in seeing a genetic cause for schizophrenia and depression. He called the critic of those theories, R. D. Laing, 'that crazy Scot – I think it's vicious, that he should go around unloading a burden of guilt onto the shoulders of unfortunate schizophrenics and their parents, making them think that they're responsible for their child's schizophrenia.' He was equally firm that the cause of depression lay in the genes.

We can find good scientific evidence to support whichever view we prefer, but no amount of scientific evidence can protect us from the implications our search for causes has for our own lives. If we hold to the environmental view, we must then feel guilty when our lives and the lives of our children go wrong; but we can feel some hope that we can repair the fault. If we hold to the genetic view, then we do not need to shoulder a burden of guilt; but genetic faults allow no repair. Our genes can be our tragic flaw.

Alcohol is not only a wonderful way of avoiding your own depression, but also, if you drink enough, you can get other people to concentrate their attention on your drinking and so not do anything that will confront you with your depression. Siegfried had good reason not to acknowledge his depression. His family history showed that pattern which geneticists see as supporting their theories of the inheritance of depression, but Siegfried would say, 'I don't think the gene is in me', and remained loyal to that school of psychiatry which, while allowing for the importance of 'social factors', sees the cause and cure of mental illness in the metabolism of the body. Loyalty, obedience, and trust in leaders were very important to Siegfried, no less important in psychiatry as they were in the Navy. True, he was now at the head of the hierarchy, in a position to have his orders obeyed, but the leader in the hierarchy is as much a part of the system as the lowliest minion. The leader can express his individuality only up to a certain point; beyond that he must fit within the framework, the rules of the hierarchy. If the leader can manage to do this, then he can enjoy the delicious combination of the exercise of personal power within the comfort of a group. Siegfried was like very many people in striving to achieve this and, like many people in a hierarchy, he found that one of the great advantages of being in a hierarchy is that one does not have to relate to many, if any, people as equals, but only as subordinates and superiors. When we relate to another person as an equal that person is not in our control, and therefore may behave in ways which we cannot predict and which may in some way hurt us. The relationship of a superior and a subordinate, whether it be doctor and nurse, teacher and pupil, manager and apprentice, parent and child, is a limited relationship, with each member being able, within the rules of the relationship, to predict and control the other member (subordinates can control their superiors, as every experienced nurse knows). Such relationships allow intimacy without risk. But intimacy is not love, and love is a risky business.

When Siegfried and I were talking about love I challenged him on this. 'When you're in love you're not in control of your life, are you? You said something earlier about not wanting to be emotionally dependent on anyone, so that being in love, or loving someone enormously, you really put your life in that person's hands.'

'Yes.'

'All I'm noting is that your decision to become a consultant and your decision not to love deeply again, both of these decisions were based on the premise of "It's dangerous to put your life in other people's hands" or "For safety's sake I want to control my own life".'

Siegfried laughed wryly. 'Inside this husky tough there's a frightened little boy.'

To the adjectives 'frightened' and 'little' Siegfried could have added 'bad', but it was a badness that he was quite attached to. One day Siegfried was talking about a schoolmaster who had encouraged him to read. 'He was a kind and gentle man,' he said, 'I envy him.'

'You don't see yourself as kind and gentle?'

'Only sometimes – and it soon vanishes.'

'Are you saying that this schoolmaster was kind and gentle right through, at his very centre, while your kindness and gentleness is just something on the surface?'

'Yes. He would never have threatened to shoot one of his men – and meant it. I did.' At first he looked as though he might feel guilty about this, but as he talked, it became clear that he took some pride in this aspect of his character.

People who are devoted to duty are not always kind, and

Siegfried talked a lot about duty. I asked him if duty was an important concept in his life.

'Yes, enormously.'

'In what way?'

'If you accept obligations, you must honour them.'

'What would happen if you don't accept your obligations?'

'You'd dislike yourself even more than you normally would.'

'How much does a person normally dislike himself?'

'That's a good question. Do I know or do you know?'

'But you used it. You implied that normal people or people generally disliked themselves to a certain extent.'

'There are different degrees to which we accept this. Even psychopaths dislike themselves. That's why they kill themselves. They have a faint glimmering from time to time that they can't make normal relationships.'

'But what about people who don't dislike themselves?'

'The ones I know, or I think I know, are amongst the most dislikeable people one could meet.'

'So people who like themselves are disliked by others.'

'I'd put it differently. They don't have many likeable qualities.'

'What you're saying, and this links with what you said about boasting, you said that most people to some degree dislike themselves, and it's right to dislike yourself, because if you don't, you'd be the kind of person that other people don't like.'

'Yes, or more important, the person you don't like is yourself.'

'What you're saying is that for you to live with yourself, you've got to dislike yourself.'

'Got to find a few decencies here and there.'

'But to be able to like yourself you've got to dislike yourself. You've got to see within yourself dislikeable characteristics for you to be able to live with yourself, because if you stated to see within yourself wholeness and goodness, see yourself as a good person, then you would be in danger.'

'Put myself on to lithium. Wouldn't you?'

'If I said to you, well, people like Carl Rogers say that all human beings are at centre good, and suppose I tried to follow the Rogerian approach, and got you to recognize within yourself your natural goodness, which was your real self, then that would be unacceptable to you.'

'I think it would. I think his basic thesis is untenable. We're born with very nasty instincts, aren't we? Aggression, fear, reproduction (I suppose the seeds are there), appetites which we're prepared to satisfy regardless of anyone else, these are the basic things we're born with.'

'And you see them as basically bad?'

'We learn to become nice people. We learn this happy gift, when we have it, by being able to give and receive affection.'

'This is something that comes later, through learning?'

'If we're lucky. And our genes colour this too. I don't think we can remove our genes from the total sort of person that we are. If we've inherited brown eyes, diabetes, tendency to dement, I don't see why we shouldn't inherit a basic kind of brain structure, a basic neurone pattern.'

'But what you're describing is a model of a human being as – a child comes into the world –'

'A complete savage.'

Later I said to him, 'There are some people in the world who feel that their value lies within themselves, that they are valuable people to some degree, and they place that value in their essence, their being, and then there are some people who believe that their value doesn't lie in what they are but what they do.'

'Are the two different? You do so because of the sort of person you are.'

'I was watching a programme on Paul Robeson the other night. When he got into his sixties, he started to develop arteriosclerosis and got depressed. His friends who were being interviewed for the programme, one of them was describing how in the last ten years of his life, Robeson retired to his sister's home and saw nobody, and when his friends would say to him, "Look, you're such a figure in the movement, people just want to come and sit at your feet. They don't want you to do anything", he would say, "No, I won't have people do that. I can no longer do anything. I can't sing, I can't talk. Because I can no longer do anything, I'm of no value." And he wouldn't accept, even understand, that people would look at him and say, "There is a good man and we will gain something just from being in his presence. He doesn't have to do. He just has to be, and we're enriched just by his existence." Robeson couldn't see this at all. He was a man who placed value in what he did and when he could no longer do, he saw himself as valueless. You come across to me as being like that. That you place a lot of emphasis in what you do, and the way you describe yourself as being in essence not a good person, not valuable. You have certain qualities which you see as good, but if one of your friends or one of your patients said to you, "I benefit from being with you. You don't have to say anything or do anything, but just your goodness helps me", that would be something you would find very difficult to understand or accept.'

'Yes, to some extent, I think I see what you mean, but I think status, a doctor, a consultant, not anything particularly good about me.'

'You create a problem for yourself straight off by the way you define a human being. You define all human beings as carrying within themselves something bad, their instincts, and with that kind of definition, if that's how you see yourself, to be good is a constant struggle. You have the feeling that "The moment I relax, then this terrible badness inside me will get out of control".'

'I don't think so now, because I think that at an early age I saw this badness, unpleasantness, nastier features, and by accident or by luck I disliked them. Difficult to change one's mind after fifty or sixty years, isn't it?'

'If you define yourself as being born bad, with bad instincts, and then you define life as the process of bringing these bad instincts under control and in some way working hard to counterbalance the badness in you, you've immediately defined life as a struggle, and then when you get to a stage where there's no more work for you to do, and you're also getting older and more tired, then you are in a terribly vulnerable position because you start to see yourself in danger, that all this badness is going to become more apparent, less controllable. Whereas, if you start off with a definition that a human being is born good, "trailing clouds of glory", and that throughout life bad things can happen to a human being which fill his life with misery, but if at his centre he feels goodness, however this might have been got at by the passage of time, then when that person comes towards the end of his life, he's got something good at his centre which resides in him and in which he can reside, then it's possible for him to find some degree of peace and acceptance.'

'Do you find any evidence that human nature was born good?' There was scorn in his voice.

Death, he said, was the end and he did not fear it. What he did fear was what lies between then and now. I asked him how he would be remembered after he died.

'For perhaps for two generations, nothing else.'

'And what kind of memories will people have of you?'

'Pleasant chap, sense of humour, quite good at his job, drank too much.'

'How would you like to be remembered?'

'Mm – I don't know – it would be doing Shakespeare good now to think that here was the greatest poet of all time. What does one need? Nothing.'

'Some people would be quite happy to be remembered in the way that you expect to be remembered. I was asking if you would like to be remembered in some way different from that, as a great poet.'

'Mm – loyal, I think, a friend one could rely on, basically, "I'm sorry the old devil's dead".'

'That people would regret that you'd died.'

'Yes.'

I asked him whether he believed in God.

'No.' He said this very quickly.

'Have you ever believed in God?'

'I'll tell you of a slightly emotional occasion I had when my uncle got the chop in the Air Force – a man I was really very fond of. He was the only chap I used to write to regularly. I was about twelve, I think. He was a marvellous man. He was very interested in books, and he used to write to me and tell me about books he thought I might like to read. He put me on to Jane Austen when I was twelve. I used to write reviews of the books I read. They must have been terribly bad reviews, but if he thought they were good reviews, he'd send me sixpence or a shilling. In those days that was really something. And then his aeroplane came down a bit too fast. And, up to that time, twelve, thirteen, I'd had some vague sort of concept of God – I sang in the Church choir every Sunday. My last memories of any contact with God was that particular night when I called Him all the filthy language I knew.'

'So God was a person for you up till then?'

'Very vaguely. Even then I thought, if He exists, He's a shit.'

'And how do you feel about Him now?'

'If He exists, He's a shit. When that happened, I felt I'd been rather foolish and went through all the filthy language I knew. With regard to God this had been rather a waste of time. This was rather childish, but I felt a bit frightened after I'd said all these things. Thought perhaps I'm wrong. Perhaps I've made Him angry.'

'And that He'd punish you?'

'No, that He'd make it all different.'

'What did you think He'd do?'

'I'd get a telegram to say it was all a mistake and that the bloke hadn't got the chop after all.'

'That didn't happen?'

'No.'

'So getting angry with God didn't do any good?'

'I didn't expect much. One hangs onto straws.'

'And then what happened? Did you continue to go to Church?'

'Yes, because we were fairly hard up and at the end of each four months I used to get my choir money. That was a large part of my income and I liked the music and I liked the Bible. One can still read the Bible with great pleasure, surely.'

We talked about the parts of the Bible that we liked and suddenly he said, 'I've got a Louis Armstrong record. Do you like Louis Armstrong?'

'Yes.'

'I thought you would. Louis and the Good Book – he sang a song about Nebuchannezzar – God didn't approve of Nebuchannezzar altogether, so He wrote something on the wall. I've forgotten the Jewish, "But Nebuchannezzar, thou hast been weighed in the balances and found wanting" and Louis says, "Hey there". Having been weighed in the balances and found wanting by God, there isn't anything else that you can say, except "Hey there".'

We laughed and then I said, 'But that's how you feel about yourself – that you've been weighed in the balances and been found wanting.'

'It's not quite as bad as that. I'm a good deal more ordinary than I thought I was, and perhaps not even very exceptional.'

'Do you still feel that if there is a God, then God's a shit?'

'Oh, yes, He must be, yes.'

'Why?'

'He couldn't intentionally and with the ability to do something about it, run the world like this, surely.'

'I'm not arguing the point one way or the other. I'm just trying to see how you see it. Your feeling is that if there is a God, then He's a shit. He runs this world in a terrible way, does terrible things.'

'How can He tolerate man being so intolerable to man? What end can possibly be served by Auschwitz, the IRA, this wretched business we read about this morning? I could do better than this.'

He went on talking about the horrors of our contemporary world in a way which reflected how he saw God as betraying his trust, and I was reminded of Mark Twain's tirade against God:

> We brazenly call our God the source of mercy, while we are aware all the time that there is not an authentic instance in history of His having exercised that virtue. We call Him the source of morals, while we know by His history and by His daily conduct as perceived by our senses that He is totally destitute of anything resembling morals. We call Him Father, and not in derision, although we would detest and denounce any earthly father who should inflict upon his child a thousandth part of the pains and miseries and cruelties which our God deals out to His children every day, and has dealt out to them daily during the centuries since the crime of creating Adam was committed.

Siegfried doubted that I really understood the nature of life. One day, when he was telling me about the other patients on the ward he said, 'A lot of them suffer from your basic defect.'

'What's that?'

'Optimism.'

'Why do you regard that as a defect?'

'Because you're liable to be disappointed.'

'So it's better to expect the worst and that way you're not disappointed so often.'

'When I climb out of bed thinking, "Oh God", and then something marvellous happens on that day, then I think, "My God, what a marvellous day!"'

'Have you always felt that it's best not to expect good things to happen?'

'Yes.'

'As a general rule of life?'

'Yes.'

'So if you balance it out, if you expect good things to happen, then you get disappointed, so you have that pain; whereas if you don't expect good things to happen and you go along feeling a sort of low level misery, thinking that everything is going to happen for the worst, and then something good happens, you get this wonderful feeling; but if nothing good happens, you're still on this sort of low level of misery, and a low level of misery is better than the sudden pain of disappointment.'

'Yes, of course.'

When we were talking about love I asked him, 'Are you sorry now that you did not fall in love again?'

'Well, yes. God, isn't it frightening?'

'Why is it frightening?'

'It hurts – I was telling you what a brave man I was, I don't get frightened. My God, I'd be frightened of that. Can happen only once, I think. That first time of overpowering emotion, all the buts and fears that life imposes, one wonders what goes wrong. Like nothing can be too good. You'll trip over something soon, mate.'

'You feel that when life is good, something bad is sure to happen?'

'Yes.'

'Why should it?'

'I don't think I can answer that question. It seems to be a fairly popular habit.'

'You feel this is a fair description of the way the world is?'

'Yes.'

'But if you live in a world, your world, where you see people, including yourself, in essence, right at centre, being in some way dangerous and bad, and in a world where the probability of the way in which things will turn out is more likely to be bad than good, and you see yourself as unable, unwilling to have a close relationship with anybody, and you see the end of life as the end for yourself, and if there is a God, then He's a shit – if you define your world on those parameters, you haven't left a great deal of space for joy and hope have you?'

'No. So I'm back to Beethoven, Bach, Leonardo, Shakespeare, and the Bible.'

'Are they your sources of – what?'

'Beauty – truth.'

'Why is beauty important?'

'It's just there, it exists, to be looked at again and again. Or listened to, again and again.'

We talked about beauty and I tried to relate this to how he saw the human race. 'If you operate with a model of the human being as being essentially evil, then you've got a model which makes it impossible for you to become reconciled with yourself. Freud's model of the human being was the same as yours. In his life he showed great personal bravery, but he saw the human race as damned.'

'I don't think I go along with the idea of the human race being basically damned. Surely Shakespeare taught us this – the essence of tragedy is that a man of decent qualities destroys himself by having a failing in one or two small respects. Macbeth was a superb character, but he destroyed himself, didn't he?'

Siegfried saw the idea of tragedy applying 'to quite a large extent' to his life. He held to the tragic, not the romantic, vision of life, as George Steiner has described it:

> In authentic tragedy, the gates of hell stand open and damnation is real. The tragic personage cannot avoid responsibility. To argue that Oedipus should have been excused on the grounds of ignorance, or that Phedre was merely a prey to hereditary chaos of the blood, is to

diminish to absurdity the weight and meaning of the tragic action. The redeeming insight comes too late to mend the ruins or is purchased at the price of irremediable suffering . . . Where the tragic conception of life is in force, moreover, there can be no recourse to secular or material remedies. The destiny of Lear cannot be resolved by the establishment of adequate homes for the aged . . . In tragedy, the twist of the net which brings down the hero may be an accident or hazard of circumstance, but the mesh is woven into the heart of life. Tragedy would have us know that there is in the very fact of human existence a provocation or paradox; it tells us that the purposes of men sometimes run against the grain of inexplicable and destructive forces that lie 'outside' yet very close. To ask the gods why Oedipus should have been chosen in his agony or why Macbeth should have met the witches on his path is to ask for reason and justification from the voiceless night. There is no answer . . . And beyond the tragic, there lies no 'happy ending' in some other dimension of time and place. The wounds are not healed and the broken spirit mended. In the norm of tragedy, there can be no compensation.

Siegfried would allow himself no compensation. He told me about 'a special envoy sent to see me from the States. This chap – something of an evangelist – came all the way here to see me and said, "I want you to fly back to the States with me now. I'll put you inside for a month. I'll get this cleared up." Well, bloody hell. He's a nice man, but I can't join a bunch of evangelists.' To me he used the standard criticism of traditional psychiatrists, 'Your kind of psychotherapy takes far too much time. It's not on,' and when I persisted he complained, 'I think you're doing a terrible thing. You're starting to make me think again.' He used many diversive tactics to stop this happening and warned me, 'I think you do a lot of good to a lot of people, but aren't you perhaps in danger of infecting them with your optimism?'

I persisted with my foolish optimism. 'I think that human beings are neither good nor bad but simply are. Attributes of good or bad are the opinions that we hold. The universe just *is*. Goodness and badness is something we create, our own ideas.'

'Can I suggest a more fanciful compromise? There is a God and He's given us a thread of cotton by which we can haul ourselves up there, if we don't strain too hard and if we don't break it.'

'How's your thread of cotton holding out at the moment?'

'Pretty tatty. It hasn't broken, I think, but there's a knot in it.'

'What sort of knot?'

'It's a granny knot, and they come undone.'

4

The Philosophies of Those
who Cope with Life

When I first came to England in 1968 I went to work in a psychiatric clinic where I spent much of my time talking with patients suffering from depression. Many of these patients were women the same age or older than myself, and many of them, far from living in circumstances to which depression would be a natural reaction, had secure, comfortable homes, devoted, reliable husbands, and loving families. I had come to England jobless, with two hundred pounds and a child to support. My marriage had ended in a welter of painful events which even today I prefer not to contemplate. Yet, there I was working, coping, though not always as efficiently as I would want, talking to women whose lives had followed the pattern I had wanted and who sat there depressed and often weeping at their misery. I was puzzled as to why this was so. I knew that if I put this problem to the psychiatrists at the clinic they would say, speaking from within the framework of their belief in the biochemical basis of mental illness, that I was fortunate to enjoy a non-depressive metabolism. If they stepped outside this framework and spoke as people who shared a common space with me, they would have said (though not to my face – they were too kind for that) that I was a tough, aggressive, non-conforming, insubordinate, contentious colonial. It was the second verdict which I came to see as the true one, although I would, of course, have described myself in more agreeable terms. I was angry and I felt justified in being angry at those people whom I saw as having deceived and used me, and at myself for being so stupid as to have wasted so many years and so many opportunities. I had always seen the possibilities of life as infinitely varied, splendidly exciting, precious beyond price, but limited by a final death. I knew that I had to make the most of what time I had left. My depressed patients did not share my view of life. For them, even when they were not in that state called 'clinical depression', life was an intolerable burden, a punishment for past sins, a testing ground where failure was inevitable, a sunless, narrow path to an abrupt and joyless end. It was not my metabolism that protected me from depression. It was what Siegfried called my 'foolish optimism'.

So when I came to write this book I thought I should talk to people who I knew coped with their lives and see whether they had philosophies which gave them courage, hope, and optimism. I would need to have known these people for some time to be able to be sure that they did cope with their lives. Many people present a good front to the world while at the same time leading lives of 'quiet desperation', or supporting themselves by an addiction, or maintaining their own integrity at the expense of their family and friends. Who were the people I knew who, in the face of life's difficulties, coped? The first person I thought of was my friend Mollie.

Mollie was a social worker and I had met her through our work. We soon became friends, and I often visited her home and got to know Bill, her husband, and their children. They seemed to me to be a close, happy family, a family who laughed a lot. This did not surprise me. One of Mollie's clients, a bed ridden old woman, described Mollie as 'coming into my house like a ray of sunshine', and this phrase, sentimental though it sounds, did describe Mollie exactly. I knew that this was not a mere professional cheerfulness. I had seen Mollie, at home and at work, in situations which would have irritated me enormously but in which she would simply laugh, brush aside the provocation to anger, and pursue the right and proper course of action. Her life was far from easy, but she looked on each problem as a challenge to be met with courage and mastery. When Bill took a promotion in his firm and they moved away to another city I knew that Mollie would be greatly missed. She and I kept in touch by letter and phone and the occasional visit, but as usually happens in such friendships, time has the habit of rushing by and months elapsed between contacts. I knew that she had been ill at Christmas time, and we had talked on the phone after she left hospital, but summer went by without us being in touch. As autumn approached I thought I would write to her to bring her up to date with my family news and to ask her if I could come for a visit and interview her for my book. She telephoned me the day she got my letter. 'I've been thinking about you,' she said, 'I've been wanting to phone you but I know you're busy. I'd like to talk to you. Dorothy, Bill's left me.'

I was so astounded all I could say was 'You're joking.' But she was not. Bill had packed his bags and gone. So I went to visit Mollie. We talked a lot, walking beside the river, over the kitchen table, in the sitting room late at night. Mollie insisted that she should fulfil my request and talk into my tape-recorder about her philosophy of life. I was glad that she did this because what she said showed that the advice I had come armed with to give her, advice along the lines 'Men are bastards. Take him for every penny he's got', was for her quite irrelevant.

What I discovered straight away was that Mollie was not angry with Bill. She was hurt, bewildered, and very sad, but not angry. In the painful days of the break-up she had got angry with him once, and of this she was very ashamed. The problem that occupied her mind was what had she done wrong, how had she failed to meet Bill's needs, had he needs which she had failed to perceive, much less meet.

In the conversations we had had over the years, the concept of meeting another person's needs figured often in what Mollie said. So the first question I asked her in our recorded talk was 'Why is it important to be needed?'

Mollie replied, 'I suppose I don't really feel I'm a complete person unless I'm needed. I've got this need inside me that I've got to have somebody to care about. I find this very difficult at the moment with the children being at the age they are, and they don't – they're ready, nearly, to make their own lives – and I'm suddenly going to find myself without having anybody to do things for. I feel as though, one's always had a purpose in life, and my purpose has been my family and my work, but my family being always foremost. To me, family life is extremely important. I suppose in time it will take on a different meaning, if the children marry and have a family, and then probably I'll start feeling needed again because the role becomes different. You become a grandparent and you're needed because you're a grandparent. But I feel that at this particular stage in my life the role of a parent – apart from providing a home – my role as a parent is probably over.'

'When you say that needing people makes you complete, what would happen to you if circumstances were such that there was nobody in the world that you felt needed you?'

'I think that me being me, I would probably, in that sort of situation, go out and try and find some way of providing – well, for instance, when I first came to live here I felt that I needed to do something – with the children at school and Bill at work – I needed to do something that was giving me some sort of satisfaction, and so I helped the agoraphobics, and I think that if I had no one at all this is one channel, one area where I would say I've got to find some particular group where I could try and find a niche, and try and fit into it and help people who were not quite as well off – not money-wise, but not well off in being able to cope. I think this is where I would probably channel – well, not my affections – to satisfy my own needs, really – to feel that I was doing something useful, really.'

'Why is it important to do something that is useful?'

Mollie thought about this. 'I think that if I don't do something that's useful, if I didn't do my job, I'd just find that sitting at home, just doing housework, doing the sort of normal chores that women do – they have to be done, it's mundane, you have to do them, it's expected of you as a female that you look after the house and see that things are clean – but I do feel it's – I like to feel that I'm helpful to somebody, to be of use in some way, to feel that I'm giving something to somebody, and I think that that would probably give me some satisfaction in myself, make me feel better.'

'Is it the most important thing in life to give to someone else?'

'Yes. I feel that I have this need to give and to be needed to give.'

'What would happen if – suppose you ended up as a patient on a chronic ward with multiple sclerosis, how would you feel about yourself then?'

'I think at first I would probably feel like a lot of people feel – "Why has this happened to me?" But I would hope that I would be able to overcome this and be able to – well, you would, in that

100

sort of situation, identify with your fellow patients and probably be able to gain strength from each other. I would expect that this would happen on that sort of ward. You would be able to help each other, support each other, really you're all in that ward knowing that your days are really numbered. You would all know that you were all there for a certain length of time, and I would be able to contribute something to the other people that were there and not become too engrossed with myself. And probably seek support. I think I found it when I was in hospital earlier this year. One tends, when you're in that situation, to be suddenly thrown into a group where you all feel that you're in it together, and you're all facing an operation or not knowing what the diagnosis is going to be, and you do tend to support each other. You do tend to have this feeling, well, you need each other at that particular time, even though you've never known each other before you walked through the hospital door.'

(Later I pressed Mollie more on this question of what would happen to her if she was completely alone. 'That would be terrible,' she said, 'I would crack up.' Horrible though this fate might seem to her, Mollie was not one of those people who believe that their very identity would dissolve were they removed from the gaze of other people. In another context, speaking of her work, she said, 'I'm not just Bill's shadow. I'm not one of those women who only exist as their husband's wife.')

I used Mollie's mention of death to ask her what death meant to her.

'It's not something I've really thought about,' she said. 'The only time I've thought about it was when I was very poorly and I thought that it might have come when I was in hospital this time. My general reaction was "Well, I don't suppose anybody would really miss me." Was it going to make them feel "Oh dear" – and had I made them feel that – I don't know, it's difficult to say, but there were times when I felt so very, very ill that I really thought I was at death's door – but I can't really put into words how I saw it or how I really felt, apart from thinking "I wonder if they'll really miss me if anything happens to me now?".'

'Did you hope that they would miss you?'

'Yes. I hoped that I had made some impression on them, that they would miss me.'

'You wanted them to go on remembering you?' (This reminded me of Mary, about whom I had written in *Choosing Not Losing*, who did not want her family to remember her after her death since this would upset them, and upsetting people was the thing that Mary feared most. But, of course, if they did not remember her, it would be as if she had never lived.)

'I felt that I'd want them to think I'd contributed something.'

'To what?'

'Well, particularly with my own family, I'd have hoped that they thought I'd contributed something, and they'd remember me with affection.'

'There would still be love coming towards you even though – '

'I was dead, yes. I can remember feeling very much alone at that time, lying in hospital, relying very much on my fellow patients for support and hoping. Because you do feel terrifically isolated, and when you go into hospital – I think this is a fear that a lot of people have – are you going to come out again, and the longing that you have, you begin to think that you are never going to see your own home again. This is something that happens.'

'So, when you think about death, you think that when people go on loving you, you sort of go on existing.'

'No, not go on existing, I suppose you hope that you've made enough mark in your life that people will think of you, and think, "Oh well, I remember her because of this – " or "I miss me mum – no one makes a cole slaw quite like her" – or things like that.'

'Do you believe in life after death.'

'I think there are some spirits after death. I do feel that.'

'In what way?'

'I can't say in exactly what way except that I have had a sitting with a spiritualist who told me that my father was always watching over me and I do believe that this probably happens. I do believe that there are people who probably give us strength, because very often when you face a crisis in your life, I think it's often been said that you get strength from somewhere to face up to it. I think when my father died I coped reasonably well. I was the one that did the catering after the funeral, even though I was one of the main mourners, and I felt that, I don't know, you feel as though you're given something – in certain situations one is given strength from somewhere, whether it is some sort of spirit that gives you this, I don't know, but I think that it could be.'

'Do you feel that your father is watching over you now?'

'I think that probably he is, yes, I think he is.'

'What does he think of it all?'

'That I can't answer. Can't really say. But knowing my father as I knew him, I don't know how he is now, but as I knew him, I would think that he would be supporting everything I would be doing.'

'So that in some way he's giving you strength now?'

'Yes.'

'He's on your side?'

'Yes.'

'That's a nice thing to know. Earlier this evening when you were saying you're not getting much help from your kids I was thinking that, apart from your friends, you're not getting a lot of support, but you're getting more support than I was aware of.'

'I think – I don't know, I can't say for sure this is happening, but I do feel that my father would be there, saying, "I'll stand beside you, no matter what you did". Yes.'

'Do you feel that when you die, you will still be available for people who need you?'

'I would hope I would be. I would hope I would be of some use. Once again, it's something very mystifying because we don't really know what happens, but I feel I'd like to feel that I was being of some help in this way – as giving my family, and friends, the help, the strength they needed.'

'So you see it in terms of being in some way connected with this world? Not in terms of going to heaven?'

'I find that difficult to answer. I think that everybody has a spirit. I can't answer that – I can't get in tune with that.'

'I asked you that because I was going to ask you about your religious beliefs. I've got the impression, from other conversations that we've had, that you believe in God.'

'Yes, I do.'

'How would you describe God?'

'I can't describe Him, really. I think He's up there, and that very often, rightly or wrongly, one sort of says, you need some

103

help, and one expresses one's thoughts to God and you ask for help. I think an instance of what happened to me last Sunday was interesting because when Bill came in the morning to take the children out – he didn't come into the house – he just said, "I'm taking the children", and I was standing feeling very hurt, very injured, and he drove off, and I felt so very, very sad, and I sat down and I said, "Please, please, God, make him come back and show that he cares a bit", and I said this half a dozen times, and at twelve o'clock he drove back and he came in the house and he said, "I'll ring the insurance company about the car. You'd better sit down, you look a bit pale." He got the insurance papers and then he went off again, and I just felt as though I'd asked for this and it had been – He's answered, and I just couldn't believe it because that Sunday I felt everything was against me, that I was losing out, that everything was going right for Bill and nothing was going right for me. Most peculiar that.'

'You felt that was an adequate answer to your prayer? You didn't think that God should have made him come in and say "Mollie, please, take me back"?'

'Well, at that stage, no, that wasn't what I was asking. I just wanted him to show that he had some concern for us at that time. That was my main thought, that he'd been so cold and aloof, that if only there was just one glimmer of light to show that he had some caring in him which I thought he had lost completely.'

'So you weren't asking for a lot.'

'No. For I felt when he drove away first that he was so cold and aloof – he was going and I was left, and I thought, "Well, that just proves he doesn't care two hoots." He's gone.'

'When you describe God as someone you can turn to for help, and when you describe yourself, you say you want to be a person who can help – it sounds that the terms by which you describe the most important part of yourself are the terms by which you describe the most important part of God. Do you see God as being entirely good?'

'No, not always. Because one cannot always come to terms with the things which happen. Therefore you don't always accept that. No, I don't think God is entirely good because you can't always justify why things happen. Many's the time when you go out to visit clients and you look at them and you think "Goodness, fancy that happening. How tragic. Is there a God?" '

'How do you answer that?'

'Well, the only way I can answer that is by saying like I say sometimes about myself, "I wonder what I've done to deserve what's happening to me" – because I've tried to – one of the things I've always tried to live by, it sounds a bit silly, but I try to do unto others as I wish to be done by – and I wouldn't go out of my way to hurt anybody deliberately, and I've always been like this. I think this is one thing that I've always felt – that I – it's just one of my moral codes – I wish to do unto others as I wish to be done by, and yet there are times when one has to face up to certain things, particularly in the sort of job we're doing – when I've had to take someone's children into care and I've thought, "Gosh, what would I have felt like if somebody had come and done that to me?" What torment would I have gone through and how I would have hated that person for doing that. But in my everyday life I would try, I think I do try, to understand and care for people. But I don't know. What's that saying, you can't be all things to all men.'

'But when things go wrong for you you look into yourself and say "What have I done wrong?" '

'Yes. This is bad, I realize that, but I do. I sort of say to myself, "I must have done something awful." The times I've said that over the last few weeks. What have I done?'

'You don't feel that this is random bad luck?'

'Well, I suppose not because of Bill's attitude. I don't feel he was having such a bad life that he had to turn against me, so therefore it must be something, I feel, that I've done to make him resent me so much, and hate me, not want to know me. Because I can't live with unhappiness, with aggro. If I have chastized the children I've always had to go to them before they've gone to sleep to tell them that I love them, but they had to be told they were naughty.'

'Do you tell them you love them so that they will go on loving you?'

'Oh, no, no. I just want them to know that I love them, even though I've had to be cross with them. They've got to learn that there's right and there's wrong. And so therefore I find it difficult that somebody – like Bill's turned against me – I find it difficult to accept.'

'When you became ill, did you see that as something that was a message that you were doing something wrong or was that just bad luck?'

'Well, no, I never looked at it in that way at all. It just happened and it was something that I had to go through with – something's gone wrong and it's got to be put right. I didn't look at it as bad luck. I just thought it's happened. It was a traumatic experience and I didn't relish the thought of going into hospital.'

'So you didn't feel that that was some kind of personal failure like with Bill?'

'A personal failure – with Bill – yes.'

'What do you think you should have done with Bill?'

'I think I shouldn't have been so complaisant – I should – although he's not the sort of person you can argue with. When I look back now, I really don't know, apart from trying to talk to him. I feel that probably he didn't feel I gave him enough encouragement. I don't really know what he wanted and I don't honestly know now what he wants. I do so much soul-searching, trying to decide what I've done because all I've ever wanted was for him to be happy, and yet he never was contented because he was always searching for something more. He could never sit down and think "I've got my health, I've got my family, good job, what more do I want? Aren't I lucky?" And yet he did resent the fact that I could do this. He felt that because I wasn't saying "Where do we go from here?" that I wasn't ambitious. It's a funny thing, life, isn't it?'

'When we want to help somebody, we have to be able to work out what kind of help that person needs. It seems that you're finding that you don't know what kind of help Bill needs.'

'No.'

'In general, in work, in relationships with your friends, and with your children, do you feel that, on the whole, you know what people need?'

'Yes. That's why I found it so difficult to accept where I've gone wrong, because one can usually assess what a person is actually looking for, but Bill's always striving for the one step ahead, in any case. I must have fallen down somewhere as a wife, because I can't believe it's all his job that's made him like this, unless it's this drive that he's got that's made him become emotionally flat, and that his work and all the other extra activities that he's done have taken over, and this driving force within himself has flattened his emotions and relationships have to go by the board. That's the only way I can think that he – that's the way I'm trying to understand it, but then am I looking too deeply when all it is in black and white is that he doesn't love me any more. At the moment I feel destroyed, destroyed in myself because I can't – I've always – if ever I've hurt anybody, if I'd felt I'd offended them, I would go up to them and say "I'm sorry". I'd try to do something about it. Whereas with this I feel I can't do anything about it, and because I can't find out about it, I wish it was something I can't do anything about, yet in some way I do blame myself. It's something I shall never find out about – I suppose I shall never get to the bottom of the reason why.'

Mollie never doubted her ability to make friends. Ever since she was a little girl starting school she had lots of friends who sought her out and who cared for her. She could always feel reasonably sure that she could perceive the other person's needs and so she could help that person. She had thought that the support and love she had given her husband, even when his career ambitions made little sense to her, had been what he needed, but now all she could do for him was to feel pained and baffled by his evident unhappiness. He had withdrawn from family life and gone to live elsewhere. Mollie wondered if he had another woman, but she wondered this, not out of jealousy, but out of concern for him. For Mollie, being on your own is the greatest terror and deprivation, a fate she would wish on no one and certainly not her husband. All she wanted for Bill was for him to be happy. Now he had refused her love and help, and he had told her that he no longer loved and needed her. Such a rejection attacked her very reason for being. But even in the midst of her distress she did not feel totally destroyed. In her work she knew that she was loved, needed, and competent. She did not doubt her ability to make friends, to join a group where she would be loved and needed. She felt that her father was with her in spirit, supporting her, wishing her well, loving her. She knew that God to whom she had turned all her life for help was up there still listening, guiding, supporting her. She felt, too, that while the meaning was still obscure, eventually she would see this experience as in some way beneficial. Tragedies only appear as tragedies because God's purpose is not clear to us. 'Perhaps there is a reason,' Mollie said, 'We just can't see it.'

'If there weren't any tragedies,' I said, 'there wouldn't be anyone who needed help.'

Mollie laughed.

When I began asking people about their beliefs about life and death I was surprised to discover just how many English people had some sort of belief in reincarnation. I, in my ignorance, had thought that this belief was confined to those who had grown up in the orbit of the philosophies of Hinduism and Buddhism. Now I found that there were many people who interpreted their lives in terms of the karma that had accompanied them into this present life. They might not have used or even known the word 'karma'. Instead they would say, 'I must have committed some horrible sin in a previous life to be punished like this.' 'This' was a life of heavy blows accompanied by the misery of depression. The person would feel overwhelmed by guilt and, finding no adequate cause for such guilt in this life, attributed the cause to sins of an earlier life, or he would look back at the series of misfortunes he had endured and, instead of attributing them to life's random unfairness, hold to some notion of justice by accepting responsibility for crimes committed in a previous life. Thus the mixture of the Western notions of sin, guilt, and punishment and the Eastern notions of death and re-birth produced a philosophy of life that was black and heavy in the extreme.

Not everyone interprets karma in such a way. My yoga teachers, Eric and Christine, interpret it in a positive and joyful way. I have known Eric and Christine for four years, ever since I began attending their classes. They would talk about their philosophy in class, and, as I met them socially in other circumstances, I knew that what they said in class was not a facile recitation of some of the tenets of yoga but rather represented the way they lived their lives. They were past retirement age, but both looked much younger. They had had, and were still having, their share of life's woes, yet they remained courageous and cheerful. Karma, it seemed, could be interpreted optimistically. So I asked them if I could visit them with my tape-recorder, and they agreed.

First of all I asked Eric, 'What do you believe will happen to you when you die? How do you see your death?

He replied, 'For me, I see waking up in another place, whatever that may be. What happens over there I'm not very clear. From what I've read there are numerous things that can happen, but I think probably it will be something like a period of rest and then a chance to look back on what I've done in this life – re-run the tape, learn from it, and in due course, I don't know how long that would be, I shall come back. It's an opportunity for me to build on my experience of lives to date and, I hope, move on from where I am now. What, I mean who I come back as I'm not at all clear and I don't think that matters. Whether I come back as Eric moved on, or as an entirely different personality of which only my inner spirit is the same, continuing entity, I don't know. I don't think it matters.'

Christine said, 'Don't you think you come back with some part of your personality the same, because otherwise – I mean, look at a group reincarnation – I think we come back in groups. For instance, I think we've probably done exactly this before. Although I may not be a woman next time and Eric may not be a man. I think we've swapped over many, many times.'

'Oh, I'm sure,' said Eric, 'I'm sure for myself that I've been a woman because I feel very sympathetic to women and I think I understand them better than I understand men. I expect we shall swap and change as our experience requires.'

I asked, 'Eric, do you see it as a progressive thing in that you're in some way refining yourself or part of yourself so that you're moving along, or do you see it more as a cyclical thing?'

'I would hope it was a progressive thing, but I quite see that just as in one's ordinary life, this life now, one can slip back, not make much progress, I find when I look over my life I find I've gone in fits and starts. There are periods when I feel I've progressed and got on, and periods when I've either marked time or even slipped back a bit, and then that's followed by a period that I would call progression. I think that's what happens in one's series of lives. There are lives when perhaps you mark time and lives when you even slip back a bit, but in general, taken over a sequence, I would hope that I've progressed.'

'Do you see this reincarnation going on forever and ever or do you see the progression leading to a final stage?'

Eric replied, 'I think that given time one will reach the end of that, what happens after that I'm not sure. It may well be something like the Buddhists say, that one merges with the greater consciousness and loses to some extent one's individuality. I don't know, but I would have thought that it wasn't endless for ever and ever.'

'How do you feel about the loss of your individuality?'

'It used to bother me terribly,' said Eric, 'and I found it very difficult. Now I can see that it doesn't matter. Looking at myself today, that's a long way off.'

'So you still see your individuality – something that is intrinsically you – still coming back again.'

'Yes,' said Eric, 'I find myself more and more attracted to Buddhism – Buddha discouraged all forms of speculation, and I'm coming round more and more to thinking that this is it, that one has to get on and do the best one can according to one's life. But I can't help seeing that as part of this progression of life. That eventually we'll end up somewhere, but at the moment I'm not bothered where that is. I'm content to enjoy the journey without worrying about where I'm going.'

'Do you have any recollection of past lives?' I asked.

'No,' Eric replied, 'I've no memories that way. We know a lot of people who have very clear memories of what they were. The only thing that I can say is that I have one clear picture of a place. This may be something I've just imagined, but I feel it's a long distance memory. But, I don't know. The mind's such a funny thing. You can kid yourself into believing what you want to believe. This is something that's been with me all my life, a picture of a place, a snapshot almost. It's a cloister bathed in sunlight, nobody about. I can't even see myself or what I was. I've never come across it. I've a feeling it was very long ago so it may not even be there now. That's no proof, but I recognize that I could, long ago, have seen a picture which attracted me.'

110

I asked, 'How far back in your present life have you held these beliefs?'

'From my late twenties,' he said, 'that's thirty years, thirty-odd years.'

'What sort of beliefs did you have before then?'

'Well, I was brought up in the Church of England. My parents were C of E nominally. My grandmother was very strongly Church of England, and eventually I ended up in the choir. I couldn't sing but I looked very nice. Later in my life when I went to college, I took up chemistry and for some time I didn't become atheistic, but I became very agnostic. I thought that there probably wasn't much else but molecules and atoms. And then, after I met Christine, I came in contact with a little fellowship called the Order of the Cross, which is a mystical fellowship. It was founded in 1904 by a chap who had been a Congregational minister, and he had a series of memories from past lives which were all connected with the Christian belief. Implicit in his teaching was reincarnation and implicit also was being a vegetarian. I've been a member ever since. I'm one of the trustees of the Order. On top of that I've always read more widely than that and I've become very interested in yoga and the Hindu beliefs and Buddhism and Taoism and Zen. I find myself very much attracted to that.'

I asked, 'Can you see the roots of that going back to your childhood at all?'

'No. My family were orthodox Church of England. My father and mother were not regular churchgoers. No, none of those things were known about. To my grandmother that would have been paganism. I didn't really accept these ideas until I came across the Order's teaching. The older I got the more sensible it seemed, and I would find it impossible to throw over that idea since it seems to me the only idea that gives meaning to what you see around you in life – law of karma and being responsible for one's actions so that what happens to one is not a result of outside forces or germs or accidents or other people cheating you, but what happens to you is one's own direct choice and responsibility. The central core of my philosophy is that one is responsible. If I fall downstairs, it's not just that I fell downstairs, but for some reason or other my consciousness allowed me to fall downstairs. In other words, the lack's in me. If I suffer from some disease it's because I've allowed that disease to take hold of me, or it is to teach me something. I go along with one of the Stoics who said I look upon everything that happens to me in life, whether it is good or bad, as an opportunity of learning. And I think that's a marvellous way of looking at things. Everything that happens, whether it's bad, whether it's tragic – the biggest tragedy you could imagine only stays a tragedy if you cannot draw a lesson out of it and learn to do differently in future.'

'When you say "You learn something from it", you could be saying "Something happened and I drew some conclusions from it", or are you saying "Some things happen to me because there's a power beyond which is using these things to instruct me"?'

'Both. Isn't that the same thing. If you said there is a power beyond me – that may not be some guardian angel pushing me, or even tripping me up, but the workings of the law of karma. You see, I see life as an interlocking web, a network in which – almost like great marshalling yards where there's an enormous amount of lines with branches and points which we travel through. Now, if we have to stop at a station to pick something up, which might be good or might be bad, it's because that's the way the points are set for us. We have set the points. The working of the law of karma is the resultant of our actions, our words, even our thoughts. So, every moment as I'm sitting here thinking, my very thoughts are setting the points ahead of me, like ripples going ahead of a boat, and eventually I have to sail through that course. Now my thoughts at the moment aren't going to make that much difference, but if I go out and kick the cat' (and in that household there were a lot of well-fed cats) 'I've made a major reshuffle of points, and sometimes that new track I'm having to take because I've done something that was basically an infringement of another creature's life, then I shall have to do two things. Either I shall have to know what it's like to be kicked for no reason at all or I shall have, at some time, to make it good – helping someone else or some other creature that's in a bad way – to balance the books. Everytime I do something which is morally wrong – and don't start asking me what's moral. Let's say there are moral, amoral, and immoral

112

standards. If I do something which is a good action, I put something on the credit side of the ledger. If I do some wrong deed I put something on the debit side. Sooner or later these have got to be balanced, and if there's a red entry, a debit, then I've got to cancel it by a credit entry.'

I asked, 'How do you see your entries standing now?'

'Well,' said Eric, 'one has to endure, suffer is what the Buddhists say, the law of karma, until one can become so unattached to the results of one's action that one escapes from the law of karma, then it no longer has an effect upon you. And this is the probable, of course, that whatever we do, and for whatever altruistic motive, most of us – one in a million is unattached, the rest of us are attached for a greater or lesser degree. Until one can do that one is bound to the law of karma and to the wheel of rebirth. One's incarnations stop when one can genuinely become non-attached to everything. It doesn't mean that one has no place, but that one can do things from the real, true meaning of altruism. One does it because one wants to help, because it is good and not for what one is going to get out of it. One may not have a material reward but one tends to feel good – now that's a reward. It means you're still attached.'

'Are you saying you're still feeling a good deal of attachment?'

'Of course I do,' said Eric. 'Don't we all? If I didn't I'd be a saint. And there are a few saints. One hears of them, mostly in India, who are genuinely unattached, and that's why they're saints. They can do good without knowing that they're doing good. People get benefits just from being in their company. I've got a long way to go.'

I told Eric and Christine about the people I had met who interpreted karma in such a fearful way. 'You don't give me any sense of fear,' I said.

'Oh, good heavens, of course not,' said Eric. 'This is a great misunderstanding. People talk about karma as if it was something bad. But there's good karma.'

'If you assess yourself as a bad person,' I said, 'then if you believe in karma you would see your reincarnation as not being the best.'

Eric replied, 'There are very few really bad people. There are very few good people. We're all a bit of a mish-mash in the middle. You know, some of the most cruel and monstrous people in history have had a good side to them – they loved their dogs or their children, or they kept a garden, yet they could do monstrous things. 'There's nobody who is wholly good or wholly bad.'

'So when we're born we're a mixture.'

'Yes, of course, because if we were wholly good we wouldn't be born, we'd have come to the end. The fact that we are born shows that we are a mixture. I think it's the only thing that gives meaning to life, and I don't think it's a thing to be frightened of. All it tells me is "Eric, you're responsible". You can't blame the government, your father and mother, your upbringing, a germ because you caught a cold, you've got to blame yourself. When I say blame myself, that's the wrong term, because I can look back and see the good things that have happened to me and think "Eric, you gave those to yourself". Because we're not punished for our sins or rewarded for our virtues, but we are punished by our sins and rewarded by our virtues. If you look at it that way you've something you can get on with. What's the use of complaining about something when you know it's your own fault. The thing is to make sure you don't do that again.'

'So you see yourself as possessing virtues and also possessing the ability to do better next time, ' I commented.

'Oh, yes,' said Eric. 'You've got to. I've always – a lot of my colleagues in the Order are very hesitant about doing anything in case they make a mistake. I always say I can think of very few decisions that one can make in life that if it is not the right decision cannot be put right or turned to good. There's very, very little in life, except, perhaps, swallowing cyanide that's irrevocable. Nearly everything else, if you find you've made a bloomer, you can either retrace your steps or go off at a different angle. You try to tell people that, oh dear, don't you dare do that, they say, just in case.'

I asked, 'How did your grandmother present religion to you – as something that was painful and threatening – '

'No, not at all. She was a nice old girl. Not one of those fundamentalists that said if you didn't go to church you'll go to hell. Not at all. She just invited me to go along and I liked her and went.'

114

'It was a pleasant experience?'

'Yes. I used to enjoy it. I think probably because of my long history in the church. For instance, if I hear a Gregorian chant, it does something to the hair on the back of my neck. And I'm sure this wasn't the first life that I've been involved in religion. And I think it was probably in the West, in Christianity, and I think that in this life that's what I'm breaking free of. No proof, of course, just a feeling.'

'Do you have any belief in a personal God, or a trans-cendent God?'

'Well, yes and no. My own belief is that the whatever, the great mystery, is not an old man sitting on a cloud. It's something of which we cannot have the slightest understanding of until we merge with it, and our understanding will become its understanding. At the same time I'm absolutely certain that because we have finite minds and finite understanding, that this infinite does on occasions present itself in a finite form which we can understand. Hence some of the visions that some of the mystics have seen, which have been of tremendous meaning for them but has been presented in the visual form that they would expect, so that Christians see Christ, Buddhists see the Bodhisattva, Hindus see one of their three hundred and thirty thousand gods. I feel that this is really the way in which, for purposes of watching and helping a human soul, the whatever presents itself in a limited form which one can contemplate. You see, there are very few people who can contemplate a mist, an all-over mist. You've got to be fairly well on the path to be able to do that. And therefore I think that this is one of the reasons why mankind through history has created symbols – a Cross, a Virgin Mary, or a Kali or a Shiva or a Buddha – something which they can sit and look at and which can mean something to them and they can relate to. So, as Jung said, man needs his symbols, and those are very potent symbols. Many people will have to employ them for many lives to come, until you can start and have some relationship with something that is informulate. People have to reach a stage where they can see beyond a symbol to what it symbolizes and place no actual sacredness or intrinsic power in a symbol, but only see that that power comes from the reality which the symbol symbolizes.'

We talked about death and Christine in her usual enthusiastic way said, 'I love it here.'

'You don't want to go?' I asked.

'I want to see what it's like on the other side, but I want to come back again. It's a nice place, in spite of all its peculiarities.'

'You don't fear that you might come back to some terrible place?' (I had often pondered upon why I had awoken to self-consciousness in the nineteen thirties as an Australian in Australia and not as a Jew in Warsaw or a Russian in Leningrad.)

'You'd have chosen it,' said Christine, 'when you're up there, when you're looking down from your rest place and you're reviewing your life and saying, "Well, really, this soul needs such and such an experience" and therefore you would choose, say, Australia.'

'You feel we choose our suffering?'

'I'm quite sure we do. A conscious choice, knowing what is necessary,' said Christine.

'A degree of understanding,' said Eric.

'I think sometimes one has it chosen for one,' agreed Christine.

Eric said, 'I feel it's a little like school. When you were a youngster, you hadn't much idea of what school is about, your parents push you there and say that's where you're going. When you've got more understanding of what you've got to do, the things you've got to learn, when the time comes for you to go to university you choose yourself the university. I think it's a bit like that with reincarnations – souls of little understanding are directed, but as one gets older, spiritually speaking, one is consulted and eventually one makes one's choice oneself – this is the experience I must have to round me off. Sometimes one chooses a very difficult experience.'

'This implies some knowledge of the future,' I said.

'Yes, sure,' said Eric. 'There is a pattern which is changing. It is laid down. We know that in three years there'll be a General Election, unless we have a nuclear war. The pattern is fixed over a large area. Life is to a large extent predestined, not in everything, but in a lot. Whether we've got free will or predestination, we still have to get on and live it. We act as though we've got free will because that satisfies our ego. "I am

116

the master of my fate." That sounds good and gives one a nice feeling. I'm getting round to seeing that there's no free will. That doesn't mean anything mechanical.'

'We have free will within a circumscribed position,' said Christine.

'The more I think about it,' Eric said, 'the more I think it is more circumscribed than what we think it is. All our choices are determined by our character which is determined by things like what our parents were like, how we grew up, and so on.'

The question of free will and determinism in human behaviour was one which Eric was currently pondering upon, trying to relate personal responsibility to the causal connections of the law of karma. He enjoyed working on problems like this, but now was not the time to discuss the different arguments. Instead Christine went on to tell me about herself.

'I'd been into isms and ults all my life. My mother was a primitive Methodist and I started life being dragged along to chapel three times on a Sunday and I didn't like that one little bit. But I think I always had the feeling that I needed something because I went through the whole lot, Congregationalist, Church of England, even got to the point of signing on to be a Roman Catholic. But all the time I had this feeling that this wasn't quite what I wanted. My own teacher was a member of the Order of the Cross and that's how I got into it when I was about sixteen or seventeen. The idea of karma and reincarnation just seemed so obvious that I couldn't think why I hadn't thought of it before. Like Eric, I've got more and more drawn to Buddhism over the years of doing yoga and meeting so many of the marvellous Indians who are such marvellous people and so full of fun. That's what I like about them. They find the whole of life as one huge joke.'

'How do you see your next life?' I asked.

'I haven't the faintest idea,' said Christine. 'I hope it's where it's warmer. I'm jolly sure this is the first time I've been in a damp, cold country.'

'Where do you think you've been before?'

'I think India. I remember when I was at Art College, donkey's years ago, having my eyes tested for colourblindness because they said that no Westerner would ever put the colours together that I always put together – pinks and oranges and yellow – no, India, China, Japan have always fascinated me.'

'Have you any memory of such places?' I asked.

'No. One thing I'm sure of, I was never in a convent or a monkery or whatever you call it.'

'Christine, in class you come over as more – well – childlike and magical than Eric – like you don't have to worry your head about it.'

'No,' said Christine, 'that's a feminine attribute. Men are terribly logical and they'll work things out and get there in the end whereas a woman goes whoop and she's there, and not knowing how she got there between whiles. I can't argue with you or discuss as Eric does in a logical way, but I *know* without having to be bothered with all the logic, and how could I be wrong?' She laughed.

Eric said, 'I think actually she's touched on the right word there – the magical side of life. I think we both feel that life has magical properties, there's far more to it than we know about. Don't you think so?'

'Oh, yes, absolutely,' Christine said.

'It's becoming more certain to me – it's always been that way for Christine, me having spent my life in science and industry, always been hampered in seeing the poetic side of life, but I must say of recent years, since I left industry, I've become much more that way – haven't actually seen fairies at the bottom of the garden, but they're probably there if I could look well enough.'

'How do you see that as fitting into your philosophy?' I asked.

'What, the fairies?'

'Well,' said Christine, 'don't you think that everything – animals, plants, landscapes, stones – everything has got its particular being and – ' She looked at Eric.

He said, 'I just want to refer back to what I said earlier. I'm sure that just as the great mystery has to make itself recognizable if it wants to approach an individual, so I think it has to take on a form which we associate with it.'

'Have you read *The Magic of Findhorn*?' Christine asked me.

'No,' I said. I knew nothing of Findhorn.

'Oh, you must, Dorothy. It's a gorgeous book. Have you put

118

the kettle on, Eric?' Eric went out to make the tea and Christine told me about Findhorn. 'Now you have to take it with a slight pinch of salt. It was written by an American when he was absolutely skyhigh about Findhorn. Findhorn is a community in the top right-hand corner of Scotland which was founded about sixteen years ago by Peter and Eileen Cady who went there willy-nilly, they had no idea why they were going there and over the years it has become a community, a spiritual community which I feel is one of the most important things that is happening on this planet in this generation. It's a marvellous place. Eric and I went there a couple of years ago and our immediate reaction was to come back, sell up, and go back there to live. It's a fantastic place and the Cadys are fantastic people, and it started by them growing a garden. A friend who was with them, Dorothy Maclean, was one of those people who could contact the spirits of the plants, and it was through Dorothy and Eileen that Peter was able to produce a garden. They grew huge cabbages and roses, marvellous on soil that was not much more than sand and pebbles. And then after some years came David Spangler, another American, who altered the direction of Findhorn slightly. He said that by the time he arrived Findhorn had ceased to be a place to grow gardens and became a place to grow souls. David had a tremendous influence on the development of Findhorn and has written some fantastic books.'

I asked Christine, 'Do you see magic as a word to cover all these things – do you see that as good or bad?'

'Oh, good.'

'Entirely good?'

'No, not entirely good. It can be used – if it's used selfishly, it can be bad.'

'So the badness comes from the usage. You don't see the badness as being outside in the magic forces themselves?'

'No. It's the way one uses it, I'm sure.'

When Eric returned with the tea Christine said, 'I don't see magic as a thing, do you, Eric? It's just sort of force fields.'

'That's right,' said Eric. 'Good magic is the power of positive thinking, bad magic is the power of negative thinking.'

Over tea I asked them, 'How easily do you think you could change your beliefs?'

'Oh, I couldn't,' said Christine, 'I think they could be enlarged.'

'It depends,' Eric said. 'I think if something came along and was presented to me in such a way that it made sense, I would embody that in my belief and cast out things which did not fit. That happens all along.'

'Yes, I think it's a growing thing,' Christine said.

'Looking back on my life,' said Eric, 'I've changed out of all recognition. I'm sure I could change if I was convinced that something came along that was better. I can't see, quite honestly, a complete and utter reversal. I can see an expansion and extension.'

'When you were a small child,' I asked, 'did you feel you were a good person?'

'Just cannot remember,' said Eric.

Christine said, 'I can remember very plainly. It's taken me a good deal to overcome one aspect of my mother's treatment of me. She was the most incredibly beautiful woman, and she always used to say in my hearing what a pity it was she had such a plain daughter, and it took me until, well, even now it overcomes me sometimes – that I was hideous and it took me a long time to realize that I wasn't all that bad. However, I think I've got a bouncy nature.'

'Did you think it was just outside that was bad and inside you were all right?' I asked.

'I've always been quite pleased with myself inside,' said Christine. 'That's not quite true. I've always known that I was all right inside. Other people might not think I was but I knew I was.'

Eric said, 'Right up into my twenties I had the most colossal inferiority complex. If somebody said good morning to me I used to blush and stutter and hardly could say good morning back.'

'That's something I cannot understand,' Christine said.

'Well, it was,' said Eric. 'Why it should be I don't know.'

'Well, it was your mother, dear. She kept you right smack under her thumb. You had to do just as you were told.'

'I found it very difficult to stand up for myself,' said Eric.

120

'But even if you could not stand up for yourself, did you have some areas where you felt all right?' I asked.

'Oh, I think so,' said Eric. 'I've always been pretty sure of my own abilities. I hope that I've got a reasonable assessment of my own abilities. I don't think of myself as completely good. There are areas where I could be very much better, but I've always been fairly confident of myself intellectually and practically, the use of the hands.'

'Eric's never said he couldn't do a thing,' said Christine.

Eric agreed. 'Even if I'm not sure how a thing could be done. I've always said yes, I can do it, and then found out – and have always found out.'

'How far back in your childhood can you remember feeling that?' I asked.

'Oh, far enough. I've always been extremely good with my hands.'

'This links with earlier when you were showing a feeling of confidence that whatever situation you were presented with, in whatever life, you could use this situation in some way to improve yourself, and you were always capable of improvement because you had the confidence that you could do this. If you make a mistake you have the confidence that you can repair it. You can do better next time.'

'Yes,' said Eric. 'My difficulty always arose in my relationships with other people. I always felt embarrassed in public, but I seem to have overcome it. One of the formative things in my life was when I went into pharmacy. I was apprenticed to a pharmacist and he taught me the art of salesmanship. That got me talking to people.'

We finished our tea and Christine remarked, 'I think that life is completely fascinating. I get frightfully fed up with it occasionally and I get depressed sometimes, don't I? I get gloomy rather than depressed – '

'Who doesn't?' said Eric. 'We'd be fools if we said we never get down.'

Christine said, 'But I usually reach a point in my gloom when I come to see the funny side of it and start to laugh, but, by and large, I think life's marvellous.'

'Yes,' I agreed, 'I always feel that there are so many wonderful things to do.'

'Isn't it a blessing that you have plenty of lives in which to do them all?' said Christine.

I said, 'But when I get terribly tired I think "Oh, I couldn't go through all this again".'

Christine laughed. 'Oh, yes you can. Of course you can.'

When I surveyed my friends and acquaintances it seemed that everyone I knew was in some way involved in health and social services. They were psychologists or doctors, teachers or social workers, nurses, natural health practitioners or theologians. Was everyone I knew in the business of making other people better? Then I remembered Richard. He was a farmer and he knew that worrying about the state of our minds and souls is something we can do only after we have made sure we have enough to eat. When I asked him if he would talk to me about matters of life and death he protested, 'I'm a very, very ordinary farmer. I won't be able to give you the intellectual answers that you require.' But I knew that Richard was concerned with more than making his farm pay. There are many farms in Lincolnshire that are run as business concerns and, despite the advantages that nature may have given them, such areas of land have all the charm and loveliness of a bare factory. Richard's farm was a successful business; it was also a place of great beauty, enhanced by his loving care. The passion with which he spoke about the trees he had planted and the woods we walked in made me believe that I had found someone who shared my feelings about trees. I find it very difficult to put my feelings about trees into words. All I can say is that I could manage to live in a world without books; I might manage to live in a world without people; but I could not live in a world without trees. Years ago I met a teacher who told me that when she was nineteen and just out of teachers' college, she was sent far from her home to a one-teacher school in the outback of Australia. Such schools stood alone in the bush, and the handful of pupils would come from a scattering of homesteads often miles away. The teacher would be given board and lodging at one of the isolated homesteads. So lonely and difficult were these teaching posts that only young men would be appointed, but in the war years such posts had to be filled by young women. This teacher described to me how lonely and frightened she was, and then she told me of her long walk to and from school each day along a bush track that wound its way along a river bank where great white gum trees stood. 'In the years I was there,' she said, 'it was only those trees that kept me going.' I knew what she meant, and Richard would have known too, though he described his passion for trees in terms of how he was more distressed by the destruction of some saplings through a car accident than he was by the injuries to the people concerned.

So I prevailed upon Richard to talk to me and my tape-recorder. He poured us both a good measure of his own sloe gin, and I asked him, 'What do you expect will happen to you when you die?'

Richard said, 'I very rarely think about it. I don't believe that there is something like an afterlife, I don't believe that there isn't, and I feel I try and lead a reasonable sort of life – I don't suppose that makes any difference about your life after death. I never think about it. Do I think there is? I suppose one hopes there is. I just don't know and I can't really see much point in thinking about it because I shall never know about it till I die. When you talk to religious people about life after death they say oh, yes, everybody has a life after death, dogs and cats, well, I believe that some people on this earth have no right to have a life after death because they behave so badly, and why should they have a life after death? I know there are a lot of different views, that life is a preparation for death. I don't ever think about it. If there is a life after death, well, that's a bonus. But I don't think it would make any difference to the way I behave in my business or the way I treat my children or anything else. I'm not conscious that I would. I haven't given you a very good answer. I just don't think about it.'

'When you say that some people oughtn't to have a life after death – '

'Well, one reads stories in newspapers about how people have tortured animals. I read a story in a newspaper about a dog that had had knives put in it, and if you look back in history, one day a year in a certain village, the people used to let a bull go in the streets and the idea was that people in the village used to stick knives in it. Eventually the bull would fall to its death and they'd cut it up. No, I feel, should there be a place for people who don't know how to behave – in the next world – I don't know. I don't think we're good enough to go on to another place. Now you can say I have thought about it to have thought that far.'

'It's impossible to make these things entirely separate because the whole business of the purpose of life and the nature of death is part of the nature of morality, isn't it?'

'Yes. I was brought up in an atheistic household where religion was never talked about and my father, when I said I wanted to be confirmed, said, "I'll disown you if you get confirmed." But I've never stolen or done anything I've thought was wrong. That was the way I was brought up, but religion never came into it. I don't think I've spent enough time thinking about it. Perhaps I will when I'm older. I imagine older people when they get near death, they do think about it.'

'But you've thought a lot about how you ought to live your life now – your present life.'

'Well, I suppose one is influenced by the way one's brought up and so on. Yes, I believe one should be kind to people and animals. I would think hard about doing anything that I did not think was in my code of conduct.'

'Why is it important not to be cruel to animals?'

'Because they're defenceless.'

'It's wrong to hurt defenceless beings?'

'Yes, I think so, because they can't fight back. They can't say anything or do anything – completely defenceless.'

'Now some people see defencelessness in human beings and animals as an opportunity for themselves, but you see it as a restriction – you must pause and think what you are doing.'

'Well, I feel very close – I suppose it's the job I do. I'm very involved – we have a lot of livestock, and if you want to get the most out of an animal you've got to be kind to it. Like the cow. The cow, the kinder you are to it the more milk it will give you. You hit it or do something to it and it won't give you anything – which adds up. It's sensible, isn't it? And I love animals. I like animals much better than I do human beings.'

'What is it about animals that's nicer than human beings?'

'Because they don't answer back, I suppose, and they're not

unkind. I've never met an unkind animal in my life. If an animal's unkind, you've made it unkind. That's right.'

'What's so bad about answering back?'

Richard laughed. 'Well, it's inconvenient, isn't it? Yes, I suppose it is. I don't like being answered back, I suppose.'

'I feel perhaps I should ask you whether your kids do.'

'Oh, yes, of course they do. I would be horrified if they didn't, or question the things that you tell them. But I think that's one of the reasons I'm a farmer. I don't come from farming stock at all. It was animals that drew me into farming. I think because I love them so, and we're lucky, we've been very successful with them. But I haven't answered your question about – because I really don't know. I don't really want to think about it or talk about it before I get involved in it because I can't think it'll make any difference.'

'How do you see yourself spending the rest of your life?'

'Do you mean the next ten years, next twenty years – I don't know how many – it might end tomorrow.'

'How old do you think you will be when you die?'

'I always used to think that I was going to die young, but now I think I won't be quite so young when I die. I don't know. I think I shall die when I have had enough. I would think I might make eighty. I wouldn't want to live an awful lot longer than that. How do I see myself spending the rest of my life? Well, I think once my eldest son starts to farm – I think he will – I know he will – then I shall take less of a part in the farm. Do you mean spiritually or – '

'No – if someone said that to me I'd say, well, I want to do this and this.'

'Oh, I see. Oh yes, there are all sorts of things I want to do but I've got to persuade Jennie to do them with me. I would like to spend two or three months abroad every year because I don't like the climate in England very much, or not in this part of England. I'd like to see more sunshine. I'd like to see a lot more of the world. I'm a very shy person. I can't take a very active part in the community because I don't really like getting up and talking and being involved with people. Much as I would like to take a part, more of a part in the community, I don't think I'm able to.'

125

'When you say you're shy and when you say you don't like people answering back, does this mean you've often found people to be hurtful?'

'Mm, well, in business you can't afford to have people answering back. If you say something then it's got to be done that way, I have a very good foreman who does answer back, and I have to slap him down. I don't like doing it but I have to. He argues about what we're doing and what we should do, and I'm a little bit dogmatic, a little bit arrogant at times, but I have to in order to – he's a strong chap – but he's very, very good. If he wasn't I should have got rid of him.'

My question had come from my experience of depressed people who were terrified of anyone who might be less than gentle with them. I could see that this was not Richard's problem and so I changed the subject. I asked, 'You said that when you were a child you wanted to be confirmed?'

'Well, actually, my best friend at school was going to be confirmed and I said to my parents that I was going to be confirmed and would they come up for the confirmation and a letter came back saying that – well, of course my father wouldn't disown me because we've always got on terribly well, but words to that effect. He didn't approve so I didn't get confirmed.'

'Did that matter very much to you?'

'Well, I think I missed out a bit when, on Sunday morning, all my pals used to go to the service and come back and tuck into their breakfast. I think it was a great pity that I didn't. I think I missed something. I certainly missed something socially, and probably spiritually as well. And from that sort of time I suppose I didn't really bother about religion any more.'

'One thing about the Church of England, it certainly provides a social framework for life, doesn't it?'

'Yes, it does.'

'What did you feel you missed spiritually?'

'I don't know. I think if I'd been encouraged to go to church and I'd been encouraged in a religion – well, there you are. I don't really know. I think perhaps it is a bit of a facade. I mean, the idea of people going to church on a Sunday in a village is very, very attractive, isn't it? And it's very much a part of the way of country life, going to church. I think I do miss something there. I do occasionally go, but I feel uncomfortable because I've not been part of the church for the past twenty-five years.'

'When you say uncomfortable, do you feel that part of you wants to be part of the church?'

'I think it does, yes, but I think it's too late. But I don't think badly or laugh at anyone who goes to church. If the children want to go to church, that's fine. I would encourage them to go. But it's very difficult to be religious when you've been brought up in an atheistic household.'

'How does the idea of having another life appeal to you?'

'It depends on what it was like.'

'Do you see yourself as being good enough to go on to another life?'

'No, I don't, I'm sure I'm not. I wouldn't qualify.'

'What do you see as your deficiencies?'

'You're asking very, very deep questions, aren't you? I've never talked to anybody about things like that. I've thought about them. I don't think I can answer that question. I don't think I'm a nice enough person. I think I'm too aggressive, I'm not kind enough. I don't really know but I don't think I am. It depends on how many. If you said, well, ninety-nine people out of a hundred go there, then I think I would make it, but if you start getting under fifty out of a hundred, then I don't think I would make it. There are degrees. I think I'm better than some people but – '

'Being kind or unkind, that's important.'

'Yes. Well, I would say that Jennie is a hundred per cent kind. I don't think I fall into that category. I tend to say nasty things about people. It's worse – if I said things to their faces, that's all right, I suppose. I'm not thoroughly nice, like many people are.'

'In your job, you can't be a hundred per cent nice, otherwise people will take advantage of you.'

'Yes, I do have to be hard, very hard. It certainly went against the grain when I started working, whereas now I don't mind. When I say hard I don't mean unkind. One has to be hard in order to be – if you make a mistake you can go out of business. There's a lot of money tied up in it, and I would think that my reputation of being hard – not that I want to be that, but I've had

127

to be. I've taken over a farm which I think I've made fairly successful, but I haven't done that by being unkind to anybody, but I've had to be tough. I haven't been ruthless. But I've had to be a little bit tough. Whereas now I've reached a point where I delegate a lot, and therefore I don't have to make the immediate kind or unkind decision, not to human beings anyway.'

'Would you rather make unkind decisions to a human being or to an animal?'

'Oh, to a human being. Oh Lord, yes. If it was justified I don't mind making an unkind decision. If it's justified I don't mind that at all. But an unkind decision to an animal is physical, whereas to a human being it would be mental. Oh no, I can't bear being unkind to animals at all.'

'How do you see human beings? Do you see them as basically good or basically bad?'

'Well, I think you could divide the world into two, the good ones on one side and the bad ones on the other. I don't think you can say people are basically bad. I think there are an awful lot of bad people in this world and I think there's an awful lot of good people in this world.'

'Do you see good people as being born good?'

'I think if you put it in a percentage – you mean, is it environmental or is it breeding? I think it's both. Of course environment is terribly important. I think there's a lot in breeding. I wouldn't like to put a percentage on it either way. I think if somebody comes from bad parents and had an idyllic upbringing they should have every chance of being good people, and the other way around is much more difficult. I don't think there's a cut and dried answer to it. Provided you've got them young enough.'

'Some people see human beings as being basically bad, dangerous.'

'Well, they are.'

'In what way?'

'We can talk about Hitler or Arthur Scargill – to me he's somebody who is bad, completely bad. I think he's the most evil man in this country today. He's anti-establishment – anything to do with the society we're living in at the moment. He wants to change society. He's going to have a jolly good try to do it, and if he got assassinated, then I wouldn't shed a tear. He wants to change society into a communist society. A nineteenth century Arthur Scargill would have been a very different sort of person, but a twentieth century Arthur Scargill is to me a very dangerous man. I don't want society to change. I mean, it will do, and I know we're gradually moving to the Left and it bothers me. I see him as a desperate chap. So long as he sticks to his miners, then that's all right, but once he gets involved in politics which he inevitably will do, then that's where the danger will start. I think one of the saving graces of this country is that we are a sort of moderate people, and people can be whipped up overnight by somebody like him. He's a very bright man. He's got a chip on his shoulder . . . I think the more you have the more you want to keep hold of it. I'm not worried about me, but I would love to keep it all together for the next generation and for the good of the country because it would be very detrimental to break up what we've done, and by God, we've worked hard for it. Everything we've made we've put back . . . All I want to do at the moment, I want to send my kids to the schools I want to send them to, I would like to have a nice holiday each year, spend a little bit of money on the house, and as long as I can do that I'm happy, very happy.'

Richard poured me some more sloe gin and said, 'I had a very, very happy childhood, a lovely childhood. I was brought up in the country which I absolutely adore. I'm completely a hundred per cent at home in the country. I don't like towns or people. I'm a bit of a loner, perhaps, although I love company. I love to have lots of nice friends. But I had an idyllic childhood. My mother's a real country bird, that's where I get it from. I absolutely loved the country and I spend a lot of time thinking about my childhood. I could go into minute details of days at home, spent in the holidays. I do spend a lot of time thinking about my childhood and how happy it was. We lived miles from everywhere and we went everywhere on bicycles. I do spend an awful lot of time thinking about my childhood, probably literally hours a day, because it was so happy, which is marvellous, isn't it really? Not that I'm not happy now. I am, but I don't live in an area where I was born and brought up. I like this area. My kids have been brought up here and adore it but I don't feel completely at home here. I spend a lot of time thinking how happy I was. I don't think about unhappy times. Everybody's got unhappy times. I did my National Service in the Army, and I had some unhappy times in the Army, but I think I've had such a happy life that I can overcome that, and I even think about the unhappy times and laugh about them because it's past and it's gone and I've overcome it. But I've been very lucky. Very few people have the opportunities and the luxuries that I've been able to have, at least I know that.'

I had heard so many middle-class English people talking of their guilt about their privileged position in life that I had to ask, 'Do you feel guilty about that?'

Richard said, 'No, of course I don't feel guilty about it. I open my curtains in the morning and feel very grateful. I feel very fortunate. Why should I feel guilty? If I felt guilty then I would start feeling miserable and life's too short to be miserable. I love being happy. The only things that make me unhappy is when the weather's bad and I can't do the things I want to do on the farm. The weather does make me miserable, but not for long. To enjoy the good things in life you've got to see the bad side. If you haven't seen the bad side, how can you possibly know it's the good side? Life goes so quickly.'

5

Laying the Foundations
of our World

I. The Discovery of the Axioms of Life

In constructing our world we have to deal, however ineptly, with the issues of life and death – the purpose of life, the supposed existence and nature of God, the possibility of annihilation or life after death, guilt, sin, punishment and reward, expiation and propitiation, fear and courage, forgiveness and revenge, anger and acceptance, jealousy and sharing, hate and love. Struggling with these issues is not a solely adult and intellectual activity. We each began to learn about these issues when the world we were born into began to make demands upon us – when we had to lie in our cots until the appointed hour when we would be fed, or when we were made to understand that we should ease the pressure in our bowels only according to some external decree, or when we were forced to accept that this was not a world which we were free to explore. It was then that we learned that the world contained the possibility of sadness and joy, freedom and coercion, justice and tyranny. As small children we knew our world as exact, certain, and real. We were like Henry James's little Maisie: 'She was at the age for which all stories are true and all conceptions are stories. The actual was the absolute, the present alone was vivid.'

At such an age *we learned certain truths about ourselves and our world, truths which remained absolute and unquestioned, despite what other experience later life might bring us.* Of such truths Camus wrote, 'A man is always a prey to his truths. Once he has admitted them, he cannot free himself from them.' Many of our truths came to us as rules about how we should conduct our lives. We saw these as axiomatic rules, no more to be questioned than we would question that the sky is above us when the earth is beneath our feet. Since some of the axiomatic rules we learned in childhood continue to be true throughout life – rules like 'Fire burns', 'Don't run on busy roads' – we expect that the other rules we learned will continue to be true and useful, when in fact they may no longer apply. As we get older we do not always inspect our axiomatic rules to see whether they still apply. We may neglect to do this because we are lazy or lacking the skills of self-inspection, or we may resist doing this because our childhood rules are no longer rational rules but have become metaphysical beliefs. And metaphysical beliefs always carry a load of fear.

When we were small babies we looked at the world with uncritical interest, but our world, however pleasant and secure it might be, soon taught us to be careful. Not only were there places where we should not go and things which we should not touch, but there were people whom we should fear and never trust. Some children manage to retain a delight and interest in the world around them, but others are taught that their physical environment is full of terrors, that they should fear all kinds of things – animals, insects, birds, rain, hail, thunder, sunshine, shade, stairs, buildings, many kinds of food – and, most of all, that they should not explore. Curiosity is dangerous. *Many children are actually taught by their parents to fear anyone who is not a member of the family*. A mother may not put this attitude into words, but she shows it in the way she never allows neighbours into her house, or she refuses to let her child play with the immigrant children across the street, or she sends the child to a particular school to avoid him mixing with working-class children or children of another religious faith. Such experiences in childhood not only form the basis of the social class, racist and religious prejudices which bedevil our society, but they also serve to isolate the individual in our changing society. It always saddens me when in conversation with a depressed person I hear that person say that he has never acquired the knack of talking easily to people whom he defines as not members of his social class, or when he describes his terror that all he holds dear will be engulfed in a remorseless tide of black strangers – strangers whom he can never recognize as individual human beings like himself. As small children we absorb the prejudices, the cultural metaphors, of our society. James MacManus, writing in *The Guardian* about the policy of apartheid in South Africa, reported, 'At Ministerial level one senses a revival of the old Dutch dyke mentality that stamped the thinking of the Afrikaaners' forbears. Living beneath the level of the North Sea, the Dutch knew better than to tamper with the marine defences in stormy weather – and so the thinking goes now in South Africa's twin capitals of Pretoria and Cape Town. The imagery of floods and storms, the fear of being swept away by a "black tide", occurs constantly in conversations with Afrikaaner politicians, civil servants and academics.' Some of us like to feel that we have outgrown the narrow-mindedness of our early environment, but our earliest attitudes, though hidden under recent accretions, are still available when necessary. I pride myself on my liberal and enlightened attitudes, but I have discovered that I still carry the illiberal and anti-English attitudes of a native Australian. In my first year in England, when I felt harassed and lonely, I found myself responding to something which I had labelled as an act of treachery with the thought 'What else could you expect from a middle-class Pom?' The thought came into my mind with all the comfort and reassurance of an illuminated Truth.

Attitudes such as these, passed from parent to child, can be argued to be unrealistic. But a child who is born into a world where he is wanted by no one, where he finds himself to be an intruder on his parents' lives, or where he is passed from one home to another as adults come and go in his life, makes for himself a very sensible and realistic rule, 'Trust nobody'. Such a rule is necessary for survival. However, in the long term, it has a devastating effect on all relationships. The child who has made this rule axiomatic and never modifies it grows up completely incapable of making affectionate relationships. Sometimes the child learns to modify the rule slightly, to make it, 'Trust one or two people slightly'. He manages then to make some relationships, but the lack of trust lurks like a worm in the bud. He expects to be disappointed and he is.

The axiomatic rules that we learn as children contain predictions of what our life would be. Some children learn to expect little. 'Keep out of trouble and you won't suffer much pain' is the bleak rule on which many people fashion their lives, eschewing joy, and being thankful for an absence of pain. Some children learn to relish small pleasures and so find happiness in simple, unambitious lives. Some children are taught that if they meet certain standards of behaviour rewards will follow as night the day. For some fortunate children this proves to be the case. But not all children are so fortunate. Some parents, often loving, caring parents, set their children standards which are nearly impossible to live by. Aurelia Plath, the mother of Sylvia Plath, wrote in her introduction to a volume of Sylvia's letters to her family that 'As soon as my children were old enough to comprehend it, I shared with them the belief my husband and I had held concerning the importance of aiming and directing one's life toward an idealistic goal in order to build a strong inner life.' This was a lesson that Sylvia learnt well. She strove to achieve and did so brilliantly. But, as Sylvia said of herself, 'I just can't stand the idea of being mediocre.' Neither could she stand the idea of failure, and when something did fail, her marriage, she had few resources with which to combat the distress which led to her suicide.

It is the nature of human thought that as we learn a proposition like 'I can be a good girl' we also, by implication, learn its opposite, 'I can be a bad girl'. Aurelia Plath taught her children some fine principles, but in teaching them she also taught that if one did not have a purpose in life, a goal, then not only would something bad happen but there would be something wrong with oneself. A child who accepts this doctrine wholeheartedly may make something of himself, but he can never just be – just live accepting himself and his world. In all our lives there are times when we can follow a path of striving and achievement, and times when we can do no more than live within the cycle of the rising and setting of the sun, in the cycle of the seasons. In some of our activities, such as to be close to another person, to love, to make love, the essence is just to be and not to try to achieve. In seeking perfection, the person tries to gain control and power. Such forces are incompatible with the development of a loving relationship between equals. For the child who learns to see life as a series of goals to be achieved, the ultimate goal is perfection. It then becomes a hard lesson to learn that life, in this world at least, never admits of perfection. Moments of bliss are possible but perfection always eludes us.

Aurelia Plath, like most parents, believed she was acting in her daughter's best interests when she defined the importance of having goals in life. But when we give a young child advice, whether it is 'Work hard at school and pass your exams so you'll get a good job', or whether it is 'Have a good time while you're young', we are implying something about the fundamental nature of life. Our advice carries a metaphysical implication – perhaps that in this world hard work is rewarded or that pleasures must be snatched in a world where life is transient. We cannot be sure what implications a child will read into our advice. A young woman, called Julie, who came to see me said that she had been depressed from the age of sixteen. She described to me how, all through her childhood, and especially at school, she did everything 'well', and, oh, the scorn she put into that word 'well'. She said, 'I've been conscientious all my life. When I was a little girl at primary school I got reports where I was "conscientious, serious and hard-working".' Now she feels that her parents have betrayed her trust. As she said to me, 'I think they used me. They saw me as an extension of themselves. I felt exploited by many people, by the school, by them.'

Parents often do try to get their children to achieve in areas where they themselves have wished to achieve and failed, and this may be the case with Julie's parents. They certainly had advised her of the desirability of gaining educational qualifications, but they may not have realized that in doing so they were, in Julie's ears, making her a promise. As Julie said to me one day, 'I really hate myself for being so depressed. It's so pathetic. It does make it worse that I think we should be happy all our lives. I feel really bad that I'm unhappy. I'd always expected to be happy. My parents built me up. They used to pay me a lot of attention and say, "You're going to have a great time." I just thought I would. I thought everything was going to come to me and I wasn't going to have to do anything. I had one hell of a shock.' Julie was like the character in the Thomas Mann story who said 'I repeat with emphasis of desperation that happy I must and will be. For I conceive too profoundly of happiness

135

as a virtue, as genius, as refinement, charm, and of unhappiness as something ugly, mole-like, contemptible – in a word, absurd – to be unhappy and still preserve my self-respect. I could not permit myself to be unhappy, could not stand the sight of myself in such a role. I should have to hide in the dark like a bat or an owl and gaze with envy at the children of light. I should have to hate them with a hatred which would be nothing but a festered love – and I should have to despise myself.'

Some parents, wanting to protect their children from the cruel truths of this world, paint for their child a picture of a sunlit, joyous land, where evil is always punished and virtue always rewarded. If the child identifies himself with virtue, then he may sail through childhood and adolescence secure that his reward will come, but if, like Julie, he thinks that his reward will follow like night the day and that he does not have to work for it, then he is in for a rude awakening when the vicissitudes, the random bad luck of the big world crash in upon his small world. If, on the other hand, he doubts that he is one of the virtuous and that he has the guile to avoid his just deserts, then he feels helpless in the face of the future his parents have created for him. Parents who determinedly create such a sunny picture, a world where 'everything happens for the best in this best of all possible worlds', are often protecting not merely their child but themselves as well. They find it intolerable that life contains so many random events, the ground that suddenly shifts beneath our feet, the clot of blood that appears and blocks an artery, the two aeroplanes on converging paths. The randomness of happiness perturbs them just as much, since as happiness can come, so it can go. Unable to deal with the uncertainty of life, they fail even more to deal with life's most certain uncertainty, death.

Of course it is not possible to give a child an explanation of death which is entirely comforting and reassuring. The child who is taught that life ends in death has the problem of trying to establish a sense of identity in the face of the expectation that he could well lose it at any time. The child who is taught that life continues after death now has to accept and cope with not just the rules of this difficult world, but the rules of the world to come, which may include not just heavenly angels but a Day of

Judgement and the possibility of Hell as well. The belief in continued existence in the form of spirits and ghosts can bring terrors in its train, while those of us brought up in the Calvinist traditions know what a keen and subtle knife the Protestant conscience can be.

A child may be five or six before he discovers death and has to find a meaning for it. By then he already knows a good deal about himself. He has learnt from those around him not simply whether he is a boy or girl, but also what are the standards of behaviour expected of boys and girls, rules like 'Boys don't cry' or 'Nice little girls don't make a mess'. So when he cries or she makes a mess they know that they have in some way failed. Very early in life the child has to work on that endless problem 'How much in life am I responsible for and how much is not my fault?' Sometimes a child feels responsible for his mother's death or his father's leaving home, and his guilt haunts him for the rest of his life. Sometimes the child takes the credit for being 'the cleverest, most beautiful child in the whole world', the accolade of doting parents, and for the rest of his life he basks in the security of his worth. From such beginnings come the two groups of people whom William James described: 'There are men who seem to have started life with a bottle or two of champagne inscribed to their credit; whilst others seem to have been born close to the pain threshold, which the slightest irritant fatally sends them over.'

Children learn early in life of the existence of good and evil. Goodness is pressed upon them by the adults in their world, and evil (even when disguised as naughtiness) is punished. A child may learn to see evil in William James's terms, as 'only a maladjustment with *things*, a wrong correspondence of one's life with the environment', or he may learn that evil is 'a wrongness or vice in his essential nature, which no rearrangement of the inner self can cure, and which requires supernatural remedies'. A psychotherapist, lacking a supernatural remedy, has to do battle with the patient's idea of having a 'wrongness or vice in his essential nature'. Julie once put this into words when she said to me, 'When I was a child my mother used to tell me I was critical even before I knew what critical meant. Mother's always irritated me. I don't know why. She said it's because I

137

just wasn't a lovable sort of child. She makes me tyrannize her. Because of this I have this vision of me as a little devil – just unlovable – that I will destroy anybody who comes near me.' We discussed this little devil and I asked her how much this little devil interfered in her relationships with other people. 'Almost totally,' she said. 'People shouldn't get near me because I'm just going to destroy them. I feel like I'm standing with a dagger in my hand. I'm a dangerous person, or rather, that's the feeling she's given me.' I asked her how she destroyed people and she said, 'In the way I destroy my mother, by tormenting her because she irritates me constantly. But with other people I'm not a tyrant. I'm very unassertive. I suppose that's because I'm afraid that if I assert myself I'll destroy them, so it makes me very timid with people.' And then later she said, 'If I get feedback from somebody that they don't think I'm unlovable and horrible, I just think they must be stupid because I am. I don't believe anything people say. While I've been coming to see you I've been listening for things which I could twist like that, but you haven't said anything.' The word 'yet' hung unspoken in the air.

Sometimes a child learns to see himself as intrinsically evil because this is what his parents tell him he is. Whenever he transgresses his parents' rules they say, 'You're a bad boy.' Other parents distinguish between what a child is and what he does. When he breaks a rule the parents say, 'That was a bad thing to do.' *When we are told what we have done is wrong, that the wrongness lies in our action and not in our essential nature, then we have the option of doing something different next time. We have some choice, some control. But when we are told that the reason we behave as we do lies in some unchangeable portion of our body or soul, then we are helpless. We can no more change our intrinsic evil than we can change our chromosomes or the colour of our eyes.*

Sometimes the child is not told that he is evil, but events in his life lead him to think that he must be so. Jules Feiffer, the American cartoonist and superb chronicler of the vicissitudes of life, described how this can happen in a cartoon of a little girl talking to herself. She said: 'I used to believe I was a good girl until I lost my doll and found it wasn't lost. My big sister stole it. And my mother told me she was taking me to the zoo, only it wasn't the zoo, it was school, and my father told me he was taking me to the circus, only it wasn't the circus, it was the dentist. So that's how I found out I wasn't good. Because if I was good, why would all these good people want to punish me?'

This sense of having a basic fault was described by 'Buzz' Aldrin, the astronaut, who as a child felt that he had to live up to his father's extremely high standards. 'I can look back and, even in the various aspects of my personality as a child, I can see the beginnings of the traits that later in life produce the characteristics known as the alcoholic personality. A sensitivity, an obsession with performing goals to perfection, a desire to do the best that you possibly can do. And I think another very strong characteristic of the alcoholic, which goes back to early life, is a feeling of just not belonging, of feeling uncomfortable and wanting to do something about it, of thinking that other people exist in a state of comfort that somehow you don't have. So you try to do things or take actions to make that better and, later in life, you find that the inhibitions that are removed by the consumption of alcohol make you feel the way you think other people feel all the time.'

When the child learns about good and evil he also learns about guilt and the feelings that accompany guilt. Very often it is the parent who is trying to be a very good parent – not merely the 'good enough' parent that Winnicot advocated – who helps to create in his child an overwhelming sense of guilt. Julie told me, 'My mother is very unselfish and as a consequence I'm constantly guilty.' Sylvia Plath once wrote to her brother, 'You know, as I do, that mother would actually kill herself for us if we calmly accepted all that she wanted to do for us. She is an abnormally altruistic person, and I have realised that we have to fight against her selflessness as we would fight against a deadly disease.' Altruistic people can be very controlling. To spurn a person's altruism can only make one appear selfish, so the person who is being done good to is forced to behave as the altruistic person wishes him to. Of course, for this ploy to work the person who is the object of the altruism must construe being selfish as bad. Fashions in what is considered the rightness or wrongness of particular emotions change. Many parents have taught their children that it is correct to follow a wrong action with a feeling of guilt, and so many people endure the pain of guilt, secure in the knowledge that the mere existence of the pain is a testimony to their general worth. Now, alas, there are schools of psychotherapy which teach that guilt is bad, and so instead of feeling guilty about not feeling guilty we now can find ourselves feeling guilty about feeling guilty. This demonstrates yet again that human beings, as rule-makers and rule-breakers, cannot entirely avoid the painful emotions of guilt and shame.

The link between frustration and anger can be seen in tiny babies, and the small child knows about anger long before he has a word for it. He knows not only that he gets angry but also how the people around him view his anger – whether they see it as a legitimate response to his situation or whether they see his anger as unacceptable, bad, even as evidence of the evil that he contains. The child who is taught that anger is absolutely and completely wrong has great difficulty in learning to deal with his anger successfully. He grows up fearing his anger and the anger of other people. His anger can become the most important thing he knows about himself. As Julie once said, 'It's exhausting being angry, but if you subtract the anger there's nothing there.' Unresolved anger is an important part of depression, but often the depressed person is unwilling to resolve his anger, any more than he is willing to forgive and to relinquish his desire for revenge. The sweetness of revenge is often a prospect which the depressed person would rather die for than relinquish – and he often does. Christ may have taught that we should forgive our enemies (and even He was not prepared to forgive a sin against the Holy Ghost) but who will accept His teaching if, by forgiving, we see ourselves left vulnerable to further injury or, worse, we feel that the act of forgiveness in some way diminished us as a person. Hugging our hurts to ourselves, we feel stronger. We can, of course, learn that the one person we must never forgive is ourselves. Of this Julie said, 'I've seen my father never forgiving himself and I'm the same. I never forgive myself for anything.'

In constructing the rules by which to live his life, the child has to take into account the ways in which he can win the approval of the adults around him. We all want our parents to appreciate and approve of us. We also want them to love us. A child soon senses the difference between love and approval. Approval involves the setting of some standards, whereas love, true love, encompasses everything, the good and the bad, the satisfactory and the unsatisfactory. Happy is the child who grows up in a home where his parents applaud his successes, sympathize with and encourage him in coping with his failures, and love him for himself and not just for his achievements. But the child who feels that he is loved only when he is approved of knows that he is not truly loved. He has some fault, some essential badness for which he has to mak up in order to be allowed the privilege of living in this world. Such a child fears that he is unlovable, and as he gets older he suspects, like Julie, that anyone who claims to love him is either a fool or a liar. Where love is concerned he is as disabled as the child who has suffered so many disappointments in love that he resolves never to love anyone completely.

The word 'love' covers a multitude of human emotions, and when I spoke of 'true love' I meant that warm and benevolent emotion which is unlimited, generous, unselfish, and clear-sighted. Not everyone would agree with me that true love does have these characteristics. Some children learn to see love as something that comes in limited supplies – if mother gives so much love to my brother, she must necessarily have less to give me. This is the assumption of the romance of the Eternal Triangle – that it is not possible to love two people equally. Of course, what is involved here is not the nature of love, but the problem of jealousy, sharing and control. 'If you really loved me,' the lover demands, 'you'd do what I want.' When I gave Teresa a repertory grid she described herself as someone who 'likes people to see things her way'. This, she explained, meant that people understood her, and this was very important, for, as she said in the mode of Revealed Truth, 'If people want you, they understand you.'

From this she deduced that a person who did not understand her did not love her, and since none of her relatives understood her, none of them loved her. Wanting to be understood is, as Rilke once pointed out, wanting to control others. If someone really understands our innermost being then that person will never do anything to distress or thwart us. We can be cruel only to those people we do not understand.

As small children we became aware that different people

followed, or professed, different rules, and that we, to some extent, could choose which rules to make our own. I had an optimist for a father and a pessimist for a mother, and so the notion of alternative construing came early to me. Some children see the alternatives but know that to survive they have no choice. Beryl, who became exceedingly anxious and depressed after her young son died of cancer, told me how, 'I like to feel that whatever I do, I'm the best at it. I feel such a failure, this sense of guilt . . . I should have been a boy – for my mother's sake. As a child, I could never sit on her lap and have a cuddle. Instead of a cuddle she'd pass me a penny. I had everything except that. My father was easy going. He would cuddle me. My mother expected me to be perfect.' I asked her why she had accepted her mother's rules and not her father's. 'Because she was dominant. I wanted to please her. She was immaculate, my mum, and she expected me to be the same.'

Even though, as children, we saw the alternative, the inconsistencies of the rules that were presented to us, there were still some rules, some beliefs, that had an axiomatic, unquestionable quality. These rules, beliefs, related to our perception of ourselves, our place in the scheme of things and our future. Such beliefs had come to us with the immediacy that only the perceptions of childhood can bring.

II. The Intensity of Childhood Experience

There was a time when meadow, grove, and stream,
The earth, and every common sight,
To me did seem
Apparelled in celestial light,
The glory and the freshness of a dream.
It is not now as it hath been of yore –
Turn wheresoe'er I may,
By night or day,
The things which I have seen I now can see no more.

Thus Wordsworth described the special vision of childhood,

where the world comes to us new, vivid, and immediate. Not everything we saw was beautiful. Some of the original perceptions of childhood are indescribably horrible, but whether beautiful or horrible, or simply intriguing, what the child sees conveys a reality and knowledge that say to the child, 'This is what the world is.' Some of our childhood perceptions are particularly heightened and real. They comprise what Edward Robinson called 'the original vision'. Robinson, who succeeded Alister Hardy as Director of the Religious Experience Research Unit, undertook research into the religious experiences of childhood. When Alister Hardy had first asked people to give him accounts of experiences which he had described as 'a deep awareness of a benevolent non-physical power which appears to be partly or wholly beyond and far greater than the individual self', no mention was made of childhood. Yet, as Robinson reported, 'some 15% of all our correspondents (they now number over 4,000) started by going back to events and experiences of their earliest years'. His subsequent research led Robinson, a botanist, not a psychologist, to be somewhat contemptuous of Piaget. He wrote, 'The starting point of all Piaget's thought about childhood is the incapacity of children to see the world as adults see it . . . Piaget is in fact continually setting children an exam in a subject that adults are good at and children bad.' Robinson concluded that there were some perceptions which showed the child to be wiser than the adult. He wrote: 'I believe that what I have called "the original vision" of childhood is no mere imaginative fantasy but a form of *knowledge* and one that is essential to the development of any mature understanding . . . I believe that many of these childhood experiences are *self-authenticating*: they have in themselves an absolute authority that needs no confirmation or sanction from any other source. I believe that they are also self-authenticating in another sense: they bring to the person who has them an awareness of his true *self* as an individual, with identity, freedom and responsibilities of his or her own. I believe that his vision can only be understood, either by the person who has it or by the outside observer, in *purposive* terms: there seems to be no substitute for the old-fashioned word "destiny" – which must, however, be clearly distinguished from "fate".' 'Destiny', as

Robinson uses it, comes close to the transactional analysis concept of 'script'.

One of Robinson's subjects wrote:

> On the first occasion (aged 8–10) I was in the garden, muddling about alone. A cuckoo flew over, calling. Suddenly, I experienced a sensation I can only describe as an effect that might follow the rotating of a kaleidoscope. It was a feeling of timelessness, not only that time stood still, that duration had ceased, but that I was myself outside time altogether. Somehow I knew that I was part of eternity. And there was also a feeling of spacelessness. I lost all awareness of my surroundings. With this detachment I felt the intensest joy I had ever known, and yet with so great a longing – for what I did not know – that it was scarcely distinguishable from suffering . . . The second occurred a good while after the first. It was an absolutely still day, flooded with sunshine. In the garden everything was shining, breathless, as if waiting expectant. Quite suddenly I felt convinced of the existence of God; as if I had only to put out my hand to touch Him. And at the same time there came that intensest joy and indescribable longing, as if of an exile, perhaps, for home. It seemed as if my heart were struggling to leap out of my body. How long I stood, or would have gone on standing, I do not know; the tea-bell rang, shattering the extra dimension into which I had seemed to be caught up. I returned to earth and went obediently in, speaking to no one about these things.'

Children soon learn that it is unwise to tell adults about these experiences.

We can all recall experiences in childhood where we saw and knew in such a way that we knew we had looked directly at the nature of reality. Not all of us would label these experiences as religious or spiritual. Virginia Woolf called her experiences 'moments of being'. She wrote, 'If life has a base that it stands upon, if it is a bowl that one fills and fills and fills, then my bowl stands upon this memory. It is of lying half asleep, half awake in

144

the nursery at St Ives. It is of hearing the waves breaking, one, two, one, two, and sending a splash of water over the beach . . . It is lying and hearing this splash and seeing this light, and feeling that it is almost impossible that I should be here; of feeling the purest ecstacy that I can conceive.' (The image of the wave appears often in Virginia Woolf's work, and she chose to die by drowning.)

Virginia Woolf described other moments of being which occurred when she was a child. Fighting with her brother, she became aware of the futility of aggression and of her own powerlessness; hearing of the suicide of a family friend, she found herself dragged down into a pit of despair from which she could not escape. The third moment led not to despair but to satisfaction. She was looking at a plant in the garden and suddenly thought, ' "This is the whole." It suddenly seemed plain that the flower itself was part of the earth; that a ring enclosed what was the flower, part earth, part flower.' As an adult Virginia Woolf still experienced these sudden shocks, the moments of being, and she concluded that 'the shock-receiving capacity is what makes me a writer . . . I feel that I have had a blow; but it is not, as I thought as a child, simply a blow from an enemy hidden behind the cotton-wool of daily life; it is or will become the revelation of some order; it is a token of some real thing behind appearances; and I make it real by putting it into words. It is only by putting it into words that I make it whole . . . from this I reach what I might call a philosophy . . . that behind the cotton-wool is hidden a pattern; that we – I mean all human beings – are connected with this; that the whole world is a work of art; that we are parts of the work of art.'

Virginia Woolf made it very clear that she did not see her 'moments of being' as religious experiences. 'Certainly and emphatically there is no God,' she wrote. Others of us can recall experiences which had that peculiarly striking and revealing quality but which did not relate to a non-physical power beyond and far greater than the individual self. I recall that one day when I was six or seven I was walking home from school along a hot, dusty road, and, just at the point where the road divided, the realization came to me that I was I. I stood there in the heat and dust and marvelled at my discovery. I told no one – I was already aware of the necessity of shielding myself from adult laughter – but the knowledge and certainty of me as me became my central core which was often troubled but never shaken or destroyed by the turbulence and uncertainty that my later life was to bring. Nowadays, when someone says to me 'I don't know who I am', or 'I am empty – I only exist in other people's eyes', or 'I don't know whether I'm angry or not', I can accept such statements as another person's truth, but I wonder to myself, 'How can you not know yourself?' I suppose that the person who has had an experience of God must be equally amazed when I say I have no belief in God.

The vivid perceptions of childhood fade as we get older. This is of necessity since, as George Eliot said, 'If we had a keen vision and a feeling of all ordinary life, it would be like hearing the grass grow and the squirrel's heart beat, and we should die of the roar that lies on the other side of silence. As it is, the quickest of us walk about well wadded with stupidity.' From time to time the memory of certain childhood experiences and their message comes back to trouble, comfort, or inform us. Marina Warner, who learnedly and lucidly argued in her study of the meanings given to the image of the Virgin Mary 'that in the very celebration of the perfect woman, both humanity and women were subtly denigrated', revealed that, despite her adult loss of faith, 'The Virgin, sublime model of chastity, nevertheless remained for me the most holy being that I could ever contemplate, and so potent was her spell that for some years I could not enter a church without pain at all the safety and beauty of the salvation I had forsaken. I remember visiting Notre Dame in Paris and standing in the nave, tears starting in my eyes, furious at that old love's enduring power to move me.'

When we consider the vivid original visions of childhood and realize that these experiences carried an import, a statement about the nature of ourselves and our world, we can see that as children we *knew* certain things long before we could understand or explain them. When we consider the *kind* of knowledge that these experiences gave us as children, we can see what St Augustine meant when he wrote, 'Understanding is the reward of faith. Therefore do not seek to understand in order that you may believe, but make the act of faith in order that you may understand; for unless you make an act of faith you will not understand.' The faith of which St Augustine speaks is a special kind of knowledge, the knowledge which allows a person to say 'I know that my redeemer liveth', or 'I know that I am part of eternity', or 'I know that there is a hidden pattern', or 'I know that I exist'. Of this kind of knowledge F. C. Happold in his study of mysticism wrote, 'A great deal of our knowledge is *about* things. Yet, within our normal experience, there is another sort of knowledge. When we say we *know* someone we love, we are describing a different sort of knowledge than when we say that we know that it is ten miles to X or that if we mix certain chemicals together we shall blow ourselves up. This other kind of knowledge is based on something which can only be called "union". The more the subject and the object, the observer and that which is observed, merge into each other, that is, are "united" with each other, the more profound and illuminating the knowledge becomes.'

This kind of knowledge is that which arises from a special kind of perception, what Cassirer called the symbolic form of mythical thought. Cassirer considered that myth, art, language, and science are the symbolic forms by which we know reality. As he wrote, '. . . the special symbolic forms are not imitations, but *organs* of reality, since it is by their agency that anything real becomes an object for intellectual apprehension, and as such is made visible to us.' In contrast to scientific thinking:

> . . . mythical thinking . . . comes to rest in the immediate experience, the sensible present is so great that everything else dwindles before it. For a person whose apprehension is under the spell of this mythico-religious attitude, it is as though the whole world were simply annihilated; the immediate content, whatever it be, that commands this religious intrest so completely fills his consciousness that nothing else can exist beside and apart from it. The ego is spending all its energies on this single object, lives in it, loses itself in it. Instead of a widening of intuitive experience, we find here its extreme limitation; instead of expansion . . . we have here an impulse toward concentration; instead of extensive distribution, intensive

147

compression. This focusing of all forces in a single present is the prerequisite for all mythical thinking and mythical formulation. When, on the one hand, the entire self is given up to a single impression, is 'possessed' by it and, on the other hand, there is the utmost tension between the subject and its object, the outer world; where external reality is not merely viewed and contemplated, but overcomes a man in sheer immediacy, with emotions of fear or hope, terror or wish fulfilment: then the spark jumps somehow across, the tension finds release, as the subjective excitement becomes objectified and confronts the mind as a god or daemon.

Such is the experience of the moments of being, the original vision. Cassirer was writing here about the evolution of religious ideas, ideas which relate not just to gods and daemons, but to all the kinds of beliefs that we can create and discover in our search for the meaning of life and death. The meaning that we do acquire, the beliefs that possess us as much as we possess them, become the myth by which we live our lives. Now the world of myth is, as Cassirer said:

. . . a dramatic world – a world of actions, of forces, of conflicting powers . . . Mythical perception is always impregnated with these emotional qualities. Whatever is seen or felt is surrounded by a special atmosphere – atmosphere of joy or grief, of anguish, of excitement, of exultation or depression . . . All objects are benignant or malignant, friendly or inimical, familiar or uncanny, alluring and fascinating or repellent and threatening.

So in childhood we arrive at some understanding of the purpose of life and the nature of death, but whatever set of beliefs come to us as faith and truth, there is no set of beliefs that can give us total certainty, security, and comfort.

III. Death and Doubt

A child cannot be protected from the knowledge of death. Even if none of his relatives or acquaintances die, he sees animals and insects die. Even if his parents regulate his television viewing so that he sees no pictures of the dead and dying, he comes to know that when his loving parents say, 'Don't run on the road', the unspoken reason is 'Because if you do you may die'. Sylvia Anthony, in her study of the discovery of death in childhood, showed children of two or three observing death and puzzling on it. She recorded, 'A little boy (2.2), after nearly killing a fly on the window-pane, seemed surprised and disturbed, looking round for an explanation, then gave it himself: "Mr F'y dom (gone) to by-by (sleep)." But he would not touch it or another fly – doubt evidently remained and he continued to be uneasy about it.'

By the age of five a child has elaborated a myth about death, 'Richard (5.5) on a summer holiday, walking up from the beach with M – a thunderstorm obviously approaching – talked at great length, beginning with a rational discussion of bad weather, and then: "Thunder is drums of soldiers in the sky – we shall go up in the sky if a war comes, so you needn't mind – the angels will let down a rope with a hook on the end and catch you up on the hook (this was addressed to M personally) and then you'll turn into an angel, and it will be lovely, because you'll be able to fly, because angels can fly, they have wings . . ."'

But as the child gets older alternative explanations of death become available. 'Catherine (9.10), returning from a walk with M, a younger sister and a baby brother, asked, apparently *a propos* of nothing: "What happens to people when they are dead? Are they eaten by worms? Or do they go and dance about in heaven? I'll tell you about it when I'm born again! Are you born again?"'

Sylvia Anthony reported the words and actions of the children as described by adult observers, and her interest was in intellectual development of the child in dealing with the concept of death. Thus she did not reveal the powerful impact the awareness of death has on the child. Edward Robinson's subjects wrote of their memories of their childhood experience, and their accounts emphasize that the discovery of death is not merely an intellectual problem:

> A lady in the village died when I was 8. Night after night I cried and was too frightened to sleep. Mum sat with me and told me it wouldn't happen for a long, long time and that when I grew very old I would be tired and glad to rest. But I didn't believe her. I knew that time had a way of catching up with you. It passed.

> When I was nearly five years old I would often cry bitterly at night, particularly when it was bellringing practice night, at the realization that some day my parents would die, and indeed the overwhelming knowledge that everything in the world would die some day. I found it an absolutely terrifying thought. I can still remember the feeling of utter desolation. Although I knew then there was a life after death, I was always so afraid that there would be a journey, a long dark journey, and people would perhaps get lost or too tired before they found Jesus.

> I was afraid of death but at the same time curious because I could not believe that this was the very end. I instinctively felt that death was a new beginning in some way.

It is often said that our present society keeps death a secret. In a century which has seen more than 110 million man-made deaths as well as the natural deaths from illness and old age, the secret has not been particularly well kept. Nevertheless, children are no longer expected to be knowledgeable about death. This was not the case in previous centuries. From the Middle Ages right through to the early nineteenth century death was a public ceremony and children were expected to be present as witnesses of an edifying spectacle. This century it has been fashionable to hide death from children and to pretend that it does not exist, but such pretence does not prevent the child from knowing, fearing and fantasizing about death.

Children's fantasies about death are not simply daydreams to while away the time. Fantasies have a problem-solving function, and this is what the child's fantasies about death are concerned with, since, as Piaget said, 'the idea of death sets the child's curiosity in motion, precisely because, if every cause is coupled with a motive, then death calls for a special explanation'. The young child defines 'dead' as 'killed' or 'murdered'. The limitations of this definition become apparent as the child gets older. Sylvia Anthony, paraphrasing Piaget, commented, 'the fact that human mortality represents a limitation of adult power over events, because death cannot be explained in terms of motive consistently with *decus*, the right ordering of society, leads the child to the conception of physical causation and chance – unless the issue is confused by theological explanations'. Alas, our understanding of death is always confused by theological, or at least, metaphysical explanations. If a child knocks a cup so that it falls and breaks, the child can come to understand that while his movement was the cause of the breakage, the event itself was an accident. In fact, the idea of chance is here a comfort to him, for he can plead that the event was not his fault. But the notion that death occurs by chance is a hard one to accept, and many children and adults will resist it. Death requires two explanations, a physical and a metaphysical explanation. Death occurs through old age, illness, accident, or malice towards oneself or others. As children we came to understand that all living things die, but when death touches our lives we have to find an answer to the question 'Why did this particular person die?' Was this death just random chance or was it part of a pattern? Is this person's death a punishment for his wickedness or the wickedness of his bereaved? Was it the unfolding of his karma, his fate? Was it God's will? Or the Devil's intervention? Was this death evidence of the breakdown of civilization, of the bestiality of man? Or was this death a sacrifice for the benefit of future generations? Why (not how) did this person die?

A child is given various explanations of death and he discovers others for himself. He soon finds that there is no explanation of death which brings complete comfort and security. If death occurs by chance – if some cells in my body burst into malignant life, or if I just happen to stand next to a suitcase containing a bomb – then my life is fraught with uncertainty. If death occurs through the wishes and actions of God or the Devil, then my life is in the control of an outside power and I am in danger of committing the unforgivable sin or unwittingly becoming a limb of Satan. If death occurs as part of a grand design, then I can feel the helplessness of a puppet or resentment of being expected to play a part I do not wish to play. The lack of comfort makes us doubt and question. When Beryl was telling me about the agony she was still enduring over the death of her young son she remarked, 'Someone said to me once "God needed him more than you", and at the time it didn't make sense, but if you think about it, when lots of children are taken – like Aberfan – I think there's a reason. At least, when I feel well, I'm sure there's something. When I don't feel all that good, I don't know. When someone said, "God needs him", I said, "Why mine?" That's what I said. That was all I kept saying. "Why mine?" '

Knowledge of death brings doubt – doubt that the world is the way we have been told it is. Doubt makes some people cling even more tightly to their beliefs. Others question, and through their questions discover within themselves another belief. Simone de Beauvoir has described her strict Catholic upbringing. 'I was never allowed to hear, even at a great distance, even very faintly, the other side of the question.' Nevertheless, when she entered her teens, her faith began to waver. 'For a long time now the concept I had of Him had been purified and refined, sublimated to a point where He no longer had any countenance divine, any concrete link with the earth or therefore any being. His perfection cancelled out His reality . . . My incredulity never once wavered . . . I made another discovery. One afternoon, in Paris, I realized that I was condemned to death. I was alone in the house and I did not attempt to control my despair. I screamed and tore at the red carpet. And when, dazed, I got to my feet again, I asked myself: "How do people manage? How shall I manage?" . . . It seemed impossible that I could live all through life with such horror gnawing at my heart.'

Sometimes a child tests out his faith and then discovers that religious beliefs do not always yield the desired result. Jerome K. Jerome, who carried the sadness found in every great humourist, recalled how in childhood he lived in terror that he had unknowingly committed the unforgivable sin against the Holy Ghost:

152

When I was a boy a material Hell was still by most pious folks accepted as a fact. The suffering caused to an imaginative child can hardly be exaggerated. It caused me to hate God, and later when my growing intelligence rejected the conception as an absurdity, to despise the religion that had taught it. It appeared that one could avoid Hell by the simple process of believing. But how was I to be sure that I did believe sufficiently? There was a mountain of rubbish on some wasteland beside the Limehouse Canal. It was always spoken of locally as 'The Mountain'. By way of experiment I prayed that this mountain might be removed. It would certainly have been an advantage to the neighbourhood and by comparison with pictures I had seen it was evidently a very little mountain. I thought that my faith might be sufficient, but there it remained, morning after morning, in spite of my long kneelings by my bedside. I felt the fault was mine and despaired.

Elizabeth described how she lost her faith in Jesus. 'We were brought up Anglo-Catholic. I started school at three, and I remember the priest coming in in his robes. What they put over to us was that God loves every child. He watches every little sparrow that falls. So long as you're good, the only thing you have to do if you're in trouble or afraid, have little problems, you ask God or Jesus to help you. And of course you believe all this. You sit starry-eyed listening. I used to be a very sickly child, and in our house – if you were ill my parents were extremely angry. Well, it was winter and I knew I was going to have quinsy. My throat was so sore. I was about six, a little puny kid, and they'd sent me home from school, but I tried to dawdle, waiting for the other children to catch up, because if I arrived home early my parents would demand, "Why are you home early?" and they would see immediately that I wasn't well. So I prayed. I remember I stood at a lamppost praying, "Please, Jesus, don't let me be sick. Let me be well when I get home." Of course, I fiddled around in the cold and got worse, I suppose, and arrived home with my brothers. Unfortunately, there was celery for tea. I normally liked it, but I couldn't eat it because I couldn't

153

swallow. It was all quiet – we didn't talk much at tea – and suddenly my mother noticed and she said, "Why aren't you eating?" and I said, "Um-um", and she said, "God, she's sick again. Are you?" and my sister said, "Yes, she was sent home from school", and she said, "Why didn't you come home? Off to bed!" I thought, "That's Jesus off my list." He wasn't paying any attention to me. And then as we got older I was quite off Him. I didn't like saying all the prayers. And I think I suggested once to one of the teachers, rather about the sparrows than about me. I said, "What if one sparrow He missed, or one child?" And then the answer came that the child or the sparrow must have met with His disapproval.'

The crises of adolescence have been the subject of much discussion over the past thirty years. Such crises are usually described as being concerned with the search for identity, the coming to terms with sexuality and with the adult role. That some of the most painful crises of adolescence are religious is often overlooked. An example of such a crisis was Sarah, whose mother had contacted me to ask if I would have a talk with Sarah. 'She's never been a plump child,' she said, 'but now Sarah's got so thin I'm really worried. Do you think she's anorexic?'

Sarah was indeed thin, even for a skinny fourteen year old. She explained this, saying that she was just back from boarding school where the food was very boring, but now she was home she would eat well. We covered the usual topics. Yes, she liked school and wanted to stay on. Yes, some of her friends were getting more interested in boys and clothes than she was. She did not mind if they were not as interested in her as they had been, so long as she still had one special friend. I noticed that she talked of this friend very much in terms of security. I asked her about this, and she said, 'Well, I do get anxious – I'm an anxious person. I suppose I want to know that everything is going to turn out all right. When I wake up in the morning I always say a prayer – just ask God to make sure that I'm going to get through my test or whatever it is that I'm worried about that day.'

'Is your faith very important to you?' I asked.

'Very.' she said.

I asked her what her faith was, and she described the 'gentle

Jesus' faith that Elizabeth and many other children have been taught, that God watches over His flock and sees that none come to any harm. Sarah then revealed how this faith had become the locus of her anxiety. At that particular time our newspapers and television screens were full of the strained and hungry faces of the Boat People, and we were being told that these were the lucky ones. The unlucky had been drowned or murdered. Sarah watched this spectacle and wondered. Was God not watching over this part of His flock? Or did He not care about some people? Was her comfortable, secure home a sign of God's favour? Did she deserve this? Should she feel guilty at her good fortune or terrified that He would find her out and whisk it all away? Or, worst of all, perhaps there was no God, and all she had been taught was a fairy tale, like Santa Claus, and her parents and teachers had lied to her, and the world really was the dark and dangerous place she feared it might be. She dared not discuss these matters with her parents, or teachers, or the vicar. They all seemed so secure in their faith and they would say that she was wicked just for doubting. More than that, she did not want to put them to the test and so discover what she suspected, that there was nothing any one of them could say that would return her to the safety of her early childhood.

This story has, as far as I know, no happy ending. Sarah will, I guess, be plagued by religious doubts for the rest of her life. Anxiety had become very much her way of life. By contrast, I have always been concerned with resolving my anxieties, and so when I was fourteen and began to doubt the Christian faith that I had been taught I worked very hard to rid myself of this anxiety and to try and make myself believe. I read the Bible from cover to cover, not even skipping one 'begat'. I went to church and Sunday School and attended Methodist revivalist meetings. I think I got saved a couple of times, but each time I knew that I was only play-acting. It was not me. And yet I felt that there was something very wrong with me. Other people believed, why could not I? The critic in my head listened to the minister's sermons and jeered. It was wartime. The discrepancies between Christian doctrine and Christian action were as enormous as those described in my history books. I felt guilty because I dared not stop going to church – my social life was centred there – and I felt isolated because I was different from those around me. I struggled with this problem on my own. Writing this is the first time I have ever told the story. When I was sixteen I won a prize for 'General Proficiency' at school. The headmistress told me that I could go to the local bookshop and choose a book. The war had just ended and books were scarce. I searched the shop and finally decided upon a book about which I knew nothing but which I thought might prove interesting. It was Lin Yutang's *The Importance of Living*. Here in simple language was the philosophy of Lao Tsu, and for me it was like coming home. I felt a wondrous relief. I did not have to follow the Christian faith. I did not have to squeeze myself into a mould which I saw as meagre and misshapen. I was free to be myself. Of course, at that time and after there were other pressures on me not to be myself, but that is another story.

IV. *The Axioms That Become Our Story*

In childhood we acquire some beliefs which we hold, as it were, in transit. We hold them for a while, and then our common sense shows us that such beliefs are untenable. However, we acquire other beliefs which become so settled, so secure, that we almost forget that we hold them. These beliefs become an unseen power directing our choices and so determining our lives.

Because our settled childhood beliefs concerning the nature of life and death become the structures which we use to interpret the events in our lives, we therefore arrive at interpretations which demonstrate the validity of our beliefs. Siegfried's unhappy childhood taught him that to become attached to anyone or to depend on anyone would lead to rejection and insecurity. His first love affair ended as most first affairs do. Many people survive this tragedy by deciding that they will have better luck next time, that the next lover will prove to be more faithful and true. Not Siegfried. He simply reaffirmed his childhood vows 'never to be very, very firmly committed to anyone again'. The war years gave him many opportunities to see the wisdom of this decision. In those times not only did many friends and acquaintances die but, in the general upheavals, people travelled great distances and often remained far away from their original homes. Moreover, people changed very much during the war. Friends, though still friendly, often became strangers. So Siegfried saw no reason to change or even to look critically at his belief. He simply took it with him into the one situation where such a belief is a recipe for disaster.

August Strindberg's account of his childhood in his book *The Son of a Servant* shows the conclusions he drew from his early years, how these became the rules on which he based his behaviour, and, by the time he went to school, how life appeared to him:

In the third storey of a large house near the Clara Church in Stockholm, the son of the shipping agent and the servant-maid awoke to self-consciousness. The child's first impressions were, as he remembered afterwards, fear and hunger. He feared the darkness and the blows, he feared to fall, to knock himself against something, or to go in the streets. He feared the fists of his brothers, the roughness of the servant-girl, the scolding of the grand-mother, the rod of his mother or his father's cane. He was afraid of the general's manservant, who lived on the ground floor, with his skull cap and large hedge-scissors; he feared the landlord's deputy, when he played in the courtyard with the dustbin: he feared the landlord who was a magistrate. Above him loomed a hierarchy of authorities wielding various rights, from the right of seniority of his brother to the supreme tribunal of his father. And yet above his father was the deputy landlord, who always threatened him with the landlord. This last was generally invisible, because he lived in the country, and perhaps, for that reason, was the most feared of all. But again, above all, even above the manservant with the skull cap, was the general, especially when he sallied forth in uniform wearing his plumed three-cornered hat. The child did not know what a king looked like, but he knew that the general went to the king. The servant-maid also used to tell stories of the king and showed the child his picture. His mother generally prayed to God in the evening, but the child could form no clear idea of God, except that He must certainly be higher than the King . . . (His) education consisted of scolding, hair-pulling and exhortations to obedience. The child heard only of his duties, nothing of his rights. Everyone else's wishes carried weight; his were suppressed. He could begin nothing without doing wrong, go nowhere without being in the way, utter no word without disturbing anyone. At last he did not dare move. His highest duty was to sit on a chair and be quiet. It was always dinned into him that he had no will of his own, and so the foundation of a weak character was laid . . . He was in perpetual anxiety lest he do something wrong. He was very awake to injustice, and while he had a high ideal for himself, he narrowly watched the failings of his brothers. When they were unpunished, he felt deeply injured; when they were undeservedly rewarded, his sense of justice suffered. He was accordingly considered envious. He then complained to his mother. Sometimes she took his part, but generally she told him not to judge so severely, and demanded that he judge himself severely. Therefore he withdrew into himself and became bitter. His reserve and shyness grew on him. He hid himself if he received a word of praise, and took pleasure in being overlooked . . . Life seemed a penal institution for crimes committed before we were born, and therefore the boy always went about with a bad conscience.

Strindberg as a child struggled with the idea of God at the head of a hierarchy, but found difficulty in seeing beyond the general and the king. No doubt Freud would have seen this as supporting his dictum that 'God is in every case modelled after the father, and that our personal relation to God is dependent upon our relation to our physical father, fluctuating and changing with him, and that God is at bottom nothing but an exalted father'. Ernest Jones broadened this idea into 'The religious life represents a dramatization on a cosmic plane of the emotions, fears and longings which arose in the child's relations to its parents'. Edward Robinson asked his subjects to say whether their image of God was based on their experience of their parents. In answer one woman wrote: 'I think my earliest ideas of God must have been derived from what my parents were. They were the rock and anchor of all existence; they knew everything, were all-wise, all-powerful, always there. So what could God be but someone a little more powerful and wiser? Only He could not be seen. I think I must have been early teenage when I suddenly realized my parents were not all-wise, and not perfect, and they could go away, or die, so God was not a super-parent.' Not all parents allow the child to develop the idea of God as a super-parent. Another person wrote, 'I think that my early ideas about God were drawn largely from certain characteristics in my parents. The idea of an impassive observer, rarely giving help or hindrance except at indefinite and often illogical times, very much like my parents.' Another wrote, 'Yes, my early idea of God was derived from what I saw in my parents, but it gave me a wrong idea of God, i.e., not as a God of Love.' One man replied, 'Not at all. My father seemed either asleep or out.' Some people would say that this is the perfect description of God.

Not all of us develop the idea that God is a person and that He made us in His image. As a child I thought that this was highly unlikely, but, in case I was wrong, I worked out that if God did exist like the minister said He did, then He must be at least as good as my father, and, if that were so, I had nothing to worry about. My father was good and kind, and, while he often deplored what I did, he never ceased to love and look after me. If God could not live up to that standard, then I thought that He was not worth knowing. However, my thoughts on this matter were really no more than the exercise of my intellect. My religious beliefs were not connected with gods in human form. As a child I would have been hard-pressed to put these beliefs into words, and so I was greatly impressed when recently I read the contribution of one of Robinson's subjects who recalled the beliefs she held when she was eight:

What I now see as my *real* religious feeling I used to call (but only to myself; I never talked about it or mentioned it to anyone) 'Purity'. This was the word I used as a child. There is no word I can think of to describe this feeling. It is the coolness and texture and scent of stone, and wood, and water, the primroses; it is the movement and sound of birds, it is light playing among leaves, it is life pulsating in every living thing, from a spider to an elephant, from a blade of grass to a tulip tree. I do not know how I came by it.

This woman, writing when she was fifty-three, could no doubt trace how she had tried to build her life on her religious feeling of purity, how she had suffered when there was discordance between her religious feeling and her life, and how her religious feeling had led her to relinquish things in her life which she otherwise might have held. As adults each of us can, if we desire, trace such a thread in our lives. Simone de Beauvoir described how her loss of faith exposed her to an insecurity of which the discovery of her personal death was only one terrible part. But to be free, to be herself and not what other people wanted her to be, became her most passionate desire, and so she looked for a way of life which would allow her to be 'a law unto myself'. At first she thought that to be a teacher was the solution. Then, at fifteen, she decided, 'that literature would allow me to realize this dream. It would guarantee me an immortality which would compensate for the loss of heaven and eternity; there was no longer any God to love me, but I should have the undying love of millions of hearts. By writing a work based on my own experience I would be serving humanity: what more beautiful gift could I make than the books I would write? . . . My plan to be a writer reconciled everything; it gratified all the aspirations which had been unfolding in me during the past fifteen years.'

Sartre, in his autobiography *Words*, showed how in childhood the image he developed of himself and his experience of death combined to form the plan by which he lived his life. Sartre's father died soon after his birth, and so Sartre's mother returned with her baby to her parents' home. Here Sartre was made much of by his grandparents, but as a fatherless infant in a home where his mother was still regarded as a child, Sartre soon came to feel that he was acting a part, that:

> I was an imposter . . . I had been told over and over again that I was a gift from heaven, much longed for, indispensable to my grandfather and to my mother. I no

longer believed this, but I still felt you were born superfluous unless sent into the world to satisfy some particular expectation.

As he was realizing this:

I saw death. At the age of five: it was watching me; in the evenings, it prowled on the balcony: it pressed its nose to the window; I used to see it but I did not dare to say anything. Once, on the Quai Voltaire, we met it: it was a tall, mad old woman, dressed in black, who mumbled as she went by: 'I shall put that child in my pocket'. Another time, it took the form of a hole . . . I was playing in the garden of the villa, scared because I had been told that Gabriel was ill and was going to die. I was playing at horses, half-heartedly galloping round the house. Suddenly, I noticed a gloomy hole: the cellar which had been opened; an indescribable impression of loneliness and horror blinded me: I turned round and, singing at the top of my voice, I fled. At that time, I had an assignation with it every night in my bed . . . I lived in terror – it was a genuine neurosis. If I seek its cause, it goes like this: a spoilt child, a providential gift, I found my profound uselessness even more obvious because family ritual struck me as a contrived necessity. I felt superfluous, so I had to disappear . . . I was condemned and the sentence could be carried out at any time.

Sartre's grandfather was a teacher who revered books and writers. Sartre saw that his salvation, his protection against death, lay in becoming a writer and this he did:

My commandments have been sewn into my skin: if I go a day without writing, the scar burns me . . . My bones are leather and cardboard . . . I can see my mad undertaking to write in order to be forgiven for being alive has, in spite of lies and cowardice, some validity: the proof is that I am still writing some fifty years later . . . I had long been afraid of ending up as I had begun, somewhere or other, somehow or other, and that this vague death would be merely the reflection of my vague birth.

As a child he became certain that he would live to complete his task. At the outbreak of the Second World War Sartre's friends feared that they would die, and many of them did, but Sartre had no fear of sudden death:

> I had forearmed myself against accidental death, that was all; the Holy Ghost had commissioned a long-term work from me, so he had to give me time to complete it . . . I had killed myself in advance because only the dead can enjoy immortality . . . Between the ages of nine and ten, I became entirely posthumous.

Not everyone can, like Sartre, reflect upon and report on the development of their system of beliefs. For some, it appears to be most dangerous to look at the connection between childhood experiences and the adult philosophy of life, and so the person avoids doing this, even when his philosophy of life proves most painful in the living of it. Felicity was one such person. She was a middle-aged woman, gentle, charming, and pretty, looking like she could have stepped straight out of one of those radiant advertisements which extol the virtues of some personal or household cleansing agent. But she kept her distance, both in physical and psychological space, for she believed, without the shadow of a doubt, that she gave off some unpleasant odour. She knew that this was usually the reason why people were unkind to her. She tried to wash away or to disguise the smell, and when she felt that she was not succeeding, she grew very distressed. She was forced to acknowledge what she saw as an indisputable fact to her husband and doctor and later to me, and when each of us said, in our own way, 'But you don't smell', she knew we were lying. She believed that she gave off an offensive odour, and I could no more get her to change her belief than I could convince Ian Paisley of the virtues of the infallible Pope.

In her work Felicity was extremely competent, but her relationships with her colleagues were a torture to her. She saw herself as being 'easily swayed by people' and she minded this very much. 'I do something and then get really mad afterward. "You fool, why did you do that?" I worry about what people think, obviously. I can be talked into anything. People ask me to do something and I just can't say no. And then I moan at my husband afterwards. If I said no I'd feel I'd have offended somebody. I've found that through life that with the best will in the world you still offend people. Sometimes you say something and it's taken the wrong way and you don't realize until something comes back to you.' I asked her whether she preferred to be liked or respected. She said that she preferred to be liked 'because people wouldn't respect me anyway. I always work on the principle that nobody likes me. I always work from there, and I never make the first move in friendship. I'd never ask anybody in for a cup of coffee unless I'd been invited there first. I would never make the first move.'

Felicity described her childhood as being quite ordinary, but as we got to know one another better she revealed a far from happy childhood. 'I think my older sister, as regards my father anyway, was the favourite. I can always remember asking him something and his stock answer was "Ask your mother". He'd never give you a decision. And I seem to remember her saying once, I must have been grown up then, she must have said it without thinking, he was dead then, something about, "Oh your father thought more of you when you went teaching than he had ever done." Obviously gave me a feeling that I was definitely not – that my sister was the one.' (Felicity was a past-mistress in uncovering an insulting meaning in whatever was said to her, even when no insult was remotely contemplated by the speaker.) When, eventually, we talked about affection, she said, 'I suppose we were brought up without a lot of affection. I'd never kiss my mother and father. We had a good home. Mother made sure we had everything, but I hardly ever saw my father. My mother would do more for me. I was brought up during the war. My mother was always busy – organizing canteens and poppy days, that sort of thing.' I asked her if her mother had cuddled her as a child. 'Not that I remember,' she said. 'What about your father?' I asked. 'Oh, no, no. But don't get me wrong, my mother, we were very close, especially as I grew up.'

But later she told me of two childhood memories that still haunted her. The first was of when she was four or five and her mother one night left her alone in the house while she went on an errand. On her own Felicity became terrified. She began to cry and scream so loudly that the neighbours came running. Her

163

mother arrived home to find a crowd of people on the front porch, all trying to pacify the terrified child on the other side of the locked door. Her mother opened the door, the neighbours went away, and then her mother belted her to punish her for causing a commotion. The other memory was of when she was fourteen and she and her girlfriend were accosted by two American soldiers. During the war being accosted by American soldiers was an inescapable hazard for every woman and girl where Americans were based, and sometimes the experience could be most unpleasant. But the men who spoke to Felicity and her friend were just lonely young men who wanted a chat, and so the four of them took a stroll down the High Street. That was the extent of the encounter, but when Felicity got home her mother knew of it, and Felicity was thrashed, first by her mother and then by her father when he got home from work. Next day her mother took Felicity to the barbers and had her hair cropped short. After that, night after night, Felicity would lie in bed and listen to her parents talking together. Each night she was terrified that they had discovered some crime of hers of which she was ignorant and that they would again mount the stairs and punish her.

Arthur Koestler, in his autobiography, describes the link between his childhood experiences and his metaphysical beliefs. On one occasion, when he was four, his parents took him on an outing. They told the little boy that they would visit the doctor who would look down his throat and give him some cough mixture. Then, as a reward, he would have some ice cream. But that was not what happened.

> I was made to sit in a kind of dentist's chair; then, without warning or explanation, my arms and legs were tied with leather straps to the frame of the chair . . . Half senseless with fear, I craned my neck to look into my parents' faces, and when I saw that they, too, were frightened the bottom fell out of the world. The doctor hustled them both out of the room, fastened a metal tray beneath my chin, prized my chattering teeth apart, and forced a rubber gag between my jaws. There followed several indelible minutes of steel instruments being thrust

into the back of my mouth, of choking and vomiting blood into the tray beneath my chin; then two more attacks with the steel instruments, and more choking and blood and vomit. That is how tonsillectomies were performed, without anaesthesia, A.D. 1910, in Budapest . . . Those moments of utter loneliness, abandoned by my parents, in the clutches of a hostile and malign power, filled me with a kind of cosmic terror. It was as if I had fallen through a manhole, into a dark underground world of archaic brutality. Thenceforth I never lost my awareness of the existence of that second universe into which one might be transported, without warning, from one moment to the other. The world had become ambiguous, invested with a double meaning; events moved on two different planes at the time – a visible and an invisible one – like a ship which carries its passengers on its sunny decks, while its keel ploughs through the dark phantom world beneath.

Many adults who had had similar experiences in childhood would recount their stories in words filled with anger at their unjust and cruel parents. But not Felicity. She was like Feiffer's little girl. She had to preserve her parents as good people, and to do this she must see herself as bad. Hence Felicity came to believe that she was someone that no one could like, and when her intelligence could find no adequate reasons for this dislike in her own behaviour and in the general disagreeableness of other people, then her mythical thought created the belief in an intrinsic, ineradicable, offensive odour. Such a belief, unpleasant though it may be, provided her with a protection against further hurt. Knowing that other people would not like her, she did not have to risk liking them.

When I asked her whether she saw people as basically good or basically bad, she said, 'Basically bad, I think. It just seems to me that nobody likes anybody. I never used to feel that. But now nobody likes anybody. It's just all false.' I asked her about her religious beliefs. She said, 'I can remember as a child trying to think "How did the world begin in the first place and if it was made in seven days, and there is a God sitting up there, well,

where did God come from? Where did the space come from?"
You could go mad thinking about that.' The answer Felicity had
found in the books by Dennis Wheatley. 'It's some kind of good
and evil forces which are at war with one another, and I can only
think that the evil forces are winning because certainly the world
is not improving, is it? I think Mother Shipton's right. She said
the end of the world would come in 1982 or 3. Doesn't the Bible
say that when the Jews get their own country once more the end
of the world is nigh? . . . Put it this way, if there is just a God,
then He's not a good God, but if there's a God and there is a
Devil, then there is a battle in which God is losing.'

It is not surprising that a child who is unexpectedly and
severely punished for innocent mistakes and who lacks the
shield of secure parental affection comes to see herself as the
helpless but, in part, guilty victim of the warring forces of a
world which is itself on the brink of extinction. A different
experience of childhood produces a different kind of mythology.
Ella was a beautiful sixteen year old whose increasing with-
drawal and isolation had worried her teachers long before her
parents had noticed that there was any problem. They loved Ella
dearly, but, as they both told me, they each expected their
children, without exception or argument, to do exactly as they
were told, and their children always did obey. Ella and her sister
confirmed to me that this was the case. Their parents would
indulge their children if it did not run counter to their own
desires, but if there was a conflict of views, then the parents'
would prevail. 'I always obeyed my parents,' Ella's mother said,
'and I expect my children to obey me.' So Ella obeyed. Since both
parents would get very angry when something occurred counter
to their wishes, Ella learned to avoid spontaneous decisions and
actions. At school she obeyed her teachers and spoke only when
spoken to. She would respond to only two of her classmates and
she never joined in any social activities. At home she would not
use the phone or touch the radiogram. She spent as much time
as possible alone in her room. When the family were together
there could be a good deal of talking and family jokes. But
conversation in this family was always about objective realities,
mundane practicalities. No one ever talked about feelings. Of
course, if one wants to be a powerful, controlling parent one

must never show any weakness. Ella's parents did not regard their anger as weakness; indeed, they saw it as a right. So they could display their anger, but all other feelings which might reveal their fallible humanness were carefully concealed from their children. Ella said, 'My parents don't show how they feel. My sister never tells me how she feels, and neither does anyone else.'

So one day I asked Ella how she saw the purpose of life and the nature of death. She said that these were questions that she had been puzzling over for a number of years. 'That's where I go upstairs and think. I spend a lot of my time doing that. I just started to wonder whether I'm the only person who's really alive – the only living person. Everyone else is just a vision. I'm living each person's life in turn. Not just people, everything. It's there but it's not really real.'

'The most real thing is yourself?'

'Yes. I've often thought that what I see in the mirror isn't me. I've never actually seen my face.'

'Do you feel certain about yourself?'

'Yes. It's other people that are not really there. I've thought that I've already lived their lives or I'm about to live their lives and that as I see them they're not really real.'

'Do you feel that there is any order or relationship between successive lives?'

I'm not sure whether I would be the same person or a different person. I think everyone's basically the same, it's just different ways they act. I think when people are born they're the same people and they just develop in different ways. They don't really have any character of their own at all. They acquire it from the people they live with, the environment. I think all the qualities are there at birth – all the virtues and all the badness are there. Every person can be kind if they want to, but few people are . . . I'm the only person, but each time I live as a different person. I grow up in a different way. The way I am now is the result of the way things have been as I've been growing up.'

'Does the way you develop in this life have any effect on subsequent lives?'

'No. I forget about previous lives.'

'What will happen to you when you have lived every life?'

'I don't know. I just thought that I might go back to the beginning and live it all again.'

'How do you feel about living all these lives?'

'I never feel anything about it. I just think that's what is going to happen to me and it doesn't matter what I feel about it. I can't change anything.'

'Do you mean that the life you are living now is in some way fixed or ordained and there's nothing you can do to change it?'

'Yes.'

'When we think of our lives as pre-destined, we then have the question of how this plan got made.'

'I see it as there being a God but not outside, being in it all. I believe that everything I see is God. There's a power that made all this.'

'The totality of everything is God?'

'Yes.'

'Then you are God, or part of God.'

'Yes.'

'If you're the only person, if other people are visions, then this makes you a very important part.'

'I have never thought of that. I try to look at myself as what part I play, why I am here. I haven't thought of an answer to it yet.'

'Do you feel that there must be a purpose?'

'I've often thought that there isn't any purpose. I'm just here for no particular reason at all.'

'Does that thought frighten you?'

'No. It doesn't matter whether I'm frightened or pleased or anything. That's what would happen, is happening . . . I have thought that this world is one of several worlds, not just separate planets, separate worlds altogether. There's no way I can get from this world to another world. The other worlds are similar to this one in some ways – people of some kind living in them – but as separate worlds they're completely different in the way they've developed.'

'Would they be real people like yourself?'

'Only one real person in each one. There are countless worlds.'

'Are you able to have contact with these people?'

168

'No. They're completely separate.'

'Do you see yourself as having power over the people you see as visions?'

'No. I feel there's nothing I can do to change anything.'

'How would your life change if you, somehow or other, gave up this idea of people being just visions and you came to believe that they were real?'

'I don't think I would change. How could I change?'

'If you did change your beliefs?'

'I don't think I would – but I always treat people as if they were people.'

'So, with people who are close to you, your family, at the back of your mind all the time you feel that your parents, your sister, aren't real.'

'I think that they're not real. They just behave like real people.'

'You don't think there's somebody inside them like you?'

'No.'

'And you don't think I'm real.'

Ella smiled. 'No.'

In my talks with Peter he often mentioned his Celtic background. When I first met him he was living in a lonely farmhouse with his wife and children. He did some casual farmwork, but he had to rely on Social Security for his family's support. When he was twenty he had begun a career as an actor, but illness had interrupted his career and so he had never fulfilled his early promise. Whenever we discussed his return to work he said that he had to decide whether he should go back to the theatre or resume his training as a social worker. These seemed to me to be two disparate ambitions, but within his philosophy this was not so.

Peter had been born into an aristocratic family which traced its origins into the mists of Celtic history. He numbered amongst his ancestors men who had guided the great British nation, who had created and administered her laws, who had led her armies in far-flung places, who had defended the flag and protected the weak, ignorant, and oppressed. This was a formidable family for a young lad to grow up in, especially when he was not particularly wanted by his parents. They made it quite clear to him that his presence would be tolerated only if he showed himself to be worthy of the family. To be unruly or noisy, to get angry, or to argue with one's superiors was to show oneself to be like the inferior races. To be a member of this family one had to assume the duties of the family which were to protect and guide the inferior people who were at the mercy of their passions. Born forty years earlier, Peter might have slipped easily into a well-defined and comfortable niche, but by the time he was born the family had gone into a decline which was hastened by the war. When Peter came of age there was no comfortable niche for him. He had to make his own way in the world, but he still carried with him the ideals of his family.

I asked him to tell me about Celtic philosophy. He said, 'I think the Celtic philosophy tends to be external rather than internal. They made very distinct separations. The outside influences have an effect on one. They were very much at the mercy of omens, external influences, the gods, the ancestors, the weather, things that were superstitious. I don't think they were very advanced in a philosophic sense. In a cultural, creative sense they were more advanced.'

'These outside influences, were they good or bad?'

'About half and half. There was a lot of the old Biblical thing – though it wasn't related – that if you follow the right path and do the right things, then good things will happen to you.'

'Sort of, you can influence outside influences by being a good person yourself and if you're bad you get bad omens.'

'Yes, this is so. You create your own world. The tool you use to do this is yourself.'

'The other day you were telling me how much you hated a strong wind. When you're depressed and feel that you're full of badness, would you interpret that wind as a bad omen?'

'Yes, I think so. One tends to see it as a visitation upon oneself. I say this very cautiously because one feels the root connection with Celtic history, but I have to be careful because it included a lot of things that are a lot more modern. There is that "This is happening to me because I've done something bad". Walk on the lines and the bears jump up. I do something nasty and it's God punishing me, or one of the gods. There's a sort of instinctive feeling, "I've done something unlucky". I've been in

170

contact with a bad omen which in some way outside myself is telling me about myself and about my future.'

We went on to talk about Peter's fearsome anger. Peter said, 'The person who suffers after a row – I know other people do, don't misunderstand me – the person who suffers extremely is myself. I get shattered. I think about it for months afterwards. I suppose in a sense I punish myself for it. I'm not sure that there aren't times when I promote anger in order to lay the stick on myself. In a sense, one sort of feels that for some reason or other it's appropriate that I should punish myself. I deny myself things on occasion. Self-denial. I think it does me good – it's like "If I don't do this God won't punish me".'

'So you punish yourself as both a reparation and a propitiation.'

'Yes, absolutely. It's curious in a sense – that, like having animals around, and I get upset when they die, on the other hand, I'm quite convinced, having other things about the place to sort of take, to be, the fall guys, so to speak protects my family and myself.'

There were always large numbers of fowls, ducks, geese, cats, and dogs wandering around the old farmhouse. Whenever I drove into the farmyard I was anxious lest I inadvertently destroyed a favourite pet or a Sunday lunch. Now I realized that I could be seen as a vehicle for a Celtic god. 'You mean,' I said, 'if the animals die then somebody in the family won't die.'

'Yes, absolutely. This is an almost atavistic thing, I am sure the gods demand sacrifices and therefore if you have a lot of things around you that can be sacrificed, I mean, the chance of the closest things being sacrificed are really further removed. I know the absurdity of it, but that's not what I'm dealing with, the intellectual side – I'm dealing with the emotional side. Of course one had God in my childhood. The Old Testament, as a child, is much easier to understand and is much clearer than the New Testament. One didn't begin to understand the New Testament until one begins to understand the quality of Jesus, but the Old Testament where you behave yourself or you got punished and you were born a sinner anyway – this was crystal clear to a young mind. Because the mild side, the forgiving side, the loving side is not at all clear to a child. But you knew where you were with the gods. You knew you had to conform, you knew you deserved punishment because you knew you were a sinner and you knew the gods demanded sacrifices.'

'And that kind of picture of the gods didn't run counter to the picture you had in your home, of your family.'

'Oh, quite right. It was certainly the way my father presented himself to me. Actually he was a rather mild gentleman, but, of course, he was Father with a capital F, he was an army officer, becoming increasingly senior, and he had fought one war and was going off to fight in another. He was very authoritative – a figure who had power of life and death. He was a god-like and rather frightening figure even though he wasn't a frightening man.'

Peter went on to explain that later in childhood he came to see that 'if you're allowed to make a decision, you can't expect God to protect you . . . If one looked at what Jesus was, what He became for me, what He was really showing us was what any of us could do if we managed to attain that sort of thing. What He was showing was the potentiality that existed for all people, and this became for me much more realistic and logical, so that one had the forces of good and the forces of evil which I think really cannot be denied. Of course, one realized that whatever the example of Jesus, one was nowhere near measuring up to it. So I translate God into gods, and because of the other side – there are terrible things in the darkness, aren't there – the forces of evil which one has to propitiate.' A belief in the forces of good and evil allows a belief in magic. 'One believes or one very much wants to believe in magic, or I do – romance, magic are very important factors in life – the romantic and miraculous side of magic. The magic on one side is the balance against the dark forces. You can't have one without the other . . . There are still the demons, there are still the fairies . . . This is all part of one's identity. One has this thing that one would disappear if one took away the things that one feels make up, contribute to, bolster up oneself, one's importance – my ancestors came over in 1066 on my father's side and on my mother's side it's a long history of Scottish kings and nobles – this is all very irrelevant, bloody laughable, but it is there and one is frightened of dismissing it, getting rid of it, because one feels that these things are, rightly or

172

wrongly, for good or ill, the things on which one's own identity rests, to quite a large extent.'

I asked if he saw his identity continuing to exist after death.

'I do find this very difficult to talk about,' he said, 'It's a thing one doesn't talk about because it's ingrained not to. It's labelled with being a profound subject, and I don't think I'm a particularly profound person. For what it's worth, I very definitely don't see a beginning and end in terms of one's current mortal life. I think that one is surrounded so much by evidence of cycles, re-birth, in terms of things like trees and grass. I feel very strongly that we're in a similar sort of cyclical thing, where we, in some way, are developed – and there is a purpose. I would not say that reincarnation in personal, selfish terms is a possible rule, but I think in group terms, social terms, it is. I would see it as a sort of processing in rather the same way as you process steel. You put them through various stresses to refine, temper, improve. I feel that one belongs to a group, in the sense that there is probably what might be called an artistic, creative group, there is a healing group, there is probably an artisan group. You could invent permutations out of this. I feel that the group factor is probably more important than the individual factor, in the sense that one has a life, it is a thread spun off this group which probably returns to it. Am I being clear?'

'You feel that you must live your present life so that the sum total of your life will meet whatever the standard is, so you can proceed to the next stage?'

'Sort of. I think one ought to do the best one can and I think one often fails to do it.'

'When you were depressed, did you feel you hadn't met the standard?'

'Yes, and I was quite unable to deal with that. It's also confused by the fact that one does not really know what the standards are. You look at someone like Jesus and whether He existed or not is probably not very relevant, because what is relevant is the Example, and these do seem to be nearly impossible standards to meet, and I think also because the standards are so high there is a great temptation to say, "I cannot possibly achieve anything like that and therefore I'm not going

173

to make the effort." One doesn't want to be a committed Christian because it is very uncomfortable, and also if one is looking at that sort of attainment, one is being frightfully grand and really overambitious. If I can just succeed in leaving a pleasant feeling around as far as my family and people I know are concerned, maybe for me this is the most I can do.'

Peter had explained to me that being an actor meant being a responsible member of a team, just as it is to be a social worker. Either job could fulfil the conditions set by his family and could ensure his continued identity after death, an identity which had its foundations in his Celtic ancestry. His Celtic beliefs inspired in him great fear, but, as he said, 'There is a sort of loyalty factor. If I am a Celt, then I've got to pay some sort of service to the rules I believe are Celtic rules, Celtic laws. I've got to subscribe to some of those superstitions, otherwise I lose that identity with the Celtic background; then I lose contact with myself. I'd have nothing to hold on to. One does feel that because one has grown up in this sort of format, that it is valuable and that one's own identity, one's sense of self, will disappear if one removes the casing, the setting, in which one lives.'

6

Death Imagined and Death Real

It is said that intelligence reveals itself in the capacity for abstract thought. However, intelligent or not, we still turn the abstract concepts that matter most to us into personified images. Justice, blindfolded, holds the scales; Liberty, in passionate disarray, leads the way forward; while Beauty changes her style but remains beguiling. Abstract death becomes Death, the grinning skull, the cold and implacable skeleton, the Grim Reaper with his scythe. The wars and plagues of Europe have produced countless millions of skeletons, so it is no wonder that Death there takes such a form. In other cultures Death comes in other guises. 'Death,' says a Persian proverb, 'is a camel that lies down at every door.'

Death as a skeleton or as a camel are images somewhat lacking in subtlety. Other people have other images. Dylan Thomas warned us not to hasten into that 'dark night', that 'distant bourne from which no traveller returns'. For Emily Dickenson,

> Death is the supple Suitor
> That wins at last —
> It is a stealthy Wooing
> Conducted first
> By pallid innuendoes
> And dim approach
> But brave at last with Bugles.

Death came close to Arthur Koestler in prison in Seville during the Spanish Civil War. He was condemned to death by Franco and, every day, some of his fellow prisoners were collected by a warder and priest, marched out of the building and shot. Koestler was eventually exchanged for a hostage by the Republicans, and later he wrote an account of his 'Dialogue with Death'.

Long before I got to know Spain, I used to think of death as a Spaniard. As one of those noble Señors painted by Velasquez, with black silk knee-breeches, Spanish ruff, and a cool, courteously indifferent gaze. He must have been pretty disgusted when they shot the unshaven Nicholas; indignant, he covered the little Militiaman's face with that mask of rigid dignity which is proper to the etiquette of his court. There were thirteen hundred of us, his courtiers, in the Seville house of death. No liveried lackeys announced the approach of the noble Señor; the office of herald was performed by a greasy little priest, and the introduction of novices was carried out in a subdued whisper. I came face to face with him once or twice. He only offered me his finger-tips; 'How do you do?' he murmured. 'See you later,' and passed on, followed by the priest waving a sanctus bell. He forgot his promise and did not come back; but I could not forget it, and I thought of it the whole time – it is always thus when one associated with the great.

Philip Larkin described our experience of life as watching a line of ships, a 'sparkling armada of promises', each of which we expect will heave to and unload 'All good into our lives', but 'we are wrong':

> Only one ship is seeking us, a black-
> Sailed unfamiliar, towing at her back
> A huge and birdless silence. In her wake
> No waters breed or break.

Not everyone turns death into such an awesome image. When Philip French interviewed Charles Addams, the cartoonist who created a 'bizarre world of explorers, archaeologists, monsters, homicidal husbands and wives, ghouls and, above all, the macabre Addams family', he asked Addams, 'You had recently a couple of cycles of cartoons working, one of which turns on tombstones of translucent marble, which are rather cheerful; at the same time there is another bleak series showing the ship of death bearing people over the River Styx with the cowled figure in the stern and carrying signs. In one cartoon it is the same boat

176

where you have first-class, economy and tourist class, or, on another occasion, you have on the side of the boat which people are about to board to cross the river to death, a notice which says "Driver carries no money". Were you deliberately working on a series that are quite contrasted in their way: the themes are concerned with death, but their treatment differs?' Addams replied, 'I think I am trying to make death as pleasant as possible, especially for myself, and I think of it as a rather cosy condition that should not be too upsetting. It is something that comes to us all and I think we might as well joke about it; as long as we can laugh at it, I think we are that much ahead.'

Far from laughing at death, some people are most reluctant to talk about it, and, if pressed, will say, 'I never think about it.' But even they, if asked to say whether they would prefer burial or cremation, can immediately state a preference. An indifference to the fate of our corpse seems to be rare. The preference seems not to be related solely to the practicalities of disposing of the body in that particular locality, but rather to what the person wants, in some way, *to see being done* to his body. Sometimes this is expressed as a lack of trust of other people – that they may not have noticed or they may have maliciously ignored the fact that the person is not really dead. For some people the thought of being conscious as one's coffin slides into the flames holds the greatest horror; for others it is the thought of scratching on the coffin lid as the clods of earth fall down to cover it. Stories, perhaps apocryphal, are often told of coffins being dug up and opened to reveal the marks of frenzied fingers on the inside of the lid. Cremation leaves no mark of the person wrongly consigned, but the dread of the flames of hell is burned into the minds of many of us brought up in the Christian faith.

On the other hand, we may have no doubt that we shall be well and truly dead at our own funeral, but other matters can be important. We may want to ensure that we are properly remembered by the placing of a suitable memorial, or that we are cast to the winds and the sea and forgotten. It is as if some vestige of our consciousness must remain to witness the fate of our mortal remains and sometimes, even, to share the experience of what happens to them. The churchyard in my village is large and beautiful. In winter the snows lie heaped where the villagers have been buried since Eagle was, as its old Saxon name (*ac leah*) declared, a clearing in the oak forest. The forest has long since gone, but in spring the daffodils nod over the graves and in summer the swallows swoop under the lime trees and the long grasses blow among the headstones. Whenever I walk through the churchyard I think what a nice place it would be to be buried in – to be part of the cycle of those birds and flowers and trees. Such a thought raises in me a feeling of tranquility (though I hope that this ultimate pleasure will be a long time in coming), unlike that in Dr Johnson whose dread of death often caused him to repeat Claudio's words,

> *Ay, but to die and go we know not where*
> *To lie in cold obstruction and to rot;*
> *This sensible warm motion to become*
> *A kneaded clod, and the delighted spirit*
> *To bathe in fiery floods.*

Whenever I ask people about their preference for burial or cremation I find that they respond with great fervour. My friend Harry Weber, a retired vicar who looks forward to death with joy and longing, replied to my question with, 'I have a horror of being buried alive and suffocating. I have a horror of it! When I die I want to be comfortable and sort of go to sleep – that's death. But this thought at the back of my mind – you know Rachmaninov's *Piano Concerto* – that one where there's supposed to be somebody alive, knocking on the coffin. This is the thought that horrifies me. But apart from that, I think that death is something to look forward to.' I put the question about burial and cremation to a group of health professionals attending a seminar on depression. It was late in the afternoon and we had had a long day. Everyone sat tired and silent while I talked doggedly on. Suddenly, at my question, the whole group became lively and argumentative. One person said she wanted to be buried because 'it was natural, returning to the earth'. 'Oh, no,' said another, 'I want to be cremated. I like the idea of turning into smoke – all that marvellous freedom.' One woman who had listened silently all day said very firmly, 'Burial's to do with religion and I want none of that. Cremation is me, just me. I'd like my ashes scattered over the sea.' 'Not at all,' said a man on the other side of the room, 'cremation's so clinical and there's nothing left. But with burial, there's a gravestone. There's something there – .' 'I think burial's disgusting, horrible,' broke in another woman, 'I couldn't face being eaten by those maggots.' 'But the thing about burial,' argued another, 'I've always thought that if they've made a mistake and I wasn't dead – I'd be able to attract attention. I'd have a chance of getting out.' 'If they had made a mistake,' said one woman in a tone to end the argument, 'with cremation at least it's over quicker. You don't have a slow, lingering death.'

The preference we have for either cremation or burial derives not from a whim, a choice made idly between two equally appealing alternatives, but from the way we see ourselves in relation to our past, present, and future. In construct theory terms, our constructs about the ultimate disposal of our body derive from our core constructs. The links between the core constructs and the 'disposal of the body' constructs are not always readily apparent. I often look for them in therapy, especially with a client for whom suicide seems a strong possibility. We all have fantasies about the circumstances of our death. The successful suicide is one who has stepped into his fantasy in an attempt to make it real; so to help prevent a person taking this step it is worthwhile finding out just what his fantasy is.

Hilary was a lonely, depressed young woman who was slowly losing her grip on her life. Her marriage was ending; her job lacked all interest and motivation; her friends were drifting away. She was thin, grey-faced, a ghost before her time. I tried to find something in her that I could hold on to, and so I asked her what she valued about herself.

She replied, 'I quite like the fact that I'm orderly, organized. My husband isn't. He's always rushing about and involved in things. Sometimes I wish I was more involved in things. But if I did, I wouldn't have so much time to be organized and I like to be.'

'Why is it important to be organized?'

'That's the way I am.'

'What would happen to you if you weren't organized?'

'I worry if things aren't organized. I get anxious and I don't like to be anxious. If I'm anxious I find it difficult to concentrate.'

We examined why it was so important to her to be able to concentrate, and she said that if this inability to concentrate went on and on then she would feel that 'I wasn't in control of myself. I would feel that I wasn't myself if I wasn't in control. I'd be another person. I think that this is why I get frightened when I get depressed because it's something I can't control.'

I asked her if she ever wished to be more spontaneous, less under control. She replied, 'Sometimes. With other people I tend to be controlled – I think before I speak. I wish I could chat – be more spontaneous.' But later she showed that she did not really approve of spontaneous people. Being spontaneous meant 'putting things on to other people', that is imposing on other people.

Nothing is more spontaneous than anger, so I asked her, 'Do you get angry very often?'

'No. I don't get angry without getting depressed.'

'What sort of things make you angry?'

'I used to get angry when my husband would promise me to do something and then he didn't. I wanted him to have my values. If I said I would do something I would do it.'

'Why should a promise be kept?'

'So you can have a relationship with somebody. If you promise somebody something and you don't mean it, then there's no basis for that relationship.'

I commented, 'In a relationship where two people carry out their promises everything goes along in a nice, neat orderly fashion. But in a relationship where one person doesn't carry out his promises, then that person would be creating situations which you would be unable to keep under control.' I could also have pointed out the close cirque created by her definition of herself in terms of control which leads to anger (loss of control) which leads to depression which is both a threat to her control and an increase in control, and thus, since control is good and spontaneity bad, to be good she must be depressed. I simply remarked, 'Being depressed is the opposite of being spontaneous.'

'Yes, I think so,' she said, 'because when I feel depressed I just feel I don't want to do anything and also I want to be left alone.

When you're spontaneous you feel that you want to talk to people.'

'What for you is the worst part of the depression?'

'Feeling that I ought to be doing something – part of me is saying I should be able to pull myself together. My depression is like a fog or a cloud in your mind that stops you from being able to feel, think, and do things properly. I get in the way. It's a barrier between me and everything else – between me and what I would normally think. I have to get up, get dressed, go to work – this sort of gets in the way so that I can't. I feel I should be able to do all that, but this gets in the way of doing it.'

'What would happen to you if you gave up the feeling that you should do all these things and you stayed inside this fog?'

'I think it would be nice if you could stay inside – so you could not think and you could have a sort of blank sort of thing.'

'Why would this be nice?'

'Because it would stop the struggle. It seems such a struggle, to feel that you don't want or you can't do things and the feeling that you ought to be doing them.'

'So, if the struggle ceased, what would happen to you?'

'You would cease to be – at least in your mind. You'd cease to be.'

'What would you become?'

'I don't know. I suppose it would be like I imagine being dead – being nothingness. I suppose it would be like that. Anyway, that's how I imagine it, but you wouldn't be dead, your body would go on and on. I find it difficult to put the two together.'

Hilary had earlier said that she saw dying as a better alternative than being alive. I asked, 'If you see death as a blanking out, does that mean that you don't conceive of any afterlife?'

'Sometimes death seems attractive because there wouldn't be anything. I think if there was an afterlife I wouldn't want to go – I've struggled so much with this one that I don't want another one.'

'How do you see yourself being remembered?'

'I don't know. I'd be upset if my husband was to find me dead, but I can't imagine what he would feel apart from that shock. I'd think people would think I'd taken the easy way out – but that's my view. Other people are frightened of dying. I can feel frightened about the way of dying. But the actual fact of being dead doesn't ever frighten me.'

I asked her whether she would prefer to be buried or cremated. She answered immediately, 'Cremated.'

'Why?'

'I just think it's better. I don't see any point in having graves that aren't looked after or that relatives feel obliged to look after.'

Thus, since for her neatness and order are good and placing others under an obligation is bad, she could not lie in an untidy grave nor could she demand that others tend her grave. Cremation is neat and imposes no obligation. Cremated, she could still think of herself as a good person.

Hilary, not wanting an afterlife and viewing death as a merciful blanking-out, nevertheless saw herself as still existing after death in a form which would wish to spare her husband distress or obligation. This is the 'self-in-the-future' that we take into our consideration when we plan our action. I do the washing-up at night so that 'myself-in-the-morning' does not have to face the unpleasant spectacle of dirty dishes; I pay superannuation so that 'myself-in-retirement' can live in moderate comfort. I carry out these actions even though I know that dirty dishes require the same amount of effort night or morning and that I may not live long enough to enjoy my hard-earned superannuation. These future selves have a reality which demands a response. And for some of us our 'self-after-death' can be very demanding.

Kitty came to see me because she was so very anxious. It became apparent that she gave herself much to worry about. Not only did she fear all the ordinary hazards of life, but every hazard was viewed in its extremity – every journey would end in disaster, every illness would prove fatal. She said, 'When things are going smoothly, when things go right, I always worry that they're going to go wrong. Why am I so special that it wouldn't happen to me? I always think these things could happen to me. For as long as I can remember I've always expected things to go wrong. If you look forward to something, it's often a let-down.' Moreover, for Kitty, everything had to be perfect. Curtains must hang in exact folds, every garment must be absolutely flawless, children should behave themselves. As life is more full of potential danger than it is of actual perfection, Kitty lived in a constant state of fear and anger. Such a state is not conducive to good health, and so she suffered from frequent ailments, all of which she interpreted as leading to some terrible illness and death. 'I'm not frightened of dying,' she said, 'I don't want to be left on my own.'

'What do you feel will happen to you when you die?' I asked.

'My family laugh at me when I say this, but I've often said if I die I will be watching what Bob and the children and everybody do, and I shall be in a terrible state because I shan't be able to communicate with them. I feel I shall be looking down on them. I can't visualize dying, that's the end of it, that I won't be with the children and family anymore. It's like when other people die, people I've been close to, I imagine that they look at me. I find it quite terrifying. When I was younger I found it very frightening to think that I was being looked at by my grandmother when she'd just died. It wasn't so much that I was grieving for the loss of her but I was in a state because she was looking at me. I've always had a fear of death. The last time I saw a psychiatrist I'd had a bad spell. I'd got a very dear friend and she was killed in a car accident. Every time I washed my hair I was terrified of getting the water in my eyes in case she was looking at me and there with me and I was frightened of her, yet when she was alive I wasn't frightened of her at all and she was a good, dear friend. But I don't think of my friend in that respect now – that was a few years ago.'

I asked, 'If there is a spirit that remains around and then goes away, where would it go to?'

'I've never thought about that. Once she's left my mind – because I've always realized it must be in my mind. I don't know. My doctor who's very religious says that my God is very limited. I've always steered clear of getting involved in religion, but I do believe in something. I believe there is somebody to look after you. I wouldn't want to go to church regularly yet I do pray to God. I've also been told by two friends who are very religious that I pray in the wrong way, that I pray that I don't want anything to happen to Bob or the children or me, and I should be praying for the courage to face whatever is going to happen, and

183

I can't have the courage to pray for courage. I just want everything to be all right. I don't want anything to go wrong.'

I asked her how she saw her God.

'Just as a man,' she said, 'an ordinary sort of man. I know He's supposed to be all good and then I find myself questioning why these terrible things happen. When I ask my friends why terrible things happen to young children and He lets old people who have had a good life linger on, their answer is that unfortunately, through no fault of their own, through the fault of Adam, we've all been born into sin, automatically, and that doesn't answer my question at all. I couldn't understand what the connection was – I think if I tried to get myself involved in that, that would be something else that I would have to worry about.' (Whenever Kitty purchased a dress and later discovered that its hem was not perfectly even or one seam did not meet another exactly in line, she would return the offending article to the shop and demand a flawless replacement or her money back. Unfortunately, there was no way she could return an imperfect Adam to his Creator.) 'What makes you a good Christian?' she went on, 'How do you get this relationship that He would talk to me the way you're talking to me, which is what my two friends are saying. I don't know how it's possible. My friends say that they don't have any fears about anything because they know that God will answer their prayers in some way. Both of them have never had anything tragic happen in their families. But I've got to believe something. If I don't believe then I'd disappear and I can't imagine myself not being myself. And I don't believe you're reincarnated and come back as a cow or a sheep. I find that hard to believe. I do believe in something. This Heaven that's supposed to be so wonderful, that it wouldn't matter whether you've got your children or your husband there because you feel total contentment – I can't see my life being totally happy without Bob and the children, so that what I get frightened about is to be away from them. If I died before Bob and the children, I feel as though I would know what they were doing, but I wouldn't be able to communicate with them. I'd know every move they made, but wouldn't be able to talk with them. That would be absolutely dreadful. If my father died, I'd want him to be close to me. I couldn't bear the thought of him not being around, but again I'd feel I couldn't communicate. He would just be there. And I wouldn't be able to say anything. You wouldn't feel you were ever on your own. You'd never have – I sound stupid, but if you wanted to go to the toilet or if you wanted to be private, you wouldn't be. Somebody would be there all the time. That's how I felt about my friend and my grandmother. From way back in my childhood I've always been frightened of ghosts.'

I asked her if her husband believed in the continued existence of the spirit after death. 'No,' she said. 'When Bob's father died, Bob – he's very practical and to him, his father's dead and he was burnt and that was the end of him.'

'How do you feel about this?' I asked.

'I think he should feel like I do, and yet I can't get him to believe in something because I don't know what I believe in.'

Kitty did not want to lose her identity after death or to be separated from her family, so a belief in a continuing spirit in its familiar environment was a solution, even though such a belief had some terrifying and embarrassing implications. As a spirit, not being able to communicate with those still alive would be frustrating (and perhaps terrifying to those still alive), but if her husband did not share this belief then if she died before him he would not acknowledge or believe in her continued existence. She would become, indeed, a very lonely spirit.

Death, as she conceived of it, frightened Kitty, yet she did acknowledge death's existence. Not all people are prepared to do this. However, when we turn away from death it comes to us in other guises. Jill told me that she never thought about death and wished that I would get on with the business of curing her of her obsessional habits of excessive washing of clothes, hair, and hands, and of refusing to touch certain objects or to go into certain parts of her house. She involved her young son in all these rituals which now occupied so much of her day that a normal family life was no longer possible. Jill was a beautiful, well-educated, intelligent young woman brought up in a family where, she told me, 'My father expected us to do what he said and I always did' and mother was 'a worrier'. When she was first married she worked in the office of a chemical firm. One day when she was walking through the laboratory a small quantity of a chemical compound was accidentally squirted on her skirt. She went to the First Aid room where, she said, 'They looked it up in some book and said, oh, well, there's nothing we can do. There's no antidote. If you're still alive by nine o'clock tonight you'll be alright. I was very worried. Someone since told me they were joking because they thought it wasn't very serious, but I didn't realize that at the time. I went home and took the skirt off and put it aside because I was a bit scared to wash it and I didn't want to throw it away because it was brand new. I don't know how it got in the back of the cupboard where it was when we moved.'

This skirt became the source of the contagion. As Jill saw it, the contagion spread to all the objects in the cupboard where the skirt was. When Jill and her husband and child moved house the contents of the cupboard were shifted and the contagion spread to every object and person that touched them or even just came in close proximity to them. The only way the contagion could be removed was by washing. Some things, like books, could not be washed, and while Jill was washing what she could the contagion spread to her hair and clothes. She drew lines of demarcation in the house and made rules for her husband and child to follow, and when they transgressed the lines and rules she panicked and washed everything again. Even when all the rules and rituals were kept she would look at something and doubt. 'I opened a cupboard door and saw a cup which I hadn't used for ages. I suddenly didn't want to touch that. My husband drank tea out of it to show me it was all right, but I still didn't want to touch it. Anything that hasn't been in circulation or unusual, I get worried. There seems to be no end to it.'

I asked Jill how she saw this contagion as being able to harm her. She said, 'I don't really know what I think will happen if I touch them. If they're small things I lick them if they're suitable to be licked to prove to myself that nothing will happen. I can't really expect anything to happen. I just get this feeling that I don't want to touch them. If I do touch them I have to wash my hands or my hair as well. I washed it four times yesterday. I don't really know why I have to do it, but I can't relax until I've washed my hands and hair.'

Being a fairly obsessional person myself with certain cleanliness rituals (all perfectly sensible ones, of course) I tried to understand how Jill perceived this particular 'uncleanliness'. I told her that my mother views all 'creepy crawlies' with great distaste and how horrified she had been when she discovered that while in Bangkok I had visited a snake house and had actually touched a cobra (it was securely held by its keeper at the time). Jill said that she would have touched the cobra too, and so I asked her why she would touch a poisonous snake and not some of her own inanimate possessions. 'I suppose I'm not responsible for the snake,' she said. 'The keeper was taking responsibility for that. I would expect to be safe. Whereas I suppose I'm responsible for my things. If I go into other people's houses I don't worry about it.'

I tried to pursue this question of just how lethal she saw this contagion as being. It was not just that these objects were dirty. She agreed that they had some quality of danger about them, but 'I can't explain why'. I tried to open up the whole question of death by asking, 'How do you see death?'

She replied, 'I've never really thought about it.'

I persisted. 'Some people believe that life ends in death, that that's all we've got, and some people believe that life goes on.'

'No, the former, I think.'

'Do you see any part of yourself continuing?'

'No.'

'How does that kind of prospect make you feel?'

'I don't think about it.'

I felt I was making no progress. Jill would come and sit nervously on the edge of her chair, her scaly, overwashed hands clasped tightly on her lap, and look at me, waiting for me to produce a practical solution which she could then show me by words or deeds was no solution. She would talk about her obsession, but questions about all other topics – childhood, relationships with her husband and parents – received guarded and conventional replies. She could see no reason to discuss her childhood – it was quite ordinary – and when I explained how we carry the image and metaphors of our childhood into our adult life she said that this could not apply to her since 'I'm not an imaginative person'. Nevertheless, I thought I would try and get her to imagine the contagion as being a person and then to describe the attributes of that person. But she said, 'No, I can't do that.'

187

'Well, suppose you're standing there and you're looking into the cupboard – where do you sense the danger coming from?'

'One particular object.'

'Is the danger wrapped around the cup?'

'Yes. On that cup – inside and outside, but if the cup was broken it wouldn't be on the broken edge.'

'Do you feel that the danger is in some way radiating out?'

'It's on the surface but it only spreads by contact. It doesn't actually radiate but if somebody touches the surface –'

'So it won't come over to you through the air. It can only come by touch.'

'Usually. When my husband moved the washing line it didn't touch the garden but I knew it was windy out. I thought perhaps something had blown off, on to the garden.'

'When you say blown off – when you said the danger was all over the cup I was getting the vision of something smooth and continuous like cream –'

'No, more like a dust.'

'So it's a dust which sort of lies quietly on the objects but as soon as it's disturbed the dust will spread on to whatever's disturbed it.'

'Yes, that's right.'

'This dust, what does it look like?'

'It's invisible.'

'Is it invisible to the naked eye but would it be visible if you looked at it through a microscope?'

'It's like germs. I don't know whether you can see germs or not. I don't think you can, can you?'

'Nowadays germs and viruses can be seen through an electron microscope.'

'These are like germs and viruses but I don't think, however powerful a microscope, you could see it.'

'What you're saying is that it's a real thing but there's no machinery available for seeing it because it's so small.'

'Yes.'

'Even though you can't see this kind of dangerous dust with our eyes, it is possible to have an image of it in our mind because it is possible to imagine things we can't see. Can you bring into your mind an image of this dust? Just concentrate on it.' Jill closed her eyes. I waited a while and then said, 'Now, keep concentrating on that dust. You can see it spread around things and it can blow. Just imagine you're looking at it, you're seeing it there, spread out around this cup. There's a gentle wind blowing and a little bit is blowing off the cup. Imagine that as you're looking at it all the dust turns into a person. What kind of person do you see?'

'There's a vague shape, like you see in a fog. Nothing definite.'

'What kind of shape?'

'Sort of – dressed in blankety-type clothes, just vague.'

'Is this shape friendly towards you?'

'No, distant. Neither friendly nor dangerous. I couldn't reach it.'

'Why not?'

'If you put your hand out to touch it it would move away. It would recede as you approached it.'

'Why is it receding? Why doesn't it stay?'

'Because it hasn't got any substance – if that makes sense.'

'What would happen if you touched it?'

'Your hand would go right through it.'

'How would it feel if your hand went through it?'

'Like cold steam, if you can get such a thing. Just like gas.'

'What would happen to you if you did touch it?'

'Nothing. That doesn't make sense.'

'What would happen to the shape if you touched it?'

'It would go back and re-form.'

'How does the shape feel about you?'

'It wants to avoid being touched. It's a bit like a ghost that doesn't want to be seen or touched. I don't know why. I think it wants to be left alone. It just likes being solitary.'

'Does the shape get frightened when you're close to it?'

'No, just repelled.'

'Does it want to harm you?'

'No.'

'Do you want to harm it?'

'Just want to get rid of it.'

'Could you go towards it and make it go away?'

'No. I think it would keep the same sort of distance from me if I went toward it. If I walked away it wouldn't follow me.' She described how it might be possible to walk away from the shape and put a great distance between herself and the shape. 'I'd end up running in case it decided to come after me.'

'What would happen if it came after you?'

'It would completely surround me.'

'What would happen to you then?'

'I think I would be part of it, nothing. It would be the end of you, I suppose.'

'It would wipe you out – you'd be a nothing, annihilated.'

'Yes.'

'And this is how you see death, that death is the end. You are annihilated in death.'

'Yes. I've never thought about it like that before, but yes.'

'The fact that you can't go away and leave it – you say "If I run it might come after me". It sounds like you're saying "If I can keep an eye on this shape then I can keep it at a distance. But if I take my eye off it – "'

'Yes, I suppose so.'

'That's when it's likely to be dangerous.'

'Yes.' She laughed nervously.

'So when I set you a task of showing that there's nothing of the shape on this object or that object, you immediately have to get your eye on the shape somewhere else because it will turn up somewhere else.'

'Yes.'

We talked some more about how she felt about the shape and she said that in some way she felt responsible for the shape, 'because by choosing either to go towards it or away from it I can determine what it's going to do. I'd like it to disappear but it won't go away.' In a conversation several weeks later Jill and I worked out that in all areas of her life except one she deferred to her husband and her mother. Only in her relationship to the contagious shape did she make her own decisions. If she gave up her obsession she would be doing what her husband and mother wanted her to do. It is sad that when all we can see ourselves as owning is our death.

Jill feared for her safety, but even more for that of her young son. 'I feel he's in some sort of danger. I feel something's going to happen to him.' I asked her to imagine a picture of her son and the dust. She said, 'One of the most dangerous places is the bottom of the airing cupboard. If I imagined him there it would be with this grey dust all over him, the shape, completely enveloped in it.'

'What is he doing?'

'Just sitting there.'

'Is he happy or sad?'

Jill was silent. Then she said, 'I suppose dying, in a way, completely surrounded by this dust.'

'Is he turning into dust?'

'Yes, I suppose so. There's the outline of his shape in this grey cloud of dust.'

'Can he speak to you?'

'No.'

'What are you saying to him?'

'I think I would get in there as well – go with him, wherever he was going.'

'What would happen to you?'

'I'd be dust as well. It would be the end of us both. But I'd want to go with him.'

'Where would you be?'

'I don't know really, because in theory I don't believe in any afterlife but I'd want to go with him so I must believe I'd still be with him wherever we were.'

'What comes into your mind about where you'd be?'

'Nothing really. We wouldn't be visible – just dust again.'

On another occasion I asked Jill whether she would prefer burial or cremation. She said, 'I assume I'll be cremated. I've got no choice. I'm not very happy about it. I don't like the idea of being – a box of dust.'

'What's so terrible about being a box of dust?'

'It's so final. That's the end of you. I don't think it would be any different if you were buried, except your body would be there for a bit, even if it was decayed. I suppose I don't like the idea of being burnt, reduced to ashes, dust. My father was cremated. I didn't go to the funeral. I was protected once more from an unpleasant experience. That was all I really thought about – there he was in a little box of dust. I don't even know where that box is now. I'd much prefer it if there was a gravestone.'

'Death,' wrote James Carse, 'confronts us wherever we experience a radical threat to the continuity of our existence.' For Jill a gravestone would represent some small thread of continuity; a box of dust is a break in that continuity, and so she was afraid. But Jill, who had no belief in an afterlife, had some feeling that she would go on existing after death, even though it would be in the horrible formlessness of invisible dust. 'It is,' Freud wrote, 'indeed impossible to imagine our own death; and whenever we attempt to do so we can perceive that we are in fact still present as spectators. Hence the psychoanalytic school could venture on the assertion that at bottom no one believes in his own death, or, to put the same thing another way, that in his unconscious everyone is convinced of his own immortality.' Robert Jay Lifton, who has studied the effects of the mass deaths in Hiroshima, Vietnam, and the concentration camps of Nazi Germany, concluded that, 'even in our unconscious lives we are by no means *convinced* of our immortality. Rather, we have what some recent workers have called 'middle knowledge' of the idea of death. We both 'know' that we will die and resist and fail to act on that knowledge. Nor is the need to transcend death *mere* denial. More essentially, it represents a compelling universal urge to maintain an inner sense of continuous symbolic relationship, over time and space, with the various elements of life. In other words, I am speaking of a *sense* of immortality as in itself neither compensatory nor pathological, but as man's symbolization of his ties with both his biological fellows and his history, past and future.' Lifton noted in passing that, 'The therapeutic efforts of physicians and psychotherapists are strongly impelled, I believe, by an image of therapeutic impact extending through the patient to others, including the patient's children, in an endless potentially beneficent chain of influence. The "therapeutic despair" described so sensitively by Leslie Farber as an occupational hazard of the psychiatrist treating schizophrenic patients might well result from the perception that one's strenuous therapeutic endeavors are not animating the life of the patient and cannot therefore symbolically extend one's own.'

It is this symbolic extension of our lives that allows us to maintain the idea of the continuity of our existence after the discontinuity caused by our death. Knowing the inevitability of our death, we create a myth that denies it. 'Myth and religion in general,' wrote Ernst Cassirer, 'have often been declared to be the mere product of fear. But what is more essential in man's religious life is not the *fact* of fear, but the *metamorphosis* of fear. Fear is a universal biological instinct. It can never be completely overcome or suppressed, but it can change its form. Myth is filled with the most violent emotions and the most frightful visions . . . But in myth man begins to learn a new and strange art: the art of expressing, and that means of organizing his most deeply rooted instincts, his hopes and fears . . . In mythical thought the mystery of death is "turned into an image" – and by this transformation, death ceases being a hard, unbearable physical fact; it becomes understandable and supportable.'

Some of the attempts to make death 'understandable and supportable' have been examined by James Carse in his book *Death and Existence*. 'The challenge of death,' he wrote 'will be met only by taking its threatened discontinuity into a higher continuity. To take refuge in the present continuity is the reaction of grief. Since death is a power, what one achieves is not the elimination of death – it will not be compromised – but a higher form of freedom capable of establishing its continuity regardless of death.' We find a higher continuity by changing our construction of death. Carse looked at ten major conceptions of death: 'to learn what the *agency of death* is for each of these traditions and thinkers; that is, how they describe the way we are threatened by discontinuity. This in turn brings us to the way they conceive *grief*, and its subsequent cure by the achievement of new life, a greater *freedom* to establish an inclusive continuity.'

Socrates, believing that his soul would continue in conversation with other souls pursuing knowledge, was unafraid of death and drank the hemlock. Hence Carse 'characterized Plato's classical conception of death as *change*, and the corresponding response to life *knowledge*. To "die" is only to let the body go. To "live" is to take timeless residence in "true knowledge". But the "true" is also the *real* for Plato. There is therefore no more reality to death than to the painted scenery on the stage. If we can come to believe the scenery is real, we may also believe that we shall all perish with the last line of the final act. Plato was convinced that when the last line is spoken the scenery is removed and the conversation continues – on a different stage.'

In contrast, Epicurus and the philosophy of modern science consider death as dispersion and deal with it by disregard. It is the physical entities of the universe that provide the source of continuity: 'If life is understood strictly in terms of invariants or continuities, death is not a possibility, because what we call death can only be an event where nothing comes to an end.' If we believe that our actions have effects, then we can establish our continuity by carrying out actions while we are alive which will continue to have their effects after we are dead – our fame, discoveries, creations, children will be testimony of our continuing existence.

In mysticism and in psychoanalysis death is seen as separation and continuity in love. For the mystics life's continuity is provided 'not by self-existing substance, whether physical or psychic, but on one's own free act'. Death is 'the *separation* of the soul from its origin'. In choosing to separate ourselves from God we choose death. Death is overcome by the act of loving union with God. The Blessed John Ruysbroeck wrote, 'The first and highest unity of man is God; for all creatures depend on this unity for their being, their life, and their preservation, and if they are separated in this wise from God, they fall into nothingness and become naught. This unity is in us essentially, by nature, whether we be good or evil. And without our own working it makes us neither holy nor blessed. This unity we possess within us and yet above us, as the ground and the preserver of our being and of our life.'

James Carse remarks that Freud, being a strongly convinced materialist, might wonder at his being linked with the mystics, but Freud himself recognized that 'The theory of instincts is so to say our mythology. Instincts are mythical entities magnificent in their indefiniteness.' Carse comments, 'the ego – the individualized, time-orientated, and outward directed part of the self – is the manifestation of the life-instinct, the corpse-like worldly self of the mystics. The terrible gloom and ignorance one lives in is, of course, gloom and ignorance only for the ego, or the worldly self . . . For anyone who has knowledge of the unconscious, or Eckhart's "unknown knowledge", it becomes apparent that the hidden desire represented by the death instinct is more nearly a desire for continuity, for a more perfect existence . . . We have emphasised the fundamentally *erotic* character of mysticism and psychoanalysis. Their deepest desires are for an active, creative union with the source of their own existence. They place an exceedingly high value on happiness, bliss, and rapture . . . Freud also makes it clear that the life-instinct is the mischief-maker; it repeatedly breaks up our rapture, deprives us of blissful union. Bakan, also pursuing this theme in Freud's thought, implies that if we choose life we choose to make pain the path to growth and independence . . . Freud and his most inspired students understood the problem of death as a problem of making a fundamental human choice between happiness and history.'

In Hinduism such a choice is unnecessary. Death is an illusion. Continuity is in *being*, Atman, the real, that which truly is. In the Bhagavad-Gita Krishna tells Prince Arjuna, 'Know this Atman unborn, undying, never ceasing, never beginning; deathless, birthless, unchanging forever. How can it die the death of the body?' Thus, as Carse says, 'Those who know the inmost Reality know only that Reality is, and that it is One; they know therefore that *life is not* and *death is not*. More importantly, those who truly know the inmost Reality *are* the inmost Reality. Only of them can it be said, *Tat Tvam asi*: That art thou.' The union which the mystics seek is different from that sought by the Hindus. The mystic union is a loving act, an ecstacy. Ananda, the union described by the Upanishads, is indifferent to the act, since, as Krishna explained to Arjuna, he already is the Atman. So long as we refuse to recognize this and continue to be involved in the world of sense objects we shall be bound to the wheel of existence which repeats itself endlessly. Karma is grief. To the Westerner the belief in reincarnation can appear to offer the chance to do better next time, to repay the debt of past sins, but to the Hindu who sees karma not as the outcome of sin but as existence itself, the wheel of death and re-birth is indeed terrible.

For the Buddhist death is not an illusion but a fiction. What we see is not reality, nor an illusion screening a reality (as in

Hinduism), but the fictions we create in the attempt to find something permanent and solid in what is always flux. We become attached to the fictions we have created, and the cravings we feel for our attachments are the cause of our sufferings. When we give up our attachments to our fictions, cease to seek permanence in flux and instead accept the flux, the becoming instead of the being, then we have found a liberation which 'is not a victory over death that gives one more life but a victory over the craving that originally made life painful and death fearsome'. In the ultimate liberation, Nirvana, the state of pure becoming, there is no being, simply an act without anything as actor and object. How this could be may invite speculation, but Buddha wisely warned against metaphysical ponderings. 'The religious life,' he said, 'does not depend on the dogma that the world is eternal; nor does the religious life depend on the dogma that the world is not eternal.' What does matter is that 'there still remain birth, old age, death, sorrow, lamentation, misery, grief, and despair, for the extinction of which in the present life I am prescribing'.

In Judaism death is seen as inevitable and continuity in history. Unlike the Hindus and the Buddhists the Jews do not deny or abandon history but rather they see their continuity, their victory over death, in their history, which is not merely the story of the triumphs and failures of one people but a continuing discourse with God. Thus their history has an open future. Individuals die but the creative discourse goes on.

The Talmud teaches that evil comes from within us, our sins are punished by suffering and death, and so we must repent. Such a teaching focuses attention on life, on the present, and not on the indefinite future beyond death. This is the tenor of Jesus' teaching as reported in the synoptic Gospels. He mentions death and a place of punishment, but it is matters of life, how we relate to one another and to God that concern Him. 'Follow me,' He said, 'and leave the dead to bury the dead.' It is in the Gospel of St John that the Christian view of death as transformation and continuity by faith is clearly stated. Jesus said, 'I am the resurrection and the life: he that believeth in me, though he were dead, yet shall he live. And he that believeth in me shall never die.' This was the teaching of St Paul who saw death, the corruptible death of our bodies, as vanquished. 'O death, where is thy sting? O grave, where is thy victory?'

St Augustine spoke of a 'second death', the living death of the faithless in hell. 'The first death drives the unwilling soul from the body; the second death keeps the unwilling soul in the body . . . Only that which follows death makes death evil.' The concept of a second death is a powerful force in Islam. Only the faithful shall be saved. The wicked, who are always identified with the unbelievers, will endure a second death of an eternity in hell. The Koran warns, 'He (the unbeliever) shall endure the heat of the great fire. Then will he neither live nor die.' 'They (the just) do not taste death in it (Paradise) after the first death and He preserved them from the punishment of hell.' Life is ephemeral, 'a passing comfort', a 'sport and past time'. The only true life is that in the hereafter, the reward of the faithful, the fighters in the Holy War.

The image of death as a doorway is a common one. In the philosophies of Jung, the Neoplatonists, the Teilhard de Chardin, death is seen as a threshold and continuity in vision. Late in his life Jung remarked 'All my work is about the interplay of the "here" and the "hereafter".' Organic death is real, but there is no sense of death in the psyche. It exists outside space and time, and we have knowledge of that and should trust our knowledge. Following a severe illness Jung wrote, 'Death is the hardest thing from the outside and as long as we are outside of it. But once you taste the inside of such completeness and peace and fulfilment then you don't want to return.' Jung's studies took him into the realms of the magical and the mystical, and so he was familiar with Neoplatonism and the Hermetic tradition. This tradition developed in part from Plato's *Timaeus*, where the universe is seen as an organic whole into which the soul will blend, from Plato through Plotinus and his doctrine of the One, to the esoteric wisdom of 'Corpus Hermeticum' and the occult sciences of alchemy and magic. In this tradition, magic can be 'white' and 'natural' or 'black' and 'demonic'. The Neoplatonic conception of the connectedness of all things gave rise to the idea of white magic, that is, powers which can be used by those who understand them. When these powers are used for selfish, destructive ends the magic becomes black, demonic. The vision of the white magic was to perceive the higher unity of the soul with the universe. For Teilhard de Chardin death is a threshold, too, into a mode of being beyond mortality, a vision of wholeness.

Hegel, Sartre, Nietzsche, and Heidegger saw death as a possibility and placed against it their philosophical conceptions which James Carse has grouped together under the term 'power'. The ideas of these philosophers are not easily summarized and here it is sufficient to note that, in the way that none of the great religions have produced an explanation of death which is both logically coherent and reconciles us happily to life and death, so the philosophers who have set out on the enterprise of creating a Grand Design have likewise failed. By contrast, a less ambitious philosopher, Kierkegaard, made a more modest attempt and in doing so added greatly to our understanding of despair and hope. For Kierkegaard death was an horizon and continuity of our continuing discourse with one another. Such continuing discourse is possible only when the listener 'is infinitely interested in another's reality' and where what is said is provocative of further thought. These are, of course, the necessary conditions for psychotherapy.

All these philosophies and religions, all our private metaphors, concern death as we imagine it to be. We know death through our images – and then one day we discover that death is real. We are, in fact, like the man described by Sartre 'who is bravely preparing himself for the ultimate penalty, who is doing everything possible to make a good showing on the scaffold, and who meanwhile is carried off by a flu epidemic'. We each construct what Sartre called our 'fundamental project' which gives our life its meaning, and we plan a death which will be appropriate to the style and purpose of our project. But death, absurd death, real death, can render our plans vain and useless at any moment. Real death may come suddenly and completely or it may just brush close by us. Both experiences change us – one from alive to dead, the other from the security of the unfolding of our projects into the lonely vulnerability of knowing that *my death is real*. One never feels more alive than when one faces real death. Imagining our death, we believe it will never come. The soldier, it is said, always believes that the bullets have another man's name on them. I always knew that whenever I went surfing no shark would want me for a meal. Whenever I was involved in a car accident I was not surprised that each time I emerged unscathed. The possibility of my real death never impinged on my sense of security. But it came at last, carried by words uttered in a doctor's surgery. One day, when I was thirty, I went to consult a doctor whom I had not met before about some minor ailment. We talked, and then he said to me, 'I can tell by your voice there is something seriously wrong with your lungs.' All my life I had had a cough which I regarded as a nuisance and an embarrassment. Sometimes I felt ill and sorry for myself, but somehow this always seemed a bit like play-acting, pretending to be ill so as to miss a day at school. Suddenly it was not play-acting. This was serious and real, and no childish fancies could keep me safe. The surgeon's knife did not merely remove part of my lung; it forced me to turn away from childhood, to look death in the face, and being vulnerable in the immediacy of death, take charge of my life. As I recovered and time passed my awareness of my real death grew less acute. Then eight years later, under the total care of the National Health Service, I was sent to see a renowned specialist in diseases of the chest. He examined my cardiogram, the first I had ever had, and said, 'With your history I am surprised to see that your cardiogram is normal.' My colleagues at the hospital later assured me that it was the usual practice for this specialist to frighten his patients so that they henceforth obeyed him. Obedience was far from my mind. In the shadow of my death all I wanted to do was run and scream, affirming that I was alive.

Since then death has never gone away. Like Muhammad whose references to death in the Koran increase as he got older, I give death more and more thought, though not with fear. Time brings reconciliation. Like Stevie Smith,

> I have a friend
> At the end
> Of the world.

The first meeting with real death is a raw and brutal experience. If we survive we have then the task of trying to make sense of it, of fitting our knowledge of real death into our

199

metaphor of imagined death. The discovery that our image does not fit our reality can be very disturbing. Geoffrey Gorer, in his study of death, grief, and mourning in Britain, described how he, at the age of ten, assumed responsibility for his mother and his two young brothers after his father was lost in the sinking of the *Lusitania*. Although a number of friends and relatives died over the years, Geoffrey Gorer recalled that he was not deeply affected by these losses. Death became real for him later, when his beloved brother Peter died of cancer. Of this death he wrote, 'I was emotionally completely unprepared. I had (have) long believed that I was likely to die of cancer, since my father's parents and his brother and sister all died of cancer and a brother of my mother of leukaemia; I had accepted that I carried a diseased inheritance. But, quite illogically, I had never considered my brothers had the same inheritance as myself, perhaps because I resemble my father in features and colouring, whereas Peter and Richard took much more after my mother's family. It is probable, too, that in the same way as I had intellectually accepted responsibility for my mother and brothers after my father's death, I had unconsciously thought that I would take the burden of our cancerous heredity away from the others.'

Sometimes, rather than give up our image of death, we prefer to make the image into reality. When Lynette Phillips decided to kill herself, she sent a letter of explanation to various newspapers. In this she had written, 'I belong to an organization, Proutist Universal, that believes in establishing one human society, based on moralism and universalism (citizenship of the Universe) . . . At present democracy is the ruling body for a few capitalists and rich persons who are controlling all spheres of life – economic, social, political, educational, etc . . . Morality is dying. Law is mere verbosity for high fees and argument's sake . . . Anyone who speaks out against injustice is imprisoned or otherwise suppressed.' Lynette described her decision to kill herself as growing 'from a burning desire, an inner need to do something to help stop the criminality of our exploited lives on earth' and from her action she wished, 'May the light emanated enlighten other hearts.' The method by which she chose to die was burning, pouring petrol over herself and setting it alight.

We can only hope that as the flames took hold she did not live long enough to discover that words had played her false. A burning desire is very different from a burning body.

We can become a prisoner not just of our image of death but of the image of ideas that we associate with death – ideas like 'luck'. Mr G. gives an illustration of this.

It is not uncommon for a person to suffer a disproportionate amount of anxiety after an accident. When the accident is followed by a law suit, then the question arises as to the motivation for this manifestation of anxiety. It was for this reason that I was asked to assess Mr G. At work in a factory Mr G. had fallen on to a moving conveyor belt and was within inches of being crushed to death when the machinery was stopped. He had suffered little more than bruising and shock, but in the months following the accident he had become so anxious that he was unable to work or even to leave the caravan where he lived. He managed to obey his solicitor and come and see me at the psychiatric hospital. Afterwards I wrote the following report:

> Mr G. arrived early for his appointment. He was very nervous about yet another examination, and later in our conversation he said that he was frightened about coming to the hospital in case he was kept there. We talked for some time but, although he was more at ease with me, as soon as we started what he quickly identified as an intelligence test he became almost too nervous to do the test. On the W.A.I.S. Vocabulary I could repeat the questions to give him time to answer, and so he was able to make an average score. On the Block Design the test instructions are precise and limited and each item is timed. Mr G. recognised that the problems should be easily solved but he could not solve them and as he berated himself for his failure he grew increasingly anxious. His score on this test was well below average. This kind of anxiety made it impossible for him to carry out complex tasks at work and so he could be employed only at work well below his intellectual level which appears to be in the average range.

On the Rorschach Mr G. showed himself to be a person who wants everything about him to be neat and complete and to fit reasonably into its proper shape and position. Many of us are like that, but to survive in this chaotic, unreasonable world we have to be efficient in bringing order out of chaos and confident in our abilities. Mr G. is neither. He sets himself a high standard to achieve, but he lacks the ability and the originality to reach this standard. When he does manage to organize something in an adequate, mundane way he immediately fears that he has not done it well enough and that other people will do it better. He seeks constant reassurance that what he does is acceptable.

Further on the Rorschach, he showed that his ability to empathise with and relate to other adults is limited but that his awareness of his need for affection is quite great, so problems must arise within his relationships. He must demand affection without perceiving how to return affection in the way the other person wants it returned. He is very much aware of his needs and fears but he is unable to express them in any direct fashion. He is very much aware of what goes on around him but again he is very cautious and controlled in his reactions. In short, some men react to pressure from their needs and fears and to outside stress by being aggressive or by drinking, gambling or copulating to excess. Mr G. turns his painful needs and fears into bodily pain. Medical science has not yet elucidated how thought processes, many of which never come clearly into consciousness, transmute into physical pain, but such pain is felt as keenly as that caused by physical injury.

By turning fear and aggression into pain the problem of what to do with the fear and aggression may be solved and may even have the bonus of gaining affectionate sympathy, but the pain itself then raises anxiety and such anxiety is not relieved by assurances that the pain has no physical basis. Mr G. fears that the pain is a necessary precursor of death and it is death that he fears.

When Mr G. fell on to the conveyor belt he lay there

expecting to die. He said that he knew death was imminent and he thought of all the things that mattered to him, his life and his family. He was, he said, saved by luck. Now luck is something that means different things to different people. To some luck is a lady who may or may not grant her favours. To others, and Mr G. is one of these, luck is a commodity, a portion of which we are given at birth. As our life proceeds we use up our luck and when our luck runs out we die. Mr G. sees himself as having used up a lot of his luck in surviving a long war and a serious wound. He used up more of his luck in a car crash. In his accident at work his luck all ran out and he is left with so little that he expects not to survive the next dangerous situation into which he is thrown.

He lives in daily expectancy of death. A car journey is fraught with terrors whose presence he would not have recognized before his accident. His pains and stiffness suggest cancer or a crippling illness terminating in death. For some of us, death is merely a doorway to another life. But others cannot conceive of a life after death. For them death is final. This is all the life we have. Mr G. is one of these. He describes death as loss, 'loss of life, family, friends, country, everything'.

Mr G. joined the factory before the war and returned to it after the war. He has never wished to work anywhere else. He has never wished to live anywhere other than his home town. He was married and had a home and a family. Then came his accident and left him with a greatly heightened fear of death. Then came a series of disagreements with his wife which culminated in his leaving. A mere eight weeks later he was divorced. He lost his family and his home. This loss appeared to him as part of death and he wonders when the other parts of death will come. He looks at his caravan home and thinks that it is too insubstantial to survive. He looks at the woman he now lives with and wonders when she will leave him. She says she will stay but how can he be sure? He wonders when his firm will discard him and he knows that he would be unable to cope with a new job. He wonders if all these anxieties mean that he is going mad and he looks at the chronic patients from the hospital who work in his factory and he sees that they take tablets as he now takes tablets and he fears that he will be incarcerated in this psychiatric hospital. He fears being alone in the world, unable to work. He fears living and he fears dying.

In short, Mr G. is a man of average ability who, though somewhat over-controlled and somewhat restricted in his capacity to form adult relationships, was sufficiently stable to cope with ordinary life. Then he had an experience, the effect of which no person could master with ease. To master such an experience one would need a high degree of intelligent flexibility of mind and the kind of self-confidence which sees it as just and right that one has survived. Mr G. has neither of these, and so his accident has brought him an agony of mind which far exceeds the bodily pain of which he complains.

In contrast to Mr G., another Lincolnshire man of a different generation and different beliefs saw his own survival in a way that allowed him to go on with his life and not be overwhelmed by anxiety. Private Judson of the 1st/4th Battalion, Lincolnshire Regiment, took part in the Battle of Hohenzollen in Flanders in 1915. Of the 800 men in the battalion, 600 were killed. Private Judson survived though wounded and later, after an illness when he thought he would die, he wrote this poem.

> Why was I spared when my
> Comrades fell by the thousands
> Midst the shot and shell?
> I was no better than they,
> And yet, while they lie dead,
> I am here today.
> Was it luck?
> Some men will have it so
> But the hand that made
> Can keep, I know. A wife,
> A lover, a little child's plea

> *Maybe a mother across the sea,*
> *But someone had prayed*
> *To the great white throne*
> *And I knew it was God*
> *Who brought me safe home.*

When I talked with Mr Judson, who looked much younger than his eighty-four years, he told me how he had joined the Army in 1913 when he was seventeen and he showed me photographs of his platoon. 'All of us there,' he said, pointing to a row of fresh-faced lads, 'were in the football team. Everyone in the team was killed except me.' When he talked of his dead comrades tears came into his eyes; when he talked of the senseless destruction of the war and of the disillusionment of unemployment after the war there was anger in his voice. Yet he looked back to the days of his childhood and youth as infinitely superior to present times. Nowadays people do as they please, and joy and beauty has vanished from the world. What people need to know and accept is their place in the scheme of things. He showed me a card which he always carried in his wallet. This had been issued to commemorate the sinking of the *Lusitania* in 1915. The card was edged in black and contained a picture of the ship and a brief account of the dastardly act of the Germans which led to the loss of so many innocent lives. On the front of the card was the text on which Mr Judson had built his life. It was 'In God we trust'.

Faith in God and/or faith in the rightness of the side on which one was fighting sustains many a soldier, but when such faith is lost then death takes on a hideous reality and the survivor can feel great guilt at still being alive. Robert Jay Lifton in his study of the veterans of the war in Vietnam, drew a distinction between static and animating forms of guilt. 'Static forms of guilt,' he wrote, 'may include a great deal of numbing and resistance to feeling or, in contrast, may have a self-punitive, self-lacerating *mea culpa* quality. Animating guilt, on the other hand, always connects with an image beyond the guilt and moves towards change.' The images of struggle, confrontation, the conflict of good and evil, the individual against the crowd, the acquisition and demonstration of masculinity, all contained in the myths and stories of American history and epitomized in the figure of

John Wayne are images which foster animating guilt – acceptance of responsibility and resolve to put matters right, to make recompense, and re-establish continuity. Events in Vietnam denied the truth of the American myths, and for many American men in Vietnam John Wayne became the God that failed. Two other gods failed them as well. Lifton described how, 'the men had a special kind of anger best described as ironic rage towards two types of professional with whom they came into contact in Vietnam: chaplains and "shrinks". They talked about chaplains with great anger and resentment as having blessed the troops, their guns, and their killing: "Whatever we were doing – murder, atrocities – God was always on our side" . . . Should a soldier succeed in seeing a psychiatrist, he was likely to be "helped" to remain on duty, to carry on with the daily commission of war crimes. For many ordinary GIs, psychiatry served to erode whatever capacity they retained for moral revulsion and animating guilt.'

The static, numbing guilt that comes when one's images of the continuity of life and death can no longer be made to fit real events traps the person in a prison from which no new continuity can be established. Continuity is impossible since, in a sense, the person is already dead, like the veteran described by Lifton. He had 'crawled away from a terrible ambush with the corpse of his closest buddy, who had saved him from death not long before, on his back – after the rest of his squad and most of his company had been wiped out. He remembered "wishing for my death – I wanted to die". And he implied that there was a sense in which he did die: "I was the worst ghost they ever had out there".' He knew that he was a ghost since, like Mr G., 'I've used up all my luck.'

The coincidence of imagined death and real death does not always produce a state of confusion, anxiety, and numbing guilt. Rather, it can be an immensely liberating experience. Elizabeth Kubler-Ross, in her work with dying patients, and Raymond Moody, in his study of people who, close to death, have strange and wonderful experiences and live to tell the tale, have found that a close encounter with real death can enhance life, making the person who has such an experience both more vibrantly alive and more peacefully accepting of death. Both Kubler-Ross and

Moody believe that their findings confirm the survival of the person after bodily death. Whether this is so is debatable. Following an article in *The Observer* by John Davy on Elizabeth Kubler-Ross, Dr B. S. Weakley of Dundee University wrote to the paper to make the points that 'what is being presented is not evidence for "Life after Life" but evidence that the human brain is a magnificent and sensitive instrument, which under threat is capable of imaginative feats quite unsuspected during its normal operation . . . It is quite clear that people *have* had extraordinary mental experiences. But this sort of experience is by no means limited to people *in extremis*. Go to any hospital recovery room and ask the nurses about the experiences of patients coming out of anaesthetic after "routine" operations. These operations may be routine for the surgeon, but certainly not for the patient, and nothing brings one's life (past, present and future) into sharper focus than the threat of losing it on the operating table. Yet little attention appears to have been given to this, since these patients are not "back from the grave" but awakening after surgery. Is it the effect of anaesthetic on the brain which causes these phenomena or is it the dramatic high point of the surgical experience that produces them? We simply do not know. It is a rich field for investigation . . . If a person is unconscious (asleep, comatose, in a faint or in traumatic shock) it does not necessarily mean that he is insensate . . . The brain, particularly if stimulated to a heightened imaginative state by crisis, can interpret these signals and weave them into a tapestry of dream-reality. There is nothing magical about this. The afterlife, if any, will take care of itself. More pertinent is what happens during that span of existence that is securely ours.' Against this view can be placed the view, quoted by Moody of a woman psychiatrist who had a near-death experience and from that was convinced of the certainty of life after death. 'People who have had these experiences *know*,' she said. 'People who haven't should wait.'

Some people who have faced death in clear consciousness and lived to report on the experience have recounted how perception changes in that instance. The narrow focus of one's attention renders certain things marvellously clear, and time slows, elongates. I recall a very smooth and leisurely flight I once made from a car seat to a point on the road several yards distant, a flight which gave me ample time to observe a tram whose path I was crossing. Fortunately, we did not meet. I had had no warning that I was about to make this flight, and could only marvel at the experience afterwards. Arthur Koestler had ample opportunity to consider his imminent death. When he was arrested in a house in Malaga he expected to be shot immediately. Instead he was put in prison, in the condemned cell, from which he knew he could be taken and shot at any time. Later he wrote,

> I had found out that the human spirit is able to call upon certain aids of which, in normal circumstances, it has no knowledge, and the existence of which it only discovers in itself in abnormal circumstances. They act, according to the particular case, either as merciful narcotics or ecstatic stimulants. The technique which I developed under the pressure of the death-sentence consisted in the skilful exploitations of these aids. I knew, by the way, that at the decisive moment when I should have to face the wall, these mental devices would act automatically, without any conscious effort on my part. Thus I had actually no fear of the moment of execution; I only feared the fear that would precede that moment. But I relied on the feeling I had experienced on the staircase in Sir Peter's house, while waiting for Bolin's shot; that dream-like feeling of having one's consciousness split in two, so that with one half of it one observes oneself with a comparative coolness and aloofness, as though observing a stranger. The consciousness sees to it that its complete annihilation is never experienced. It does not divulge the secret of its existence and its decay. No one is allowed to look into the darkness with his eyes open; he is blindfolded before. This is why situations lived through are never so bad in reality as in imagination. Nature sees to it that trees do not grow beyond a certain height, not even trees of suffering.

Does our consciousness ever die? Whether it does or not, can we die our death in our own terms? Or is real death always something different from our imagined death? In that most beautiful television play *In Hiding* Don Taylor looked at these questions through the characters of Bernard and Mark. Mark is a lonely boy spending his summer holiday in the country. He discovers a house, once comfortable and lived in but now derelict and empty, and makes this a refuge from his rigid, uncomprehending aunt. He furnishes a room with objects from his aunt's attic, including a gramophone on which he plays a record of Schubert's song *Du Bist Die Ruh*. Bernard, a man in his sixties, joins him. Bernard does not at first explain why he is wandering around the countryside, apparently without a family and a home, but later he tells Mark that he is dying of cancer. Bernard had awoken and heard the song, and later said to Mark:

> I was quite convinced I was dead for a moment or so – truthfully I couldn't remember where I was, except that it must obviously be some kind of paradise, and that they *do* have Schubert there, as I always felt they ought to, if the place was to be worth going to at all . . . songs, I think, would be very suitable. Particularly that one . . . just the job for paradise. 'You are rest,' it says, 'and gentle peace. You are the feeling of longing and what satisfies it.' That's a pretty good definition of heaven, don't you think? A feeling of longing and what satisfies it. That's what it ought to be like. Yes. I would like it to be like that.

He explained why he had left his home and family.

> I don't want to die surrounded by concerned and weeping people, or drugged out of my senses. I have a *horror* of that, that seems to me worse than the thing itself. I'd much rather die alone, under the stars, in a private agony, how men died when they were animals and the world was empty. All my life I've done the right thing, the correct thing, and suddenly my life is almost over, and I don't seem to have lived like a man at all. And something seemed to drive me, something seemed to say, 'That's enough, be yourself now, what you really are, not what you've pretended to be or been told to be . . .' And if it is very bad – and it may not be – but if it is, I shall crawl

away into a field or a wood brake somewhere, and die in my own way, with my face looking up at the sky or the stars, not a white painted ceiling. Death is a part of my life, after all, it does belong to me, as much as my body does, and I want to experience it fully, for what it is, not turn my face away because it looks ugly at a distance. Who knows what it will be like when it comes? No one does. No one. And I want it to be mine, whatever it's like.

But Schubert's music rarely gives total completion and comfort. There is always joy, delight, and the sense of poignant mystery, of something beyond which does not frighten but intimates 'and yet – '. So it is with this song. Bernard says,

That song has been going through my head, ever since you woke me with it . . . how many centuries ago? I've probably been singing it here for hours. Singing and brooding, and brooding and singing. Because there isn't any peace, you see. There's never any peace, not even in the song. All that desire, and all that longing, it isn't really satisfied, it just stops for a time, and then begins again. Or is stopped. Cut off. Clean. Silence. And that isn't peace. That's nothing. To experience peace, you have to be able to feel it. And the dead feel nothing. They *are* cut off. All the feeling goes on, in someone else, not them. Just as the song begins again. Same song. Different singers . . . Listen to the house, Mark, listen to it breathing. Listen to all the lives that have been lived in these rooms, all those dead voices, whispering together. That's what our ancestors heard when they talked about the music of the spheres, not the whistling of the planets, marking out their empty circles in space, but the dusty voices of all the millions of the dead, a dissonant keening from all those centuries of silent throats. How many men and women have lived on this earth since the beginning, where have all their dead voices gone? I shall be one of them soon. One more candle for All Souls' night, one more flame guttering in the window. Behold, I show you a mystery. We are worthless material, whirling in a measureless emptiness, and death is no more than a change from one material state to another. But we are conscious of our changes, and when we change, what happens to that consciousness? Does that change too? Or does it remain, somehow suspended, like a song in the darkness? All that passion, and experience, and intensity, what happens to that? Does that die? My body is dying. I can feel it. But not my consciousness, not myself. That light is burning as bright as ever. Brighter, in fact, much brighter! Will it really go out? Complete darkness. I can't believe it.

7

Angels and Devils

Does our consciousness die with the death of our body? The idea that it does not seems to be most persistent, even with those of us who have no belief in an afterlife. Yet just how some form of consciousness or identity could go on existing is hard to determine. Bernard's 'dead voices, whispering together' sound very sad. Yet the image of perfect beings in a perfect heaven is not without its inconsistencies. I pondered upon this when my mother died and a friend, in offering her sympathy, spoke of my mother being in heaven. I immediately felt sorry for God, especially if he is male. Mother did not approve of men, and she did not approve of places other than her own home. Heaven, being a foreign place, is unlikely to meet her standards. Moreover, she will not be pleased to find herself there since it is not what she wished. Sometime before she died, Mother and I talked about what she expected death to be, and she said that she saw it as the end. She thought that the idea of heaven was illogical. 'How could there be all those millions and millions of people there?' she asked. Death as the end did not frighten her. 'I've had a good life,' she said.

Now Mother's reason for rejecting heaven fitted exactly the way she lived her life. She kept herself very much to herself, being close only to her immediate family and a few old friends. She avoided social gatherings, and large crowds frightened her, as did people of any nationality other than her own. Yet it was not fear alone which kept her aloof. It was also pride, and it was this pride which enabled her to battle through a life which was far from easy and which only in her last years she could regard as good. Her pride and fear in constant conflict, yet rooted in the same source of her childhood experiences, caused much pain both to her and to those around her. If she arrived in heaven as the person she knew herself to be, then no matter how perfect heaven was, she would suffer (and perhaps the angels would too!). A perfect environment does not produce happiness, since much of our misery we create within ourselves. If she was, through some process, 'perfected', then she would no longer be the person she had known herself to be. Her charm would disappear along with her temper.

The idea of an identity persisting is only tenable if we think of ourselves as being some kind of single unit, like a solid ball made of one material which travels through space and time but is not affected by them. However, this is not the way we experience ourselves. We know ourselves to be complex and conflictual, and we know that it is the interdependence of our inner and outer reality that allows us to create our identity. We perceive ourselves, we perceive others, and we perceive ourselves perceiving others and others perceiving us. Out of these perceptions we create a structure which we call 'I' and a structure which we call 'other people'. We may see some parts of 'I' as being the same as 'other people', and this becomes what psychologists call our 'model of the person'.

A group of psychologists came together recently in Cardiff, Wales, to discuss what they called 'Models of Man'. They had quite a few to discuss. The index of the book published about their deliberations lists twenty-four models – man as agent, ape, bio-social organism, capitalist, epistemic man, a generalized machine, logical man, machine-minder, magician, model, moral man, a natural phenomenon, a nervous system, an object, problem-solver, programmer, program-user, man the punter, rational man, man the rhetorician, rule-follower, rule-maker, and scientist. Added to that, Halla Beloff asked, 'Are models of man models of woman?', to which in answer she gave a simultaneous 'yes' and 'no'. However, models such as these are intellectual abstractions, more or less useful tools in the pursuit of knowledge. They are not the models by which we actually know and experience ourselves and others. Marie Jahoda pointed out that 'Like everyone who reflects on the human condition, psychologists carry in their minds an ontological model about the essence of being human; as scientists they add to this a conceptual model which incorporates the point of view from which they look at man systematically . . . an ontological model rests on metaphysical assumptions; a conceptual model is a tool

213

for thought . . . As a rule psychologists remain silent about their ontological and often about their conceptual models, while being explicit about their theories.' Marie Jahoda described at least part of her ontological model. 'My own metaphysical commitment on the ontological issue consists of a belief in the essential indivisibility of body and mind. I cannot conceive of psychological phenomena independent from or outside an organism, even though I realise – sometimes uneasily – that in their religious beliefs probably nine-tenths of mankind can, including some scientists.' Such a statement of ontological belief provoked no discussion thought worth recording and no other statements of ontological belief, though Professor Howarth did remark in his paper that 'All life is a struggle against the "final solution" implied by the second law of thermodynamics.' On the whole, British psychologists are more interested in conceptual tools than they are in immediate experience.

For it is our immediate experience of ourselves which is our ontological model of ourselves. Eric experiences himself as basically good with some parts in need of improvement, and so he says, 'There are very few really bad people. There are very few good people. We're all a bit of a mish-mash in the middle . . . There's nobody who is wholly good or wholly bad . . . The fact that we're born shows us that we're a mixture.' Siegfried experiences himself as bad and says, 'We're all born with very nasty instincts, aren't we?' and he believes that a child comes into the world 'a complete savage'.

The sense of goodness and badness comes in different images in different people. The writer Jacky Gillott, who killed herself in 1981, felt herself to be 'bound within the body of someone you fear, loathe and despise'. Her depression she called 'my great black owl; it roosts on my shoulders'. In 1976 she wrote in *Cosmopolitan*, 'Depression is suffered by people who see no reason to like themselves at all . . . If you find yourself loathsome, you expect the rest of the world to find you loathsome too . . . I'm convinced that many of the neat, unexpected suicides are committed by depressives who quite simply wish not to be a nuisance any longer . . . I always make sure I'm permanently in debt because I feel it would be rather disgraceful to go leaving other people to pay my bills.' By not paying bills one can confirm one's sense of badness while acquiring, at least from one's creditors, a sense of being needed. However, such a balance may be too precarious a basis for a long life.

Debt, as badness, need not be felt simply in money terms. Julie said, 'I feel as though I don't have a right to be here . . . I feel I've been running up a shopping bill for seven years and I've got to pay for it all before I can go on, instead of paying for it day by day or not paying it at all. I don't know who I'm in debt to, but I do feel in debt. I think this is the basic idea of having to suffer. You'll only gain if you suffer . . . I think I'm totally plastic. I just don't feel like a human being. I don't feel three dimensional. Like a sort of cardboard cut-out. If you look at it from the front it looks perfectly normal, but if you look around it, there's no form to it.'

Such fear and loathing of our sense of badness can seem incredible to those who live easily within themselves, and this, perhaps, explains why Elizabeth fared so badly when she entered a psychiatric clinic for treatment for insomnia. She told me, 'I like to be away from everybody and everything. I can't even cope with me. I don't think I'm good for people, so I prefer to exclude myself. I just have to be on my own, responsible for myself . . . I never let people see me as me in case they won't accept me. I just prefer not to be with people, not to be an influence on them . . . I always put on an act in front of people, and then I have to recoup on my own. I have to have the time in order to be me or I would go insane. This was the reason I would stay up at night, and however late other people stayed up, I had to stay up for at least an hour after everyone had gone, in order to be me, so I could come back into being me before I went to bed, and it took longer and longer to do that, so in the end I wasn't sleeping at all. When I went into hospital I thought, with a room of my own, I'll have time to catch up with being me and I can go out and face the world again. Instead of which I was thrown into the worst kind of situation for me, which is where I'm constantly on view, constantly on guard, constantly on duty, constantly on stage, I suppose. They would never let me go into my room even for five minutes to recoup, and this is why in the end, in desperation, I was breaking down, physically – I was developing all sorts of sores and I was completely tired, then I did break down mentally, so much so I even cried on the ward and that is just not me because whatever else I do, if I'm on duty out in the world, I try not to affect other people badly. They've got miseries of their own. There was one instance there which was totally beyond my control, and since I had no room to go to since they'd thrown me out of my room, I did break down and cry and I think I hated myself and them more for that than anything else, since I'd lost control and there was nowhere to run and hide, which is what I usually do. Do I think people don't like me? I think I'm too distant for people to notice. I'm not concerned with if they like me. I'm more concerned with what I do to them. I've got a positive genius for doing the wrong things. For some reason I don't know, I attract people to me in that they think they can come and confide in me or they can depend on me or rely on me. And I'm always terribly, terribly afraid that what I'm going to say or what I'm going to do is going to do them more harm than good.'

I asked Elizabeth what difference there was between the person she was and the person she presented herself as being. She replied, 'Complete opposites. I really don't like being with people. I'm a very private sort of person. Socially one has to mix with other people. In a sense being private is a protective measure because if I were really me, then that's what everyone has tried to change. Probably my whole life has resolved around people saying, "If only you were – " or "You've got to be more something or other", so I keep the private me in a sort of bubble and then put out the sort of behaviour that I feel they want . . . My sister and I are both interested in reincarnation. She said to me, "What's happening to us now is that we are having to pay off old debts that happened in a former life." I asked her what on earth we had done and she said, "Probably we were much too arrogant and we've been punished in this life and we've got to learn humility." I suppose I'm learning humility by being reduced to absolutely nothing, being nothing. As I am now I'm absolutely valueless and I feel all used up. There's no future and the past is useless. I don't mean that morbidly and in a self-pitying sense. I mean it totally unemotionally. If one viewed from abov the millions of people on earth, some are valuable, some are sort of half and half, and some, quite frankly, the world would be just as well without. I come into that category. There's no point. Whereas before I was working now I'm not. I've come to a standstill or retrogressing. I suppose I was just too arrogant in a former life. I can't be arrogant in this one. I haven't done anything. I haven't achieved anything at all. Either in some past life or in this present one, either we are trying to atone for what we did or we are doing it now and we're not aware of it but others are. They see it.'

Sometimes the sense of badness is felt to be a force of evil which the person experiences as being as real as toothache or an icy wind. My friend the Reverend Harry Weber described to me how 'Evil has many facets. I see evil as an influence that can take over or influence us. I think we're all having evil impinged on us in this world. I think there is holiness. In prayer and in spiritual life you are deliberately reaching out toward God. I do think there are evil influences and the world today is very much in the grip of evil. You know as well as I do that you can go to certain places which have evil associations where the atmosphere is terrible. You can go to other places which are spiritual and holy or good and full of love and friendship. I think there is an evil force and a holy force, but I think for the most part that evil forces do not take possession of a normal sort of person, though I do see some psychiatric patients as being influenced by evil. We are all buffeted by evil influences, but normally speaking we're perfectly safe. The holy influences are stronger than the evil influences. I don't think there is anything to be afraid of.' Harry spoke of combating the force of evil with prayers of healing, prayers of exorcism, and anointing with holy oil. He said, 'The priesthood has a charisma. I do believe that we can touch, we can bless, heal by spiritual means. In baptism we are all blessed with the Holy Spirit. But the gifts that God gives us can be destroyed or thrown away. You are a creature of free will. The gifts that God gives us we can always throw away at our own peril.'

Had Harry known Trevor he might have considered him to be a person in the grip of the force of evil. Trevor had successfully completed his university degree but after that could not keep a job. He would drift off into a state which he called

'Nowhere Land', a lonely, empty, and very private place. Once in Nowhere Land his perception of reality altered, and to the outside observer his behaviour could become extremely odd. At times his fear and distress were so great that one would think that Nowhere Land was a place that he would want to avoid, but I had a difficult task in trying to persuade him that it was worth keeping at least one foot in the land of ordinary, shared reality. For him Nowhere Land, which he could reach both with and without the aid of drugs or hallucinogenic mushrooms, was a land of promise and delight, and he was reluctant to give it up. But sometimes he would be unable to leave Nowhere Land and then he would discover that all other human beings suddenly appeared as dangerous, poised to attack him without warning. One day when we were talking about this Trevor said, 'I believe that we've all got this witchcraft, devil in us, all these hidden powers in our genetic code. When you take mushrooms it tends to bring them to the foreground and makes you aware of them. Normally you're not aware of them . . . It's like a closed loop system. Everything revolves around nothing. And it all revolves around nothing – nothing, nothing, zero. Everything, the whole of life around nothing. It's absolutely pointless, means nothing. This is the devil. He tortures us by making us aware of the fact that nothing is worth while, got no point to it. This potential to be the devil is within us. You can live a life of hell on earth – living the experience of the devil. Experiencing everything as futile. Being totally confused. End up in circular loops where everything revolves around nothing. Nowhere Land isn't necessarily where the devil is. Nowhere Land is a peaceful place to be. The devil is somewhere else. The devil lurks within us. He's there all the time and sometimes he comes forward and he can take over our consciousness. Nowhere Land is a place of rest away from the strains of reality.'

I asked, 'Last weekend, when you were in that psychotic state, were you in Nowhere Land?'

'I was partly in Nowhere Land to start off with and then I gave up and became the devil.'

Trevor dated the beginning of his difficulties from when he had first tried the mushrooms, but the more we talked the more it became clear that Nowhere Land had always been available.

He said, 'As a child I was positive all the time. I had direction, a purpose. There was no need to drift off into Nowhere Land – except I do have recollections of sitting round the table with the family and drifting off into Nowhere Land.'

'When you were a child, did you have any concept of the devil?'

'No. That was not until I had those mushrooms. I was frightened at discovering the devil, but at the same time I came to the realization of a God, a Godliness, and everything's perfection. I went through the two extremes. I could see life as being perfection or damnation. I couldn't see anything in between.'

'Where is the Godliness?'

'Inside us.'

'So you see the devil as being a person separate from us?'

'No, no. The devil is an integral part of us, of our minds. He's the way we think.'

'Is that one of the reasons – when you start to drift off into a psychotic state you get frightened of other people?'

'Yes. I get frightened altogether. The devil and all his works. There's no means of escape.'

'You can't escape your own devil and other people who look normal have the devil inside them?'

'Yes, but it might not be obvious at the time.'

'Is it the same with God? Do you see God as separate?'

'God's an integral part as well.'

'Do you see us as having a choice about God and the devil inside us?'

'No. It's all decided by conditioning, I think. In the extremes you can't control them. But there's a gradual path to the extremes – a gradual path of events that led you to that extreme, so that there's points on the scale between the two extremes. I think that circumstances lead us one way or the other. If we're in easy company we tend towards Godliness, whereas if there's a difficulty we tend towards the devil. If we're in the company of people with similar minds the two people come together to form Godliness. Whereas if you're with people you don't communicate with – that's steps toward the devil. Nowhere Land isn't Godliness – it's an escape, a retreat.'

'Is Nowhere Land always solitary?'

'Yes.'

'So no communication and so you drift toward the devil.'

'Yes.'

'What would happen if you moved right to the extreme of Godliness?'

'All the time? I don't think it's possible. If it was possible I think you'd do the same as Jesus – teach other people how to achieve the same position, the extremes of Godliness.'

'How far along the line of Godliness do you see yourself moving?'

'About three-quarters of the way.'

'And what would you be doing?'

'Most of my relationships would be kind and loving. People would communicate with me.'

'How far along the devil dimension could you see yourself moving?'

'I could see myself moving to the furthest extreme. I would hope that something would manage to get me out of it. But – death comes at the extreme of the devil, because the devil has taken over to such an extent you can't control it anymore. You feel like committing suicide.'

'If you did commit suicide, what would happen to you then?'

'That would end everything between the two alternatives.'

'Do you see any existence going on after death?'

'No. None whatsoever. Life will go on as usual on the planet. I'll be just the molecules and atoms I'm made up of – eventually they'll make something else.'

Harry Weber and Trevor illustrate how the sense of goodness and badness can be experienced as being located either inside or outside ourselves. Harry saw goodness and badness impinging on him; Trevor saw goodness and badness rising up inside him. This difference in their experience of themselves reflects the differences in experience of those people who could be labelled 'extravert' and those who could be labelled 'introvert'. The characteristics of the introvert and extravert can be described in many different ways, as Freud, Fenechel, Jung, Eysenck, and others have shown, but the difference I have found most useful in trying to understand the construct systems of other people is the difference in their awareness of and therefore their construing of internal and external reality. As experiencing human beings we are always aware of two realities, one inside us and one outside us. Practitioners of the Rorschach technique report that it is a rare person whose consistent mode of perception allows for an equal awareness of inner and outer reality. We each have a preference, perhaps determined by our genetic inheritance or perhaps learned. Whichever, to some greater or lesser extent, the extravert sees his external reality as having the greater reality; his internal world is less real and makes him feel embarrassed and reluctant to explore its infinite possibilities. The introvert sees his internal world as having the greater reality and importance and he is not afraid to explore it. But he lacks confidence in his external world and is often unaware of its dimensions and possibilities. Extraverts and introverts who cope have developed some proficiency in dealing with their lesser known worlds, but proficient or not, we always know on which of our worlds the existence of our identity depends. Extraverts feel that their identity depends upon the regard, the existence of other people, while introverts feel that their identity depends upon their ability to create and develop themselves. Knowing this about ourselves, we know what choices we have to make if we are to survive, and sometimes these choices lead us to ways of life that cause us much pain.

We reveal our preferred reality in what we say and do. In his *Unreliable Memoirs* Clive James declared, 'Sick of being a prisoner of my childhood, I want to put it all behind me. To do that, I have to remember what it was like. I hope I can dredge it all up again without sounding too pompous.' What he 'dredged up' was an amusing account of the things that happened to him, the sights that he had seen, the people that he had met – all events in his external reality. He did consider that 'books like this are written to satisfy the confessional urge' but he concluded that 'In my case I suspect there are a thousand crimes, which until now I have mainly been successful in not recollecting. Rilke used to say that no poet would mind going to gaol, since he would at least have time to explore the treasure house of his memory. In many respects Rilke was a prick.' By contrast, Wordsworth once remarked, 'In childhood . . . I was often unable to think of

221

external things as having existence, and I communed with all that I saw as something not apart from, but inherent in, my own immaterial nature. Many times while going to school have I grasped at a wall or tree to recall myself from this abyss of idealism to the reality. At that time I was afraid of such a process.'

The attraction of 'this abyss of idealism' can outweigh the fear that it inspires. Ella could abolish all troublesome others by seeing herself as the only real person in the universe, while Trevor could escape into the peace and certainty of Nowhere Land. For Tony, such solutions to life's difficulties were unthinkable. He said, 'I only exist in the warmth of somebody else. I come alive when somebody else says "You're alive".' What life was about was, for him, other people. Relationships were 'the most important thing'; art was 'an expression of relationship'. For Mollie the whole of life's meaning was contained in her relationships with others, whether they were real people or loving spirits. Christine enjoyed the world and the company of others so much that she saw reincarnation in terms of groups of friends returning, but Eric, though well aware of the world around him, saw life and re-birth in terms of personal responsibility and the honing and refining of oneself.

It is not easy to describe how we experience and thus construe our inner and outer reality and how such constructions thus determine our behaviour, since we may never have put such constructions into words, either to ourselves or to other people. Two of the people I have talked to about this were Julie and Peter.

Julie described her depression in the image of 'just me in a desert. Other people don't exist but I do.' Try as she may, she could not people that desert. One day I posed her that problem of being respected or liked. I asked her, 'Suppose you were faced with a situation where you could act only in one of two ways. If you acted one way people would like you, but you wouldn't respect yourself, and if you acted the other way people wouldn't like you but you would respect yourself. If you were faced with that, which would you choose, respecting yourself or other people liking you?'

Julie answered immediately, 'Respecting myself. That's one of

222

my standards. I realized that at university. One thing about depression, it does make you independent because you don't care about popularity. You just function without other people anyway, so it doesn't really matter about other people. I suppose you just live like an observer, observing people, the way they live, and just get a bit cynical. I'm very scornful of people who do things just to be popular. I analyse myself and other people constantly, and 'honesty and integrity' is the byword. All the time I'm scorning myself because of that attitude – it's totally ridiculous. I can't live up to my standards, so nobody else could really, could they?'

'Why is it important to be honest?' I asked.

'Well, my aim is to be able to communicate to the outside world what I feel on the inside, not just about myself, I mean generally, and I think it is important to be as honest as possible. That way you get a clearer picture of things that are going on around you, and I think it's important to be clear. It's better than living in a fuzz. What I really mean is that you can keep channels of communication better if you're being honest with yourself and other people are being honest with themselves. Actually, that sort of honesty you arrive at only once in a blue moon. The rest of the time I'm just miserable because I don't find it. I suppose I live in a fuzz now. This is a fuzz. I can't communicate anything at all. I feel so impatient. I've got such a struggle to establish some kind of clarity. There's something propelling me on all the time. I've got to struggle to get out of this . . . I think that when you die your body decomposes but maybe your spirit remains behind. Maybe spirits return in other forms through the years. But I do believe you have to concentrate on the here and now. I've no beliefs in the hereafter at all. I don't believe in heaven or hell or anything like that. I feel really angry that I've wasted seven years being unhappy. I feel I should be happy all my life – which is just another tremendously high standard which is impossible to achieve . . . I do have the sort of feeling that there is reincarnation. I don't see how your spirit can be totally snuffed out. I have this feeling that we kind of inhabit our bodies and it's up to us to make our body work.'

'And are you failing at your task because you haven't been making your body work?'

'Yes. This is what I mean by clarity. I don't mean that I want everything cut and dried. I want to be able to express myself. That's the biggest task, the most important. You've got to struggle to express what is within you to express. I feel that if you fail you've wasted your life.' (Julie said this without knowing that in the ancient secret Gnostic gospels Jesus is reported as saying, 'If you bring forth what is within you, what you bring forth will save you. If you do not bring forth what is within you, what you do not bring forth will destroy you.')

When Peter came to see me he told me that what he found hardest to bear was his fear and depression. What his family found hardest to bear was his anger. We all know that anger is an important component of depression, so Peter and I spent a great deal of time discussing anger and exploring what were the values and implications he put on anger. For him anger was something bad, completely unacceptable. He feared his anger, and, in doing so, made it impossible for himself to come to terms with his anger, to accept it and so control it. In different contexts I would describe to him how I construe anger. To me it is a human response to frustration. It is not essentially evil, but is a facet of our vitality and creativity. Our task in dealing with our anger is to inspect critically the sources of our frustration and to develop ways of expressing our anger which are socially acceptable and creative. To this he would say, 'Intellectually I know what you mean. But in my heart I can't believe it.'

One day when we were discussing his family, he spoke of his attachment to his Celtic background and said, 'One does feel that because one has grown up in this sort of format, that it is valuable, and that one's sense of self, one's own identity, will disappear if one removes the casing, the setting in which one lives.'

This doubt about the existence of his identity was something that bothered Peter a great deal. Here he went on to say, 'One time I had a clear identity which depended on my past, my relationships, my physical being within certain perceptible reference points. Underlying this was the fact that one had a fairly good knowledge that one only existed in oneself in one way. I don't know whether I told you about this, but there was a time when I was staying with a great dear friend of mine, and when I left I went to the end of a long drive to catch a bus, and there was nowhere I had to go, nobody was expecting me anywhere. Therefore, if I didn't turn up anywhere, nobody would notice. I had just left some friends, I was estranged from my parents, and the marriage I had no longer existed, and I came to a sort of T-junction, a physical T-junction of a driveway and a road, but also in a sense a sort of, not an emotional T-junction, a life T-junction, and it didn't matter which way I went. Physically it wasn't important, it was neither here nor there, but from the point of view of how I felt, I felt sort of isolated and non-me. I felt as though I didn't exist, because my existence depended upon other people's recognition of me and my perception of me.'

'What you're describing,' I said, 'is that you saw yourself in other people's eyes, like other people were mirrors of you and if there weren't any mirrors there – '

'Yes,' he said, 'I suppose you could put it like that. It's not how I saw it. I saw it, and I'm not deliberately playing with words, but I'm trying to say how I saw it at the time, was that my reference points of existence were other people – that I reacted to them and they reacted to me. In my vocabulary this would not be a mirror thing, though one could argue that it is. I saw it as a fact that I functioned in conjunction with other people and I had nobody to function with. Then I had great doubts about my own existence and I think also a great sense of loneliness because if one had nowhere to go where one was expected – I mean there were lots of places I could go where people would say 'How nice to see you, Pete', and this would have been fine, but this wasn't the point. The problem was that I had nowhere to slot into something that existed, so I felt isolated and I felt lonely and I felt, thought, I didn't feel that I didn't exist, but I felt that I didn't exist. I said that deliberately in that way because it was a double sounding thing. I knew physically that I had my feet on the ground and the sun was shining and there were leaves on the trees – '

'And you were there to think "I don't exist"?' I asked.

'Absolutely, yes,' Peter said, 'but the sort of identity thing had disappeared. It was most extraordinary. I think I've felt that to a greater or lesser extent at various times in my life, but that was particularly clear and harsh, in the hard sense of being very

225

pristine and sharp-edged, and that was the most extreme sense I've had of it. I felt there was no setting. I could have fallen under a bus or changed my name and gone to South America and nobody would have noticed and this was very odd and very frightening. Very depressing.'

Peter was a man of strong opinions, and when events challenged these opinions he would be most angry and intransigent. In this discussion he explained why.

'I can identify the anger. I can say "Yes, I'm angry about this", and the reason I am angry about it is so and so – I can and I will on occasions say to myself "Well, it's not something to be angry about", and it may make me angry, but it's an unrealistic reaction on my part because it isn't important enough. I tell myself that I can translate virtually any situation into this sort of equation and whatever it is, life is short, it's only me getting angry over something I feel and it doesn't justify anger. And then I get frightened because I think, okay, if that's the way it is, then I'm in danger on a long-term basis, and if I spread it over the whole of my outlook, my attitudes, my behaviour, maybe I shall stop feeling. I don't want to stop feeling. I want to feel pleased about things and cross about things because I feel that, without feeling, motivation goes and I don't think I'll become a vegetable, but I'd become so bland that I'm no longer a person, and I know that's not a good argument but it's again where I come to war with myself about feelings. I would like to be serene and wise and able to take everything in my stride and that would be a lovely sort of ego thing, I tell myself, I think with my heart. But I don't feel that with my gut. My gut says that I've got to care because if I don't care about this or I don't care about that, then I cease being *me*. I feel that things matter and, God, one can extend this argument indefinitely. One could say, if you like, we should stop immigration on the purely practical grounds that this is a small island and there are too many people here, and the more people we get here, the harder life is going to become, the less there's going to be for me and my family, and so I should feel strongly about this because if I don't feel strongly about it, then we're going to end up in a pretty poor state, and we're going to end up like the middle of India where there isn't enough food – I know I'm using a crude extension of the argument. Now if I get all bland and accepting of this particular situation, the results could be such and such and then I'm going to feel that I haven't looked after my responsibilities and cared about the people near and dear to me – that my acceptance of the situation, if I don't feel strongly that one needs to contain problems and deal with them, then I become the instrument for inflicting unhappiness or pain or deprivation on people I should be protecting, be it my family, be it my community, be it my country.'

'What you're saying,' I said, 'as a principle of living, is that there is always the danger that if you inquire into the causes of your emotions that inquiry may come up with answers which take your emotions away from you and make you into a bland person and this is the kind of person you don't want to be. Having that attitude to inquiry into emotion, this means that in the past you've not done this very often. You've not developed the habit of self-inspection, and so when later in life it's suggested to you that you ought to have a look at these things, you come up against two problems – the attitude that it's not a safe thing to do, to introspect, and also you haven't got the habits of it. Self-inspection is a mode of thought that one learns, and if you haven't learnt it, you're not very good at it.'

'Yes,' said Peter, 'sort of. I don't entirely agree with you. I think in some ways I've inspected myself too closely. The fear is that if I inspect and as a result of that inspection I see that there is another line I could take there are changes I can make which will defuse my reaction to certain things, the stumbling block comes when I look at the consequences of that defusing.'

'When,' I answered, 'you're talking about how important emotions, feelings are, you don't want to wipe them out, because if you make yourself into a bland person you won't be so aware of other people. You won't interact with them. Now when we were talking about your sense of identity and I said to you that you used other people as a mirror, you rejected that image and you said no, it's interaction. This ties back to now, when you talk about the importance of your emotions because it's through them that you interact with other people, and if you become a bland person, then you wouldn't have these interactions with other people and you would lose your sense of identity.'

Peter said, 'I would accept that as a fair evaluation. If I became passive and didn't have an active part in life, then I would see consequences which I would see as very dangerous, very threatening.' Thus he could not afford to give up his anger.

Marriages are often made between an extravert and an introvert, each seeing in the other a delightful novelty, a means of supplying a lack one feels within oneself. The introvert enjoys the spouse's gaiety and loquacity and effects an easier entry into society. The extravert enjoys the peace and stillness and the loving audience of the introvert, and supports an inner void with another's inner solidity. But such mutual support is sometimes confounded by mutual incomprehension. The introvert may come to distrust the extravert's dramatic presentation, such that he sees the extravert as being incapable of genuine feeling. The extravert may, on the other hand, read the reserve of the introvert as evidence of a lack of feeling. As Beryl said, 'My husband, he's so quiet, so gentle, but he never seems to feel – if only he'd cried when our son went. He used to get up in the night to our boy – if only he'd say how he felt about it. He gets on my wick. Whenever I ask something, it's always whatever I want, whatever I decide. It isn't half wearing. Then I mustn't complain. A lot of women have their husbands knock them about. He's a man withdrawn, he never complains, not really. I only wish he'd blow his top like I do sometimes.'

Thus Beryl saw her husband's quietness and compliance as both supportive and frustrating. Strive as we may for perfection, it seems that everything in this world is a mixed blessing – or, rather, we construe it as such, since our constructs always have good and bad implications. Suffering is painful, but it builds character; love draws us closer but depletes our individuality; war improves medical techniques; charity breeds indolence. Not only do constructs have good and bad implications, but the good and bad are inextricably linked, the two sides of one coin, as Rilke knew. He was advised to seek psychoanalysis to achieve peace of mind, but he refused since, as he said, 'If my devils were driven out my angels would receive a slight, a very slight (shall we say) shock, and, you see, I cannot let it come to that pass at any price.' We all have our angels and devils, our deadly virtues and our vital vices. In the pursuit of truth we may injure

228

others, while through laziness and self-indulgence we may forgive others as we forgive ourselves. Like Camus we can discover how 'After prolonged research on myself, I discovered the fundamental duplicity of the human being. Then I realized that modesty helped me to shine, humility to conquer, and virtue to oppress.' The barbarians are within us, and, as Cavafy said, they are a kind of solution. Kitty, whose violent rages terrified herself and her family, told me, 'It gives me a tremendous thrill being angry and I say and do awful things.' James Kennaway wrote in *The Cost of Living Like This*, 'Jealousy is wild and filthy, we know; is demanding, obsessive leading always to thoughts of violence; but Lord, it is a living emotion. We are never more totally alive than when the loved one is lying in someone else's arms.'

Julie clung to her anger since 'It's exhausting being angry, but if you subtract the anger there's nothing there.' Similarly she hung on to her depression. One day she described to me how she had never learned to swim because she would not relinquish the kick-board. She did not believe her teacher when she said that Julie could stay afloat without it. 'I also feel,' she said, 'that my depression is something I've grown out of long ago which I cling to for support.' Julie's depression was even more than a kick-board that kept her afloat. It was a vocation. 'In a way I see life as a big problem which we have to solve. At some stage in your life most people seem to have some terrible problem they've got to solve. Or if you don't, you tend to lead a two-dimensional life.' Thus Julie's depression was something she could put aside only when she felt that she had completed the task of solving the problem of her life, becoming a developed person, capable of formulating and communicating her message with utmost clarity.

Tony stressed how important it was for him to feel the extremes of emotion. 'I want to be right up there or right down there,' he said. 'I don't want to be right down there, but I know if you go up there, you've got to be down there some of the time. In this life you do not experience one thing unless you experience the opposite.' While Tony often despaired, he would have agreed with Tolstoy that 'In order to live decently one must exert oneself, become involved, struggle and fight, make mistakes, begin and give up, start again and give up, and constantly fight and use up one's resources. Peace and quiet are nothing more than the meanness of the soul.'

In ordinary life we tend to present our angels to the world and hide our devils. The well-organized, hard-working, reliable business man is admired by his colleagues and provides well for his family, but in the privacy of his home is a rigid, obsessional, implacable tyrant. The woman who is known and loved for her kindness, generosity, and uncomplaining self-sacrifice promotes through her altruism her family's guilts, and thus she controls the people she loves. When, however, we decide that we must complain about our situation, then we present our devils and hide our angels.

This is always a trap for the unwary therapist and explains why many attempts at therapy fail. There is the person who comes to us complaining of loneliness, an elderly woman whose family has grown up and left her, or a quiet young man who has never acquired the knack of making friends. They talk to us about how unhappy their loneliness makes them and we explore what possibilities there are in their environments to make friends. We discover that the elderly woman has neighbours, a church, a Women's Institute, whilst the young man has colleagues, sports and social clubs. When we inquire why they do not take advantage of these opportunities for contact with others, they present us with a set of reasons which rule out every possibility. If, then, we leave this subject of discussion, since it can rapidly degenerate into the 'Yes-but' game that Berne described, and start to talk about the person's construct system, how he sees himself and his world, we then hear our lonely client describing the pride which he or she takes in being independent or how his experience of life has taught him never to trust people. They say things like, 'My mother was a wonderful woman. She kept her house spotlessly clean and she looked after us children. She didn't waste her time talking to neighbours', or 'My father died when I was seven and my mother had to send me to boarding school while she went to work. I hated it and she was always promising to bring me home but she never did. My uncle was going to give me a job in his firm but then he changed his mind. People never keep their promises.' And so we discover that though loneliness may be painful, it is still preferable to not living up to your adored and feared mother's expectations or to putting yourself in a situation where you are sure you will receive yet another rebuff and disappointment. One can always comfort oneself by defining one's suffering as virtuous. Strindberg described how, as a boy, he discovered he could do this:

> One Sunday they were in the parsonage, where there were young girls. He liked them, but he feared them. All the children went out to pluck strawberries. Someone suggested they should pluck the berries without eating them, in order to eat them at home with sugar. John plucked diligently and kept the agreement; he did not eat one, but honestly delivered up his share, though he saw others cheating. On their return home the berries were divided up by the pastor's daughter, and the children pressed round her in order that each might get a full spoonful. John kept as far away as possible; he was forgotten and berryless. He had been passed over! Full of the bitter consciousness of this, he went into the garden and concealed himself in an arbour. He did not weep, however, but was conscious of something hard and cold rising in him, like a skeleton of steel. After he had passed the whole company under critical review, he found that he was the most honest, because he had not eaten a single strawberry outside; and then came the false inference – he had been passed over because he was better than all the rest. The result was that he regarded himself as such, and felt a deep satisfaction at being overlooked.

Therapists are familiar with the woman who comes to us complaining that her frigidity is wrecking her marriage. Before we rush into some practical sex therapy we wisely pause and take time to discuss other matters, and then we hear her say things like, 'I think most women don't like sex', and, in speaking of a female acquaintance says, 'I don't think people like her. She's one of those very sexy women.' We know then that any practical sex therapy will be doomed to failure. If we teach her to be a sexy woman, even if only with her husband, then she will become, in her world, an unusual woman who is not liked by others. Such a change would be unendurable.

People who get depressed often describe themselves as being sensitive and see this as an essential characteristic which defines their identity. When we explore the implications of this construct we find that it has the unpleasant implication that the client, being sensitive, suffers constant hurt, but it also has the pleasant implication that by being sensitive the client sees himself as being concerned about other people, as being a caring person. Uncaring people are insensitive. So, if I try to teach this client to be less vulnerable to hurt, it will appear to him that I am trying to teach him to be less loving. A more subtle form of the implications of being a sensitive person is often present in the client who has artistic interests. Through being sensitive he suffers the hurts which lead him to draw into a depression, but he also sees his sensitivity as being evidence of his creativity, the source of his being and his reason for existence. This way of construing oneself can be seen in the writings of Virginia Woolf and Sylvia Plath. Both thought that their creativity was worth dying for. Edvard Munch, whose greatest paintings reflect the agony and fear that he experienced, wrote in his journal, 'My whole life has been spent walking by the side of a bottomless chasm, jumping from stone to stone. Sometimes I try to leave my narrow path and join the swirling mainstream of life, but I always find myself drawn back towards the chasm's edge, and there I shall walk until the day I fall into the abyss. For as long as I can remember I have suffered a deep feeling of anxiety which I have tried to express in my art. Without anxiety and illness I should have been like a ship without a rudder.'

Thus the coexistence of our angels and devils can be not only our reason for living but also our tragic flaw, the factor that can bring us low and destroy us. The reason that we can be destroyed by our tragic flaw is because it is not some random error, a chance weakness, but it is an integral part of ourselves, part of the structure by which we organize our world. Coming to know oneself is the process of coming to know what in one's structure is both painful and essential, and coping with life is the process of creating and maintaining a balance between pain and necessity. In our relationships with one another we have to find a balance between our need to be an individual and our need to be a member of a group. We each evaluate these needs differently and if we are both wise and lucky we can find a balance that suits. When we reach a stage in life where we have to be responsible for others we have to find a balance between having the power to impose our ideas on others and having the cooperative security of being an equal member of a group. Leaders are not always loved. We each evaluate our need for power and our need for love in different ways. Richard wants to run his farm his way; he sees being unkind as the greatest sin. He recognizes the conflict, and sees that if he opts for power instead of kindness, or kindness instead of power, he will be lost. Instead he works at maintaining a balance between power and love, and enjoys both. Siegfried was not so lucky and wise. Love for him was dangerous, and so he opted for leadership. He was in control – and lonely. Of course, such a choice was inevitable, since he had already decided that the only way he could live with himself was to dislike himself. Unfortunately for those people who maintain their sense of virtue by disliking themselves, we cannot love others unless we love ourselves, and it is unlikely that others will love us unless we love them. Sometimes we can be persuaded to love ourselves by the love that others give us, but if we are really determined not to love ourselves we can deflect another person's love with the argument that Julie used: 'If I get feedback from somebody that they don't think I'm unlovable and horrible, I just think they must be stupid, because I am.'

This statement by Julie illustrates the kind of tight, closed cirque which allows no exit, no modification. In therapy I try to discover and trace the boundaries of such a cirque. Of course, the cirque, our individual world, has many dimensions, and to reproduce even part of it in a two-dimensional diagram is a gross oversimplification, but sometimes it is a useful exercise, at least in giving me the impression that I have some purchase on the confusion that confronts me. The map that we finally put together always seems to me to be like a Zen koan, and the appropriate response to it is laughter, but clients who are devoted to their cirque will do little more than give a wry smile.

Helen, whom I have known for quite a while came to see me to tell me that she had started drinking heavily and that she felt very suicidal. She had been getting along fine for several years but the loss of her job had left her trapped in a household consisting of three argumentative daughters and a quiet, conventional husband. Time away from the family seemed to be the appropriate immediate remedy, and so she came into hospital, on to the most entertaining of our hospital's wards. She improved quite rapidly and soon had to venture home for a few hours one evening. The visit was a disaster. When I asked her what had happened she said, 'Nothing, really. I said I wanted to wash my hair when I got back to hospital. Fred went upstairs to the bathroom and came down with a bottle of shampoo. It was about a third full. He said for me to take it and he'd get some more tomorrow. Then Carol said she wanted to wash her hair. There was enough in the bottle for two washes, so I said for her to use some and I'd take the rest with me. Then Kay said she wanted to wash her hair, and then the youngest said she wanted to wash hers. So then they started squabbling and it ended with the bottle being thrown on the floor and two of them rushing out of the house. I just burst into tears and Fred brought me back to hospital.' Helen would have left the matter there, but I was interested in why she let her daughters treat her with such disregard. She said she had no control over them. 'Fred has much more control over them than me,' she explained, and then, as an afterthought she said, 'I hear what they say about him behind his back. I wouldn't want them to say those things about me.' When we discussed her drinking she told me how she needs to drink to get through all the housework, but once she started to drink she needed another. Her daughters were young women, and so I wanted to know why she did not insist that they do their fair share of the housework. 'I don't like to ask them,' she said, 'If I do they all get offended and they won't speak to me for days. I'm scared that if I try to make them help me they'll leave home, and then I'll feel so lonely and guilty.' Drinking and being depressed made her feel guilty too, but in the opposition of power and love, Helen chose not to risk love, and so built her cirque and imprisoned herself.

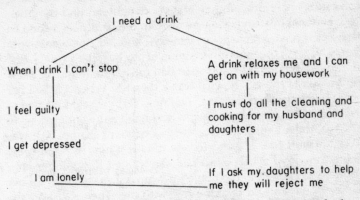

Helen's Cirque

I need a drink

When I drink I can't stop

I feel guilty

I get depressed

I am lonely

A drink relaxes me and I can get on with my housework

I must do all the cleaning and cooking for my husband and daughters

If I ask my daughters to help me they will reject me

Of course, Helen's cirque is far more complicated than this diagram shows. Helen derived some pleasure from seeing her daughters' disagreeable behaviour upset her husband whose quietness and passivity angered her in ways she did not dare express. At another level, her fear that her daughters would leave home was not merely the regret and fear that her children, once adults, no longer needed their mother. Even when the children were small Helen would consider it a real possibility that they would reject her and choose to leave her. Something that we fear very much is often something that we also desire. A fear that a loved one may leave us often contains the wish that he would and 'I shall be single again'. The bliss of freedom complements the fear of loneliness. No mother loves her children all the time. The guilt of the mother about turning her adult children from the door may cloak the guilt of the mother who sometimes wished her children dead.

Sometimes the foundation of the cirque lies in the belief that suffering is virtuous. Some of us are prepared to endure a great deal of pain in order to think well of ourselves. Tony believed in the morality of speaking out against hypocrisy and cant, but intolerance, which he regarded as a virtue, locked him in a cirque of depression.

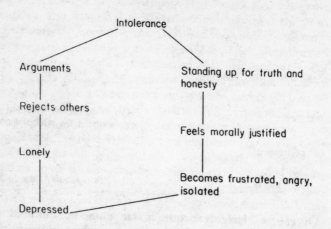

Tony's Cirque

Intolerance

Arguments — Standing up for truth and honesty

Rejects others — Feels morally justified

Lonely — Becomes frustrated, angry, isolated

Depressed

His ferocious anger left Peter feeling guilty and depressed, but by being angry he not only confirmed his identity but he endeavoured to meet his responsibilities to those dependent on him, a task imposed on him by the traditions of a family of which he wished to be a worthy member.

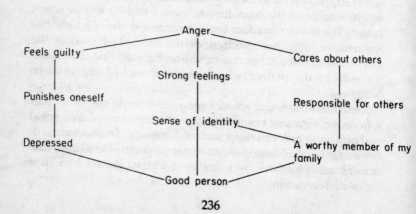

Peter's Cirque

Anger

Feels guilty — Strong feelings — Cares about others

Punishes oneself — Responsible for others

Depressed — Sense of identity — A worthy member of my family

Good person

One of the reasons that Helen gave for not wishing to anger her daughters was her firm belief that we should never forgive anyone who angers us. Forgiveness is not universally regarded as virtue. John came to see me because he was very anxious and often got depressed. He was a gentle man, 'timid' he called himself, and he apologized for not actually being depressed when he met me. He feared that I might think he was an imposter and was wasting my time. 'I'm not always depressed,' he said, 'just sometimes, but it can last for days, weeks even, and it's horrible.' We talked about what might make him depressed and he said it was anger. 'Something happens that makes me angry and I get into a terrible rage and I'm disgusted with myself.' He would try to rid himself of his anger by running several miles, but too often the black rage and the even blacker guilt would remain. I asked him what kind of things made him angry. To work this out he recalled the last time he had been angry. It was an incident at the school where he taught. Another teacher had acted on a matter without consulting John first. 'It was just thoughtlessness on his part,' John said, 'and that's what I can't stand – people being thoughtless.'

'Why is thoughtlessness so bad?' I asked.

'Because it's hurtful – other people get hurt. I don't like that.' By 'I don't like that' John meant 'I can't forgive that'.

We went on talking and John told me about his childhood. He had grown up in Leeds where his father, a silent man, had worked long hours and left the running of the household to his wife. At primary school John was discovered to be bright, and his parents were immensely proud when he gained a place in a grammar school. Until he entered grammar school John had lived a life that centred on his home, his parents, and his grandfather, an old soldier who since 1930 had 'just sat'. Home was a cosy haven where John was loved and admired because he was good, kind, and industrious. The only glimpse John had of the world outside was when he was eight and his father took him on a trip to London to visit a relative, a successful business man. John came back from London vaguely dissatisfied with his home. He realized that there were people in the world better off than he, and he also realized that the world was not as good and kind and reasonable as his parents would have him believe.

'When I went to grammar school,' John said, 'I lost my innocence. My parents were innocent. They still are. That's why I can't talk to them.'

At grammar school he ceased to be ambitious and he ceased to work. He became part of a gang of lads who were always into mischief. John could pass his exams without effort, but he slipped out of the classes preparing for university entrance and took the easy option of studying art. He kept his transgressions hidden from his parents until he was sixteen. The headmaster had asked to see John's parents and told them that John was close to being expelled. At home John's father hit him, and nothing more was said; John managed to stay on at school.

John and his friends committed no major crimes – no drugs or stealing. All they did were acts of rule-breaking which the rigid, old-fashioned grammar schools drive lively boys and girls to do in protest against the pompous stupidities of the teachers. That, at least, was my interpretation. Not John's. He still writhes in shame and guilt at the memory of his schoolboy actions. To him they were quite unforgivable.

He told me of something he had done when he was thirteen – something he had never told anyone else. He and his friends had been playing around one day, and coming to a wall they decided to lob stones over it. This they did, and were rewarded by the sound of breaking glass. They persisted in throwing stones until there were no more sounds, and then they all went home. Later that night a policeman called at John's house to inquire whether John knew anything of the destruction of an old man's greenhouse. 'Poor old chap,' said the policeman, 'he's eighty and his greenhouse is his whole life.' 'My son wouldn't do anything like that,' said John's mother, sending the policeman away.

This act lay on John's conscience, an unforgivable sin, evidence of his wickedness, his expulsion from Eden. There was evil in the world, and the evil was in him. He could not dismiss the thought of his evil or trivialize it. He must condemn it as his parents had condemned it – without forgiveness. That way he could continue to see himself as good.

The need to think well of ourselves, to keep a close alignment between our perception of ourselves and our perception of what

238

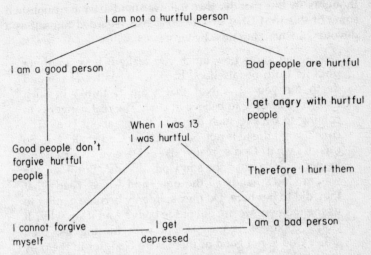

we would wish ourselves to be, is part of what William James defined as religious belief, 'the belief that there is an unseen order, and that our supreme good lies in harmoniously adjusting thereto'. Irrespective of how we define the 'unseen order' in which we believe and how we perceive ourselves, the problem is in finding an harmonious adjustment to that order. Not only do our virtues have accompanying vices which cause us pain, but the maintenance of virtue itself may be the cause of our suffering. Moreover, there is no religious belief which offers unalloyed comfort and security. If we believe in an omnipotent and benevolent God, how do we explain suffering? If we believe in a malevolent God, or the devil and the forces of evil, how are we to protect ourselves? If we believe that all the events in the universe are part of a causal pattern, how can we act as free agents, or if we see the universe as random chaos or increasing entropy, how can we feel secure? The implications of our religious beliefs, like the implications of our other constructs, are a mixture of good and bad.

When life goes along well, when we are having no difficulty in adjusting ourselves harmoniously to our unseen order, then we are often unaware of the bad implications of our beliefs. When C. S. Lewis's wife died of cancer he kept a journal of his thoughts in the months that followed and later he published some of this in *A Grief Observed*. He had regarded himself as a devout Christian, but now he wrote:

> 'You never know how much you really believe anything until its truth or falsehood becomes a matter of life and death for you . . . Not that I am (I think) in such danger of ceasing to believe in God. The real danger is in coming to believe such dreadful things about Him. The conclusion I dread is not 'So there's no God at all', but 'So this is what God's really like'. Deceive yourself no longer . . . 'Because she's in God's hands'. But if so, she was in God's hands all the time, and I have seen what they did to her here. Do they suddenly become gentler to us the moment we are out of the body? And if so, why? If God's goodness is inconsistent with hurting us, then either God is not good or there is no God, for in the only life we know He hurts us beyond our worst fears and beyond all we can imagine. If it is consistent with hurting us, then He may hurt us after death as unendurably as before it.

Eventually Lewis was reconciled to his wife's death and to God. He could write, 'The best is perhaps what we understand least.' No such reconciliation was possible for Jessica who had been found guilty of aiding and abetting the murder of her young sister. Jessica was a beautiful, gentle, simple young woman whose parents had died and left her and her older brother Luke to care for two much younger children, Angela and Mark. One night Luke took Jessica, Angela, and Mark to an upstairs room in their house and there killed Angela.

Jessica told me how she saw the world as a beautiful place but underneath it was 'all corruption and sex and violence. Like the city of Corinthians. It will always be there, through people being greedy and grasping . . . God can see it, I think. He's just letting them do it, you know. I don't know why. I'm not a religious person, really. I was on that day. We turned to God, you know.'

'Do you feel He answered?' I asked.

'I don't know whether He did or He didn't, but I know it rained on Saturday – it poured. And then we hadn't got to eat for forty days and forty nights and He was tempting us with food and we just drank water and milk for the first few days. And then I kind of came to my senses at the police station and my aunt said, "You must eat." But it's like going through hell and coming back . . . I thought we was chosen to do what we did on that day.'

'Who do you feel chose you?'

'God.'

'Do you feel that you are still chosen by Him?'

'Sometimes I do and then sometimes – I don't know. Because we love one another. There's so much love. As my brother wrote today in his letter . . . I'd love to have a good talk to him. Your thoughts and your mind's like a cobweb, it's never ending. Never ending . . . It makes me wonder why he killed Angela. Whether he loved us or hated us or what. He saw the devil coming out of her mouth. But he didn't say that to me, he just came up and did it. We thought we were going to a new land. We was going to build a boat. I think we was chosen to show people there is a God. I think He wanted her.'

'God wanted Angela to go to Him? So your brother did what God wanted him to do?'

'Yes, I think we was chosen, I don't know why, to prove that there is a God . . . My friend, we went to her for help one night, she was Salvation Army, and she said she was sure it was the devil that was in the house that night.'

'Do you feel there's a devil?'

'Yes, yes.'

'What's he like?'

'He manipulates people.'

'Do we know when we are being manipulated by the devil?'

'We should do. Being greedy and corrupt.'

'It must have been very frightening for you to be told that somebody, a friend, thought that it was the devil that made you do this and not God. Was that very upsetting when she said that to you?'

'No, because I thought it was God.'

241

'And you still feel that it was God?'

'Yes, yes, definitely.'

'So even though things aren't very good for you at the moment, you feel it was the right thing to do?'

Jessica sighed. 'God loved children, didn't He? He wouldn't have wanted her – I don't know. The more you delve, the more you get not so sure. Why did my brother do those strange things in the house? Because he was ill? We all had to wash our hands and he turned the barometer back to rain and we all prayed. It wasn't raining at the time but it poured down on Sunday, just as she died, and he felt He's answered us . . . I'm sure I'm not mad . . . I don't know what happened to us. It had to though, because we were so happy.'

'Because you were so happy you knew that something bad would happen?'

'Yes, well, we thought, you know, we woke up that Thursday night and we talked and talked out in the garden on Friday all day, round and round in circles, and just talked and talked and talked. About things. And we thought we were the only people on the earth, that evening . . . They won't let me see Mark. I think they're frightened it might happen again. I don't think it will, but the authorities, they've sent me here.'

'What do you think will stop it happening again?'

'I don't know – but knowing what went wrong last time.'

'What do you feel went wrong last time?'

Jessica sighed. 'Or did it go wrong?'

'You're not sure whether it did go wrong?'

'No.'

'Am I right in thinking that this is the way you feel – that if it was God that chose you to do this, then it went right? If it was the devil, then it went wrong?'

'Yes.'

'And you're not sure?'

'No. I don't know.'

The doctors labelled Jessica 'schizophrenic' and treated her accordingly. But there was no treatment that could resolve her dilemma. If it was God that had chosen her to assist in the killing of her little sister, then she can live at peace with herself for having carried out God's will, but what other tasks might He demand of her? Had Angela been possessed of the devil or had God wanted her with Him? On the other hand, if she had been used by the devil, then her life must be filled with endless remorse and guilt and fear of God's retribution, both in this world and in the hell which she is sure follows this life. The non-religious answer to her questions, that she and her brother were insane when they killed Angela, brings no relief of guilt, only the drugged numbing of the pain.

8

Suffering and Change

Why do we build ourselves these prisons and then tramp round and round them with such dreary regularity? It is true that some of us, with wisdom and luck, have built ourselves some fairly comfortable prisons, but they are prisons, nevertheless, and we run the risk that the comforts may disappear at any time and the punishments begin. On most days I write myself little lists of tasks to be done, and when, at the end of the day or the week, each item has been firmly crossed off I feel a glow of pleasure. The tasks that I list are not what I regard as solely pleasurable. I do not bother to list items like 'watch TV', 'read today's newspaper', 'visit friends', but I do list things which require some effort – making certain telephone calls, typing a manu-script, buying shampoo, defrosting the refrigerator. Why do I carry out these tasks? Because each one of them is part of the responsibility I feel I must meet, a responsibility to myself and to other people. What are these responsibilities? To myself they are to look after myself, to use my talents, not to waste my limited time; to other people they are not to hurt, to keep a promise, to help keep pain and disaster at bay. The discomfort I feel at carrying out the tasks I set myself is as nothing to the pain when I feel that I have failed to meet my responsibilities as well as I might. Over the years I have become wiser in choosing what I see myself as being responsible for and more efficient in carrying out my tasks, but woe betide me if my wisdom and competence fail. How can I live with myself if I cease to see myself as a good person?

It seems that there is no pain, no misery which some member of the human race is not prepared to put up with in order to think well of himself. Some of us can only think well of ourselves so long as we uphold some principle, irrespective of what obloquy we bring on ourselves; some of us can only think well of ourselves provided we are assured that we have the approval of others. To such ends some people are prepared to whip themselves till the blood runs, or pierce their flesh with steel rods, or throw themselves under a galloping horse, or set fire to themselves, or starve themselves to death, or go naked and smear their cells with excrement, all in the effort to maintain the belief that 'I am a good person'.

If only we could agree on what goodness is! I think it has a lot to do with tolerance and freedom, with understanding, forgiving, sharing compassion, and love. Goodness, for me, has no essential and intrinsic relationship with any nationality, creed, class, or race. But not everyone shares my views. Forgiveness between Protestants and Catholics in Northern Ireland can result in shattered kneecaps or worse, while for Jew and Arab revenge can be a virtue of the highest order. When the West Bank mayors were maimed by a car bomb a Palestinian resistance supporter said (quoted in *The Guardian*, 1980), 'Yesterday, Mayors Bassam Shaka and Kareem Khalef were men we looked up to and respected. Today, whether they recover from their injuries or die, we venerate them as heroes and martyrs. They are passing on the flame to our children and our children's children.' Meanwhile, in the Hebron Jewish cemetery, Mr Yossi Dayan said of the attack, 'This is only the beginning. The God of Israel is the God of revenge, and we pray to the God of Israel to be the instrument of his vengeance.'

That revenge is virtuous is a belief held not only by certain religious and nationalist movements but also by many people whose narrow prison cell is that of depression. How often have I heard a depressed person declare that to forgive a parent or a spouse was unthinkable, totally impossible. Arguments that loving parents often act unwisely through stress or ignorance, or that sometimes it is a good idea to cut our losses and start again fall on deaf ears when revenge is construed as both virtuous and sweet, irrespective of the suffering it brings with it. Forgiveness can be construed as a diminution of one's self-respect or a weakening of one's control over another person. When I dared to suggest to Tony that his wife might view their relationship differently from him and that he should accept this he was furious. He saw his anger with his wife as moral and righteous since she had not kept her part of the bargain. He agreed with me that he saw the whole point of his existence as being angry with his wife and that he would persist in this, even though it perpetuated his depression and left him with no energy to be creative. For him to leave his wife or become tolerant of her was to lose the war, and the struggle between them was a fight to the death. Nurturing and preparing for revenge can be seen as more enjoyable than actually carrying out the act of revenge with its possibility of post-revenge tristesse, while those of us who despise calm and contentment can agree with Saul Bellow that 'trouble, like physical pain, makes us actively aware that we are living, and when there is little in the life we lead to hold and draw and stir us, we seek and cherish it, preferring embarrassment or pain to indifference.'

Trouble, for Tony and many people like him, was not merely the goad which provoked reactions in him which confirmed that he was alive. It was also the means by which he saved his soul. When I told him to be tolerant I was telling him, as he said, to put his soul at risk. Now all of us have souls which we do not wish to put at risk. I do not use the word 'soul' with regard to myself, but I do use words like 'integrity' and 'self-respect', and, while I do not expect that whatever there is about me that can claim these qualities will continue in existence after my death, I know that in my scheme of things I cannot afford to put these qualities at risk, for to do so involves some kind of self-annihilation. I suppose I could have had an easier life had I been prepared to risk my 'soul' on more occasions than I did, so now I try not to ridicule those people who construe their own suffering as part of a universal plan or as part of the bargain they have struck with God. I use the term 'self-indulgence' as a term of opprobrium, so I guess I must be at least a small subscriber to the 'suffering is character-building' school of thought, even though I have plenty of evidence that there is a degree of suffering in childhood which produces, not noble characters, but mean and twisted parodies of human beings. However, I find it hard to tolerate the casuist who balances the credits of good against the debits of evil and pronounces that God is satisfied with the bargain. Yet there are many people who carry out this spiritual accounting, along with the many who eagerly embrace suffering in this world in order to store up treasure in the next. Sometimes

246

it is possible to accept present suffering as the inevitable outcome of our deeds ('I didn't study for the exam, therefore I failed') and so accept responsibility for our actions in the present world, but when we explain our suffering as the result of sins committed unknowingly by us, then we undertake an endless search for faults within ourselves, a search which allows us to demonstrate our virtue by our cries of 'mea culpa' and by our visible suffering. When the acceptance of suffering is construed as the means of gaining atonement, pardon, and forgiveness from God, then ways of relieving the suffering must not be accepted, even when the sufferer seeks them. If, in the Judaic tradition and in the sacrifice of Jesus on the Cross, we believe that the suffering of the innocent can atone for the sins of the guilty, then we are ready to join the ranks of the martyrs and to resist having our suffering taken away from us.

If we see our suffering as the means by which we assure ourselves of our virtue and also preserve and protect the people we love, then we have locked ourselves into a prison where suffering becomes the justification for our existence. Conor Cruse O'Brien told the story of how his father, an agnostic, died suddenly, a fate which to a Catholic in Ireland in 1927 meant that he was consigned to Purgatory. Friends tried to reassure Mrs O'Brien that as her husband had lived a good life he would, sometime, get to Heaven. She did not doubt that he would. The question for her was how soon he would get there and be no longer separated not just from God but from her. Conor Cruse O'Brien wrote:

I know that the date of my father's arrival at that destination was problematical. The reason for that was myself. Because my father, besides being an agnostic, and dying without a priest, had done something much worse: he had sent me to a Protestant school, because he thought Protestant schools were better than Catholic ones, which they were. My mother was told that if she prayed she could shorten my father's term in Purgatory. So she prayed like mad. But she was also told that every term she kept me on at a Protestant school lengthened my father's term of suffering. She would not take me away from that school because it had been my father's wish that I should go there, and that was that. Every day of her life was shortening, lengthening, praying and holding firm, with heroic fortitude. Years afterwards, a Pope decided that enough was enough, and closed Purgatory down. Of course, he said he *wasn't* closing it down, it had just never been there. It had been there all right, I knew, because my mother was shut up in it for more than 10 years, from Christmas, 1927, to her death at Easter, 1938.

In a similar way Felicity and Jill created and lived in their own purgatories in order to preserve their loved ones. To see her mother as unfailingly good Felicity took all the badness inside herself and identified it as an evil smell which had to be kept in check by ritual cleansing and isolation from others. Jill needed to preserve her parents and herself as good, so she located all the badness in an external contagion which could be controlled only by unceasing cleansing rituals. Neither Mrs O'Brien, nor Felicity, nor Jill could lay aside her daily task of lonely ritual, since the impulse to such ritual came as much from love as it did from fear.

Love and fear, especially when the fear is experienced as guilt, often render the idea of personal happiness irrelevant. Therapists know only too well the client who has many family problems and who has managed to become involved with a number of helping agencies but who, in one way or another, rejects the help these agencies offer. One such woman was sent to me because she was depressed. She had a very handicapped child about whom she talked to me a great deal. Her conversation had two themes. If the child was at home with her she would talk about how muddled she was and how she could not cope; if he was in hospital (a very good hospital, as I knew) she would complain about his care and say how guilty she felt about his being excluded from the family. At the same time she would subtly accuse me of not helping her while, in overt and covert ways, she made it impossible for me to give her even the simplest of help. One day, in desperation, I asked her if she thought she deserved to be happy. She rejected the word 'happy' – it was not in her vocabulary – but she did venture to admit that, 'I don't think I ought to be comfortable.' I knew I was defeated, just as I had been defeated by the client who, when I asked her how she had enjoyed a family party where everything had gone well, replied, 'I didn't enjoy it as much as I ought to have enjoyed it.'

My feelings towards my clients are always a mixture of loving sympathy and amused exasperation. The amusement and the exasperation become uppermost when I am observing how much of my client's misery stems directly from personal vanity. I can find myself equally ridiculous. Sometimes I manage to recognize that my belief that to be good is to meet my responsibilities is in fact an aspect of my vanity. Of course, one has to catch oneself as being vain. I recall feeling guilty because I had not spoken to a depressed friend when she telephoned while I was with a couple who were telling me of their marital problems. Somehow, I seemed to think that I should have dispelled my friend's sadness while creating harmony between husband and wife, yet I knew perfectly well that if my friend gave up being depressed she would be at a loss to fill in her time, while I suspected that this married couple got much more pleasure and excitement out of their battles than they had ever had from their sexual encounters with one another. Only vanity made me feel guilty that I could not achieve the impossible.

When one considers the history of the human race with all its enormous difficulties and disasters, and the lives of individuals whose persistence in surviving is an object lesson to all who despair, one can only conclude that a high level of self-esteem, even if unsupported by external evidence, is a necessary commodity to win the battle to survive. But it is not for nothing that in Christian theology pride is regarded as the deadliest of the seven deadly sins. It is pride that makes us sit at the centre of our constructed worlds, blind to the recognition that other people inhabit worlds different from our own, or when this recognition is forced upon us, it is pride that makes us label the people who see things differently from us as either stupid, mad, or bad. It is pride, vanity, narcissism, which makes us construe everything solely in relationship to ourselves. The sun is good because it shines to warm us; the rain is bad because it wets and frustrates us. That nature is indifferent to our existence and that other people have projects and concerns that are not centred on us are facts which we try to exclude from our vision, and when such facts are forced upon us we feel frightened and lonely, and we protest. We demand that the world take account of us, and when it fails to do so, we are prepared to suffer so that we can cease to be ordinary and thus stand out from the crowd. Sheila MacLeod, telling the story of her adolescent anorexia, wrote, 'While I was anorexic, I had always considered myself to be extraordinary rather than abnormal. The difference between the two concepts can be seen more easily if we convert the two words into their antonyms. To be ordinary carries connotations of being dull, boring, unimaginative, unadventurous, and, in school parlance, "stodgy". Like many a non-anorexic adolescent before and since, I despised ordinariness.' 'Ordinary people,' said Tony, 'aren't remembered.' Better a universe that is conspiring to destroy you than a universe that ignores you.

The devil tempts us to the sin of vanity in many subtle ways. Arthur Koestler records that a friend once remarked to him that, 'you have the vanity to give but you lack the generosity to take.' Many of us suffer from such a short-coming. It is much easier to give love than to receive it. In receiving love we have to risk being pitied, or accepting something which does not meet our standards, or being put in a situation which we do not control. In giving love we are in a position of strength, we can dictate the terms of our gift and all the time bask in the glow of virtue. It is vanity which forces us to present a good face to the world, even if this means we must never reveal an unworthy emotion or a less than perfect home, and so we are unable to admit a mistake and must therefore continue to live in ways which cause us constant pain. It is vanity which makes us construe our lives as a line of progress or as the saving of our soul, so that anything which is construed as an impediment in the achievement of these ends produces in us a devastating despair. The gap between self and ideal-self is filled with pride which often presents itself in the guise of humility. Thus one can, like Siegfried, 'feel guilty about not achieving and frightened when you do'.

When we consider the vast size of the universe and the

multitude of people on Earth, we can feel, as an individual, most insignificant. We may be prepared to accept our insignificance provided we can assure ourselves that we control our own lives, and, in particular, the numbers and kind of disasters that can overtake us. Our vanity can lead us to the erroneous assumption that if we bring certain disasters upon ourselves then we can avoid the unexpected disasters which Nature or God or the Devil may visit upon us. By behaving in such a way that we are certain of a degree of constant or regular suffering, or by creating our own disasters and thus finding an explanation for our sense of impending doom, we hope that we can avoid the unexpected, massive suffering which goes beyond our limits to endure. Unfortunately, life is not always so amenable. Even if disasters do come in threes, as the superstition says, manufacturing a calamity to complete the set does not ensure that a further trio does not immediately arrive.

Even if we can, without too much insult to our vanity, accept our insignificance, we need to keep the circumstances of our life fairly constant, since abrupt and vast changes can threaten us to the extent that we fear the loss of our very identity. We do not realize how much we depend on the familiar routine of our daily lives until we find ourselves bereft of our possessions, in alien places, surrounded by people who do not share our definition of ourselves. The familiar can be seen as better than the unfamiliar, even when the familiar includes our suffering. Better the devil you know than the devil you don't know. If the familiar devil gets too hurtful we can seek out a therapist in the hope that the therapist can take away the pain without changing us. Few therapists have the necessary magic to do this. Even analgesic measures produce some change.

Some of us are prepared to risk change because we do not construe change as totally fearful and unacceptable. Indeed, some of us prefer risk to boredom. But not all. Recently a friend consulted me about a mutual acquaintance, a woman who was married to a man who treated her abominably. 'Katherine ought to leave him,' my friend said. 'I'm sure she could manage to support herself and the children. She's a qualified librarian and a specialist in her field. She could easily get a full-time job and be quite independent of him.' My friend had given this advice to

Katherine but found that Katherine argued that such a plan would not work – she was out of touch, no one wanted a middle-aged woman, the job needed a responsible, organized person, and she was not very responsible or well organized. These appeared to my friend as peculiar reasons, since in her eyes Katherine was an extremely responsible and well-organized person. One day my friend, Katherine, and I went for a walk with Katherine's children. Our path ran beside a brook over which was a tiny, rickety wooden bridge, so rickety that when the younger of the two boys, preparing to cross the stream, grasped the bridge railings and shook them, the whole bridge creaked. He hesitated. His mother called, 'Damien, when in doubt, don't.' Leaving one's husband is, unquestionably, an action that is charged with doubt.

We can construe change as bad simply because we do not want to think about the life we lead. Tolstoy once remarked that, 'It is generally supposed that Conservatives are usually old people, and that those in favour of change are the young. That is not quite correct. Usually Conservatives are young people: those who want to live but who do not think about how to live, and have not time to think and therefore take as a model for themselves a way of life that they have seen.' When we are young we may resist any experience which casts doubts upon the scheme of things which we see as reality and into which we fit harmoniously. We may believe that goodness is always rewarded and that justice will always prevail, that the nation or class to which we belong is superior to all others, or that the religion or political creed in which we believe will triumph in our lifetime. Change is not welcome in such a cocoon of belief, and so we must protect ourselves from conscious awareness of any event which may reveal our beliefs as illusions. Such conservatism in youth can lead to uncomprehending misery later in life, a state which supplies not only many clients for therapists but characters for writers. In an interview with Arthur Miller, Melvyn Bragg asked him, 'In a lot of your plays, from *Death of a Salesman* almost through to *The American Clock*, the real failure of a person is not being able to face up to the truth of their own situation. Why won't they face up to the truth, do you think?' Miller replied, 'Because too much has been invested already; people make an investment in falsehood, invest a whole lifetime in it. It's not an inability to see the truth, it's an inability to start all over again. An age comes when it's impossible, so you continue on until the grave, to reinforce it and to justify it, because to overturn it is too painful or expensive.'

Sometimes the person who finds himself suffering may be prepared to risk change to seek an end to his suffering, but those around him, his nearest and dearest, may construe change as bad and so render it impossible. Individual therapy often founders because of this, and so family therapy and marital therapy have been devised to find a way around this problem. This is not easy, for it is not just a matter of getting all members of the group to construe change in one member as good. They may be happy to see certain problem behaviours disappear, but they do not want to go to the effort of major reconstruing of their own systems. If 'My wife does not go to work' implies 'I am a good provider and must be seen to be so', or 'My son prefers home cooking' implies 'My son loves me and I shall not be alone in my old age', then efforts to make the wife less depressed or the son more active and independent are likely to fail unless the husband and mother are prepared to face the pain of changing. Rather than do this, they may value and so cling to the very aspects of their loved one's character which promotes his own suffering. Tony may have despised ordinariness, but he knew that his wife did too, and that she loved him and clung to him because she saw him as extraordinary, even though she found much of his extraordinary behaviour quite painful. Later when Tony had decided that it was not worth spending his life locked in battle with his wife, he wrote the couplet,

> If you hadn't loved my devils so
> I might have sooner let them go.

Sometimes we fear change simply because we have so few ideas of what living without our suffering would be like, or because we see 'normal' life as unattractive. A friend once told me about a schizophrenic patient who preferred to remain psychotic since the common, shared reality was, as he described it, 'an iffy swamp'. I thought that was an excellent metaphor for the way in which life is so full of doubts and so resistant to any form of neat and solid categorization. Those people who wish to see their sufferings as a form of special knowledge often espouse the proposition 'Anyone who hasn't got my problem hasn't got any problems at all.' Some depressed people believe that when, if ever, they cease to be depressed, they will never be unhappy again. Some stammerers believe that fluent people sail through life without meeting as much as a ripple. Some homosexuals believe that heterosexual couples have no experience of passion, jealousy, uncertainty, and misunderstandings. The therapist who attempts to alter these views to bring them more into line with reality – to point out that most adults, no matter how well they cope, experience periods of difficulty, or that fluent speakers often have difficulty in communicating, or that heterosexual couples can suffer agonies in their relationships – may find that he has deterred his client from attempting change. Better the devil you know, every time!

Sometimes we fear change because, even though to outsiders we appear to lead a happy and productive life, we know that we have made a marginal adjustment and that any untoward movement can lead to disaster. Having made such an adjustment, it is sometimes seen as necessary to remove all conscious awareness of this state of affairs and to resist any attempts to bring it to light. The writer Elaine Feinstein told the story of how her husband and herself had become concerned that one of their adolescent sons had taken to spending many hours alone in his room. 'My husband expressed the hope that, whatever else, he was enjoying the pleasures of melancholy. He spoke in a wistful voice and was quite unprepared for the vehemence and immediacy of my objections. Melancholy, I explained to him, was a disease. There were no pleasures attached to it. It was a condition of deep gloom, anciently recognised, for which it was inappropriate to hope.' Her husband suggested that 'melancholia' had the additional connotations of 'a poignant apprehension of beauty, for instance, and an awareness that it was transient . . . By now battle was joined . . . While the running battle continued, no investigation of the reasons for my obstinate refusal to yield an inch could be expected. It was only after several months that we were presented with a clue. We had been talking about Samuel Beckett's years of staying huddled under the bed-clothes till mid-afternoon when I experienced a mild epiphany. I had understood why I could not allow any pleasure to exist in the state of melancholy. As far as I was concerned, the mood was a real threat. If it took over, I knew it could do for me altogether. I have always been a tightrope walker with darkness on either side of me. Who can afford to savour a situation like that? Sometimes I marvel at the daring of such a proposition; but it offers no pleasure to me, and secretly I suspect it remains a state of peril no one sane would bring upon himself.'

The spoken word often fails us when we wish to describe something important that is happening to us, and so, like many therapists, I often say to my clients, 'If you could paint a picture of this, what picture would you paint?' Once I am sure that I am picturing the described image as accurately as possible, we can then start exploring the implications of the image to see where the angels are welcoming and the devils are lurking, where there is hope and where despair. This is a particularly useful exercise in coming to understand how a person is experiencing his depression, and so in the talks I give to professional groups about depression I often ask them to describe their own images of being depressed. I can always be sure that in whatever group I am talking to, there will be several people who know full well what it is to be depressed. The differences between their images and the images of those people who have experienced no more than common unhappiness serve to define clinical depression with a clarity no textbook has ever achieved. The images of depression, however exprssed, are always of a person alone in some kind of prison from which there is little hope, or even impulse, to escape. They are of dungeon cells, or endless dark tunnels, or empty deserts or thick, black fog. Some images have a sense that some kind of change might be attempted – tunnels can be explored, deserts can be traversed, fog penetrated. In some images change can only come from outside – a rope could be thrown to a prisoner in a pit, prison doors could be unbolted. But some images are of situations where the slightest movement to change would imperil survival. One man spoke of sitting on an icefloe in the Antarctic as a ship vanishes over the horizon. Icefloes, as we know, melt, or, while floating, can easily capsize.

One woman described her depression as being locked in a cage which was so small that she could not sit, stand, or lie, but only crouch and remain unmoving since the cage was suspended by a fraying rope over a bottomless chasm. In such a situation any movement towards change would be disastrous.

When one young man told me about his image of depression I asked him if he had read Jacky Gillott's account of her depression. He had not, and so I discovered another person whose depression was a large black owl that sat on his shoulder. When he was not depressed he knew that the owl had simply left its perch and was hovering above him. He was certain that the bird was an owl and not an eagle – eagles are harsh, aggressive, and dominant. His owl was gently heavy and soft, dark, and silent. He feared its coming and so moved carefully beneath its outspread wings. Birds are sometimes said to symbolize transformation, and in its way this owl did so. One day, he told me, the bird would swoop silently down and gather him up. He and the owl would blend into each other and depart. From the tenor of his voice and the expression on his face it would seem that such a fate was not entirely unwelcome. I doubted if he would risk any change which might imperil his owl.

A common image for the danger which awaits us is that of the abyss. Hell is underground; depression is down into the pit at the bottom of which is madness and death. It may be a fearful thing to fall into the hands of the living God, but it is, as D. H. Lawrence said, a much more fearful thing to fall out of them.

That awful and sickening endless sinking, sinking
through the slow, corruptive levels of disintegrative knowledge
when the self has fallen from the hands of God
and sinks, seething and sinking, corrupt
and sinking still, in depth after depth of disintegrative consciousness
sinking in the endless undoing, the awful katabolism into the abyss!

We may, in the broad light of day, carry on our lives with exemplary skill and enviable contentment, but in the dark of night we may wake and find our heart and guts squeezed tight with fear as the abyss yawns within us. In the words of U. A. Fanthorpe:

This is the hushed network of nightmare.
You have lost touch with the sustaining
Ordinariness of things.

Suddenly the immense and venerable
Fallacies that prop the universe
Fail, the colossal flickering fabric
Which we must believe in so that it can be
Goes out.

Here malevolence is routine, the shadow
Is real and the world is shadow.
Here the happy-ever-after crumples
Into a rheumatoid hic-iacet.

Here the appalling and unexpected
Disaster is expected. Here the blood
Screams whispers to the flesh.

Such terror, or the faintest inkling that such terror is possible, will compel some people to remain in relationships which otherwise are stultifying and painful, while other people are engaged in an endless round of sexual adventures to blot out the terror and to assure themselves that they exist. When Evelyn Waugh chided Orwell for presenting as the solution in 1984 as that of 'finding reality with the Proles in the sexual act', he was agreeing with Otto Rank that 'sex is a disappointing answer of life's riddle'. If we have defined our salvation in terms of romantic love or sexual prowess or infinite desirability, then we are in danger when the object of our love proves to be all too human, or when age threatens our strength and beauty. We can then deny, against all evidence, that anything has changed, or we can rage with increasing bitterness against the unjust fate. Sentimentality and a sense of injustice have charms which some of us are reluctant to relinquish.

One of the advantages of sexual encounters without commitment is that they allow contact with another person without having to engage in the kind of conversations where we may not only reveal ourselves but also find ourselves in a situation which we cannot control. Those people who construe relationships in terms of control rather than love experience a loneliness which can lead to depression, but for many like Siegfried the pain of loneliness is preferable to the risk one runs in knowing another person without controlling that person. In such a relationship it is not always possible to predict what the other person will do. There is always the danger of being ridiculed or rejected, or being required to behave in unfamiliar ways. The possibilities for pain are seen as greater than the possibilities for pleasure, and so the person decides to stay in his position of lonely power. Since animals can be trained to be more predictable than humans, their company can be preferred to that of people. Richard is not alone in valuing animals above much of the human race.

Anything that offers to change us, even when such a change may reduce our suffering and increase our happiness, can be seen as a threat and as such rejected. It is necessary for us, in some measure, to be resistant to change, otherwise we would be at the mercy of our parents, teachers, employers, politicians, advertisers, and therapists. But it is one thing to resist the influence of others; it is another thing to close our eyes to any evidence which threatens our view of the world. History is full of the tragedies that occurred because certain people would not accept the evidence of their senses. Between the two World Wars, when many people hoped that Marxism would abolish poverty and inequality, the need and hope was so strong for some people that they blinded themselves to the evidence that oppression in Russia matched or exceeded that in Nazi Germany. Other people, for other reasons, refused (and some still refuse) to believe that Hitler was engaged upon exterminating all the people who did not meet with his approval. These blindnesses caused death and misery to millions of people. A similar and potentially even more dangerous blindness exists today in those people who insist that some sort of acceptable human existence will be possible after a nuclear war. When I meditate upon a vision of the aftermath of a neutron bomb, where the buildings are relatively untouched but all the people dead, I can only conclude that all our lives are, as Robert Oppenheimer said of his, not tragedy but farce.

Why do we resist having our suffering taken away from us?

Our clients beg us to help them, yet, when we speak, our words bounce back at us as if in an echo chamber. Few seem to reach the person in the chair opposite us. Freud spent nearly a lifetime analysing the forms that resistance can take, but here my answer is simply that when we offer to help a client change, we are not merely offering to help him relinquish his pain. We are also offering to help him to relinquish a valued attachment. And that he is reluctant to do.

So long as we are attached to anything we are vulnerable to suffering. Solzhenitsyn noted that 'Unfortunately for us mortals and fortunately for the powers that be, it is in the nature of man that as long as he is alive there is always something which can be taken away from him.' Is there no solution to the problem of suffering? Diogenes' advice to desire nothing, fear nothing, possess nothing, and Spinoza's *nec spe nec mutu* – hope for nothing in order to fear nothing – conjure up a bleak life. The mystics, who see suffering as resulting from the craving for an independent life and hell as the total separation from God, advise that we can escape from suffering only by accepting it and passing beyond it into a union with God. Buddha taught that 'the cause of pain is the craving for individual life', and in his Fire Sermon he described the cessation of suffering for the person as:

> . . . he becomes divested of passion, and by the absence of passion he becomes free, and when he is free, he becomes aware that he is free; and he knows that rebirth is exhausted, that he has lived the holy life, that he has done what it behoved him to do, and that he is no more for this world.

Those of us who find the commitment demanded by the mystics and Buddha more than we can manage may prefer the kindly wisdom of Lao Tsu

> There is no greater sin than desire,
> No greater curse than discontent,
> No greater misfortune than wanting something for oneself.
> Therefore he who knows that enough is enough always has
>   enough.

But it is hard to give up our attachments, especially the attachments we have to our own suffering. There are many of us like Saul Bellow's Hertzog who, when remembering a particularly happy time in his life, said, 'To tell the truth I never had it so good. But I lacked the character to bear such joy. That was hardly a joke. When a man's breast feels like a cage from which all the dark birds have flown – he is free, he is light. And he longs to have his vultures back again. He wants his customary struggles, his nameless empty works, his anger, his afflictions and his sins.' We fear the empty space that will be left if we let our attachments go, or, in letting them go, we fill the space with self-righteousness, a consciousness of our own virtue. We can glow with pride over the two thousand extra calories we have not eaten that day, or we can, like some people I have met, raise being an ex-addict to a full-time profession. We can forgive those who have hurt us, and we can go on forgiving them again and again, without realizing that real forgiveness means letting go of both the hurt and the act of forgiveness in the way that we might drop two leaves into a fast-flowing stream where they disappear forever from view. Ending attachments means releasing our constructions which then disappear into the formless, changing chaos of reality.

In the Pali language the word for 'suffering' or 'sorrow' is 'dukkha'. Ronald Eyre quotes a Buddhist monk who gave him the most succinct definition of dukkha. He said, 'Dukkha is the attempt to make reality repeatable.' We see our constructions as having a continuing existence and from this we construct the continuity of our existence. Our attempts to force reality to repeat itself or to be what it is not result in our suffering, but we may be prepared to go on suffering in order to maintain the continuity of our existence. Anything that threatens the continuity of our existence we see as a form of death. Whenever we see our continuity as being ruptured or damaged we enter a state of grief. 'The concept of grief', wrote James Carse, 'appears prominently in all great systems of thought, although it does not always go by that name. We find it discussed under such categories as ignorance, despair, karma, yearning, neurosis, or the abandonment to history. Whatever the term, each of these shares the universal characteristics of grief: lack of effective speech, isolation from others, no interest in the future, abnegation of freedom – in sum, the contradictory state of living in a way which resembles death. Grief is our refusal to recognise the fact that death has not taken away our freedom to reconstitute the continuities it has destroyed . . . (for the Buddhist) in grief the impulse of the mind was to leap off the wheel of ceaseless change in the desperate attempt to find something immovable. Attachment leads to suffering because nothing is exempt from change.' When we discover that we cannot reconnect the continuity of our lives as it was before our loss and that reality is insubstantial and changing, we make the discovery that C. S. Lewis made: 'No one ever told me that grief felt so like fear. I am not afraid, but the sensation is like being afraid. The same fluttering in the stomach, the same restlessness, the yawning. I keep on swallowing.'

How can we deal with pain and fear? We can try to find some general principle which is real and secure enough to form the foundation of our continuity. Since we can conceive of perfection we may decide that our world ought to be perfect, and when it fails to live up to our expectations we feel angry and cheated. If we reconstrue, and see that we know perfection only because we know imperfection and that our world is made up of the necessary coexistence of opposites, then we have gained a measure of peace and freedom. Since we can conceive of justice, we may decide that our world is coordinated by a Grand Plan where everyone receives his just deserts, and then we need to feel guilty about any good fortune that comes our way in case it exceeds what we are entitled to. By feeling guilty we may be able to ward off a greater punishment. (Guilt can function as both reparation and propitiation.) If we reconstrue to allow chance into our scheme of things then we are free to enjoy our good luck and to absolve ourselves of responsibility for our bad luck. We may try to maintain our continuity by striking a bargain with God, but God is deaf to the offer of bargains, as should be our therapist when we ask him to assure us that all will be well when we venture a modicum of change.

In order to change, to overcome our suffering and grief, we need to accept that reality is not repeatable. We may express this as the surrendering to the will of God, or as the abandoning of cravings and approaching the state of Nirvana, or as the recognition that in science all predictions and measurements are approximations and that the physical world at the small level is full of ambiguities (as Gregory Bateson said, 'The generic we can know but the specific eludes us'). It is only through the acceptance of uncertainty that we can realize our freedom to reconstitute our continuity and overcome our grief.

If we construe what is wrong with us, our badness, our evil – whether we see it as Adam's curse, or the Devil, or the legacy of our genes – as immutable, then we are powerless to change ourselves. The first step to change is to see it as possible in our scheme of things. The next step is to accept and cope with the anger and frustration that change brings. Linda Viney, in her study of the way in which women cope with the usual transitions of life – from primary school to high school, from high school to work or university, to marriage and a family, to menopause and the children leaving, to sickness and approaching death – remarked that 'Good coping with anxiety involves accepting it into awareness and permitting its full expression. This may not lead to a comfortable state in the short term, but in the long term it is a most effective strategy . . . Frustration is high when there is most to lose . . . These angers, like anxiety, need to be freely expressed whenever possible, in ways that are acceptable to oneself and to others.' But accepting and valuing change does not mean that we find it easy to accept anger and anxiety in ourselves and others. Usually we can tolerate one more easily than the other and indeed value one more than the other. Some people regard a degree of anxiety as a necessary spur to action and enjoy a state of anxiety under certain conditions – hence the popularity of roller-coasters and horror films. Some people regard a degree of anger as a necessary spur to action and enjoy a state of anger under certain conditions – hence the popularity of political rallies and fights at football matches. Where anger and anxiety are construed as bad and dangerous, then the person will develop ways of avoiding such painful emotions in himself and others.

Since none of us regard anger and anxiety with unreserved pleasure, the therapist has to help in dealing with the fear of the anger and anxiety that change brings. Linda Viney, like Aaron

Beck in his cognitive therapy of depression, advocates humour. She writes 'Humour is, in itself, an effective strategy. It can permit catharsis of anxious or angry feelings, provide a perspective on transition and decrease embarrassment. It is a good facilitator of inter-personal relationships. It has even been advocated as a form of psychotherapy. One reason why humour is an effective coping strategy may be that it contributes to a sense of personal competence and control.' I agree with this wholeheartedly, but I find that some people believe that if you laugh at something it means that you do not care. Indeed, for some people, to laugh at their suffering is a form of sacrilege. Yet the Jews, who have made suffering a central part of their belief, not something to be abolished, run away from, ameliorated, but something to be welcomed and accepted as part of their relationship to God, have a genius for creating jokes about their own suffering. Humour looks at the world by moving things about and showing that reality is not immutable, that things viewed from another perspective are not as huge and overwhelming as we thought. A sense of the ridiculous is necessary for survival, although I must admit that what is perhaps an overdevelopment of the sense of the ridiculous has rendered me incapable of believing in any elaborate theory or being impressed by any ceremonial, whether the theory or the ceremonial be political, religious, philosophical, or scientific. Nevertheless, I am aware that the amusement my clients provoke in me ('I can always tell when you're laughing at me,' said one, 'your face might be serious but your eyes sparkle') is related to the affection I feel for them. I have not been able to describe this relationship properly, so I was delighted when I found this passage in one of Paul Scott's novels.

And I think it was then, with Rowan sitting opposite me, showing not a trace of anxiety (carve him in stone and nothing would have emerged so clearly as his rigid proconsular self-assurance, remoteness and dignity) that I understood the comic dilemma of the raj – the dilemma of the men who hoped to inspire trust but couldn't even trust themselves. The air around us and in the grounds of the summer residence was soft, pungent with aromatic gums, but melancholy – charged with this self-mistrust and the odour of unreality which only exile made seem real. I had the almost irrepressible urge to burst out laughing. I fought it because he would have misinterpreted it. But I would have been laughing *for* him. I suppose that to laugh for people, to see the comic side of their lives when they can't see it for themselves is a way of expressing affection for them; and even admiration – of a kind – for the lives they try so seriously to lead.

(Of course we have to love ourselves in order to laugh joyously at ourselves; if we do not, we either take ourselves very seriously or lacerate ourselves with bitter wit.)

Some changes are more profound than others. Religious conversion can often appear to be most profound, but what may have happened is simply a change in the overt attributes of a metaphor while the underlying structure remains the same. (Life may be described as a road or a river. In both metaphors the underlying structure is that of a line of progression.) Thus the change from Communism to Catholicism or from Calvinism to Islam does not represent as major a change as from, say, scientific humanism to Catholicism or Islam to Hinduism. I would argue that none of us, in the whole of our lives, ever change our basic structure totally, but nevertheless some profound changes are possible.

The destructive and immobilizing effects of guilt have been so well exposed by Freud and all the people he has influenced that in some quarters guilt has been labelled as unreservedly bad, and so now people have to feel guilty for feeling guilty whereas previously they had to feel guilty about not feeling guilty. However, guilt, like all our constructions, has its good as well as its bad aspects. It can motivate us to keep on going when life is difficult instead of sinking into debility and death; it can motivate us to try again or even to try something new. Under the force of such animating guilt we may be prepared to take a leap into the unknown.

Sometimes we do not so much leap as are pushed. This can be, in Robert Jay Lifton's words, 'any experience that brings psychic force to bear upon one's existing symbolizations of death and continuous life – the loss of a particular status or belief, contact with a new principle or image that undermines previous assumptions, the perception of a different form of honour or integrity to which one can aspire. Once confrontation has occurred, there is a shaking of psychic foundations.' Here Lifton was describing the shaking of psychic foundations experienced by many American servicemen in Vietnam. Just as profound a shaking (though perhaps not so physically unpleasant) can be experienced by a person in therapy. Tony had what he described as a profound and revelatory experience when he discovered that he could contrast his intolerance not just with pusillanimous tolerance but with the assured detachment which is the essence of Zen Buddhism. This discovery, he declared, had opened an entirely new world to him.

Profound changes do not always come with startling suddenness. Sometimes we need to go through some kind of procedure by which we can atone, make reparation, and so rid ourselves of a sense of guilt, of failure by washing ourselves clean of the excrement our past experience has laid on us. The carrying out of such procedures can signify, not just cleansing, but re-birth. 'Immersion in water,' wrote Mircea Eliade, 'signifies regression to the preformal, reincorporation into the undifferentiate mode of pre-existence . . . In whatever religious complex we find them, the waters invariably retain their function; they disintegrate, abolish forms, "wash away sins"; they are at once purifying and regenerating. The scenario of initiation – death to the profane condition, followed by rebirth to the sacred world, the world of the gods – also plays an important role in the highly evolved religions . . . Sacred knowledge and, by extension, wisdom, are conceived as the fruit of initiation . . . Socrates had good reason to compare himself to a midwife, for in fact he helped men to be born to a consciousness of self; he delivered the "new man". The same symbolism is found in the Buddhist tradition. The monk abandoned his family name and became a "son of the Buddha" . . . In his turn St Paul speaks of "spiritual sons", of sons whom he has procreated by faith.' Eliade drew a parallel with psychoanalysis where 'the patient is asked to descend deeply into himself to make his past live, to confront his traumatic experiences again; and from the point of view of form, this dangerous operation represents initiatory descents into hell, the realm of ghosts, and combats with monsters . . . the patient . . . must confront his own "unconscious", haunted by ghosts and monsters, in order to find psychic health and integrity and hence the world of cultural values'.

A sense of profound change, of being washed clean, re-born, allows the person to experience simultaneously a sense of forgiving and being forgiven. It is with good reason that Jesus instructed his followers to ask God 'to forgive our trespasses as we forgive those who trespass against us'. We cannot forgive ourselves unless we forgive other people; and we cannot forgive other people unless we forgive ourselves. We can experience our sense of forgiving ourselves either as the forgiveness stemming from our conscience or from God. Compared with some of the punitive super-egos I have met, God, even in His Old Testament roles, is a much kinder character. In dealing with our super-egos we should bear in mind Archbishop Fenelon's advice to his parishioner: 'It is mere self-love to be inconsolable at seeing one's own imperfections; but to stand face to face with them, neither flattering nor tolerating them, seeking to correct oneself without becoming pettish – this is to desire what is good for its own sake and for God's.'

Change is not possible without forgiveness, and the only way to do this is to open ourselves to the possibility of the experience. Then we may discover that we have it in our hearts to forgive and that we are forgiven, perhaps in the miraculous way that one of Alister Hardy's subjects recorded:

Gradually I became psychotic, and attempted suicide. I had done something which I considered utterly dreadful, and I was being driven to self-destruction because of an intense feeling of guilt. I had only one desire – to be forgiven . . . I was visited by the psychiatrists, my husband, my brother and the hospital chaplain, but I was unable to communicate sensibly with any of them. Then quite dramatically the whole picture changed overnight. The weight of guilt had been lifted and I was myself again, quite rational and ready to go home again. This recovery was not due to any medical aid at all. Both psychiatrists and clergy were at a loss to understand this sudden change, but it was quite simple to me: I believed that God had forgiven me . . . It was not a temporary healing. I never needed treatment since that time. Looking back I still know that there was a divine intervention in my life at that point.

Alister Hardy had asked his subjects whether they had ever been aware of or influenced by a presence or power that was beyond the individual self. David Hay extended this study by interviewing a random sample of Nottingham residents to find how many had had 'the experience of being aware of, or influenced by a presence or power, what this experience had been like, when it happened, what it meant to the person'. Some 62 per cent of those interviewed claimed to have had such an experience, double what had been predicted on the basis of national surveys of religious experience. Hay reported that 'the largest group of experiences was those referring to an awareness of the presence of God' and that three-quarters of these felt that their experience had changed their outlook to some degree. The kind of changes could be categorized as 'confirming or intensifying my beliefs, making me more optimistic, giving me insight into life, encouraging moral behaviour'. A young married woman told the interviewer, 'I feel God's always with me; it's confirmed and strengthened the things I've been brought up to know; given me will-power to go on.' A factory charge-hand said, 'Well, I've certainly been a lot happier. I've been able to mix with people more. More at ease with life.' A twenty-four year old graduate revealed, 'It completely changed my viewpoint, my philosophy of living. Instead of thinking that everything could be decided on the basis of reason, I realised that the deeper things were intuitive.' A recent study of the 'religion of modern American women' by Shaver, Lenauer, and Sadd found that in a large (2,500) random sample of women 'Seventy-nine per cent were *sure* they had experienced the feeling that God had answered their prayers; 76 per cent, that God had helped them through a crisis; and 70 per cent, that God had forgiven their sins. Far fewer (53 per cent) were sure they had experienced the "feeling of being tempted by the devil".'

These studies and others like them show that many people,

perhaps a large percentage of the population, have experiences which can only be described in words like 'religious', 'intuitive', 'numinous', 'revelatory', and which exert a profound and usually beneficial effect on their lives. Psychologists and psychiatrists interested in why people change should not ignore these kinds of experience, nor should they attempt to belittle or invalidate them. A client of mine, after she had known me long enough to have some trust in me, told me of an experience which she kept secret in case people thought she was mad. Some years before she had developed a kidney stone of such dimensions that it could not pass from her body and she was admitted to hospital for an operation. The pain was so intense that she needed regular doses of morphine, but even then, when she was conscious, all she could do in her agony was to cry out, over and over, 'God help me'. The day before the operation she was lying in a drugged sleep, when suddenly she awoke to sharp, full consciousness and turned her head and saw, just beyond her, the face of Christ looking at her. She was terrified, thinking that she was about to die. She did not. Instead she drifted back to sleep. When she awoke she found that the pain was gradually abating. The next day she could get out of bed. The kidney stone had gone and no operation was necessary. In a Catholic hospital this may have been counted a miracle, but where she was miracles – except those performed by surgeons – were not allowed to happen. Instead, the doctors told her that she had been hallucinating. What she had seen was no more than the effect of the morphia. They did not attempt to explain why the kidney stone had gone and they did not pause to consider that by explaining her experience in this way they had destroyed a gift which could have supported her through the years that followed. When she was referred to me by her general practitioner she was suffering from extreme anxiety which made her feel that she was losing her mind. Although she believed in God and prayed to Him, she did not draw on her experience for strength and security. Not being a Christian, I could not assure her that she had been a recipient of God's grace, but I did, drawing on Hardy's work, show her that other people had had experiences like hers, and that these experiences suggest that the world contains mysteries which are beneficent and not terrifying.

In contrast to my client's story is that of a young woman reported in Robinson's book *Living the Questions*. She described an experience, one snowy winter's night in a birch wood, which was:

> . . . like recognizing that someone has given you a gift of some sort, something that is a true gift . . . I felt so much standing there that I had to hug the birch tree . . . Sometimes I feel I've lost my bearings and I'm very depressed about something or other or wonder if there's any meaning to life or anything, and I can't get in touch with it, I can think back mentally, think of the birch trees, and be assured that it really did happen even if I can't feel it at the moment. And that makes me feel better, it makes me feel more alive . . . My father had died . . . when I was about fourteen . . . I really felt that after that everything had peeled away, you know, all your assumptions about justice and what should happen in the world that you're taught when you're little: that if you're good, good things happen to you, and if you're bad, bad things; when all this is peeled away . . . the feeling that when everything has gone there's still something left, that's what I got from the birch tree thing. Before that, everything was gone, but after, I realized that no matter how much in your personal life is torn away, there's always something left.

Sometimes change comes slowly as we meditate upon something someone has said to us or something that we have read. When Jenny came to see me she had got over the worst part of her depression, but she had heard about me from a friend and she thought that a discussion with me might help resolve some of her questions. We talked a little about depression, and I remarked that it seemed to me that depression was not an illness but a universal experience which had the effect of putting us into a form of painful hibernation where we become aware that there is something wrong with our lives and where we have a chance to discover what is wrong and to put it right. We spent more time talking about Jenny's relationship with her parents, how she dared not disagree with them in any way, even though she knew that they loved her and wanted to do everything for her benefit. As she was married with a family it seemed inappropriate that her parents should still treat her as a little girl. She agreed, and went away saying that she would try, when necessary, to present her own point of view to her parents. Some weeks later she phoned me to arrange a time for another discussion. When she came she said she had never felt better in her life and she thought that she would not get depressed again. She had made two discoveries – one, that her parents were willing to accept her point of view even when it diverged from theirs, and, two, that she could believe wholeheartedly what a spiritualist had told her. Jenny said, 'When I first had this experience I didn't know it was depression. I was in a terrible state. I couldn't cope. I was crying – we had friends staying. My husband was so bewildered. He rang the doctor and he said, "Oh, I'll give her tranquillizers, send your friends away" – which we couldn't do. They'd come from abroad. My husband rang a friend who has a wife who's a healer, a spiritualist, and she came along and talked to me about healing, and I'd never heard anything like this before in all my life. I think what she said made me feel much happier because I'd always wondered about death. To me it always seemed that it wasn't the end of life. They say that this life is really a preparation for the next one. This seemed more real, and I felt happier about that. But I didn't get better for a long time. After I got out of the depression I read some books on spiritualism and found them interesting. Now I go to see this girl and I go to my local church. I'm sure we're here to learn certain lessons, lessons in becoming mature as a person, coping with life and growing stronger, morally, mentally stronger. You said yourself about depression being a lesson, and lessons are not always easy, they're always hard when you've really got to learn something. If there's something I haven't learned then the depression will keep coming back again. One thing I'm learning now, I've been living in a very narrow family situation which I've explained to you, and since I saw you last time, for the first time ever, I had a confrontation with my mother. We had a situation where she attacked me because I hadn't been to see her for a day or two, and later in the day we had a talk and I explained to her that I feel torn between her and the family, and she actually admitted that she is a bit possessive, and since then our relationship has been much better. So this is to me a big step. Now that I've established myself with her I can do it again if the need be. And that has probably helped a lot. Having done that with her I can probably do it with other people. Be independent, rather than just trying to please, which is the easy way out. Relationships are so terribly important – that's what I'm still struggling with. And I'm very interested in religion. Religion gives you ideas, principles on which to base your life – honesty and so forth, being good to your neighbour. But I do find the Church of England very narrow with its doctrines and set services.'

We talked about death, and Jenny said, 'I think if you've been trying to do your best in your own life then I think you carry on – it's your soul, isn't it? The you, the eternal you inside you. I can't explain where that comes from. Your body comes from your parents, but the actual person, that goes on and you carry on learning the things you haven't learnt. I do feel that if I died tomorrow – when you go through the door or to the next plane – that I should come in contact with people that I've known, people who've died and gone before me. I'd be in touch with them, I'm sure. There I think you go on striving to become perfect, like the Creator Himself. I think that everybody is trying to do that. The Creator being God, Life Force, there's a lot of different names, but it's a great spirit that is beyond and around. There's a force for good, all good. Yes, I know evil is everywhere. You couldn't have any measure of good if you didn't have bad. The bad has to be there to strive for the good on this earth. In everyday life there's that saying, "These things are sent to try us". It's testing how far you can cope with them, whatever it is. When things go wrong, it's telling you to become better, to learn from them if you can.'

Jenny went on, 'I was always frightened of death. I've always been frightened ever since I was a child, by the fact that I wouldn't exist anymore, as a person. That's always frightened me. And it wasn't until I met the spiritualist and she pointed out the proven fact that there is another life, though albeit not in bodily form, and I felt very happy and this seemed to fill in the gap. Up till then I'd always thought of death as not very pleasant. Just not to exist – it all seems such a waste of time.

What are we here for if we're all to crumble up and that's it. So that all fits in with my belief that you're here to improve yourself in some way, to overcome certain weaknesses. The healer just said, well the depression's happened for a reason and you will overcome it eventually and you'll find the reason. Well, one does want to keep on improving, growing. I think part of my depression is stagnation. I want to do more but I haven't had the guts or push or determination to do it. My parents – I've always worried about their reaction. My husband is happy for me to do anything that makes me feel fulfilled. I think my biggest restriction is being so conscious of my parents' reaction. I think a lot of it's in the imagination. Possibly if I did something they'd react quite favourably. In the past, whatever we've done with our lives, they've tended to see the snags or prevent, and that's coloured my view, stopped me from doing things.'

Thus Jenny was able to take a step into the unknown and separate herself from her parents since at the same time she was creating another relationship which gave her more security than her parents could give her. The new relationship was not entirely new. It still had elements of the old, as in the metaphor of a pupil learning lessons set by a wise adult who was there to be emulated. So it seems that the words of the spiritualist and my words had felicitously complemented each other.

Sometimes the words that are needed come from inside us. Nick came to see me because he had lost his job through incompetence. He was incompetent because he was depressed. Nick was a very handsome, witty young man, and I found his company a delight, but he considered himself the most boring person in the world, a blight on any company. It was important, he said, to make a worthwhile contribution in a social group. Anyone who did not deserved to be excluded from the group. His childhood experiences had taught him that this was the way his parents judged people and he accepted this as an axiomatic truth which he applied to himself and others. The trouble was that he did not feel that he could make a proper contribution to the group. The social life of his family and friends centred on a pub where they would meet regularly on a Friday and Saturday night. Nick would spend a long time getting himself properly dressed for these occasions and he would become increasingly tense as he tried to prepare himself to have plenty of witty things to say to his friends. Once there, he felt himself to be grossly awkward and tongue-tied, and the misery set in. But he could neither avoid these social evenings nor devalue their implications. So he stayed depressed, until one day he arrived in my office, beaming with happiness. He said that on the previous Friday, when he was getting ready to go to the pub, he suddenly decided that, 'I was going to relax and try and be myself. I did this – I didn't try to crack any witties and get in with the group, and as I did this I started to enjoy it. Funnily enough, something did come to me that I really wanted to say, when I didn't try to. When I tried to say something, force myself, I'd say something that was alien – it didn't make sense. But at the weekend things started coming to me that I wanted to say and people were listening. It was Friday night and I went through the same things – the washing hair routine, all that jazz, and it came to me in a flash that I could stop if I wanted to. I was dreading going out, and I thought, why, if this makes me feel that bad, why should I worry about other people. I'll just go out and make sure I enjoy myself, and as soon as I did that I wasn't worried. I felt like a different person in a way. I was like a different person to myself. With my parents, I've always felt that if I wanted to say anything to offend my parents I shouldn't say it, and in the end you don't have anything to say. It was like a sudden enlightenment. We went to the same pub we normally go to on a Friday night, but it seemed like a different place to me, it seemed fresher, seemed to be more exciting, everything was great.' Such a discovery rendered me superfluous, and Nick no longer came to brighten my Monday mornings.

What Nick had discovered was something which has been known about for perhaps thousands of years and which has been described in many different ways. Socrates taught that the truth is within us for us to recollect. Ruysbroeck spoke of the 'unity we possess within us and yet above us, as the ground and preserver of our being and of our life'. Knowledge of such truth and unity gives a sense that, in the words of Julian of Norwich, 'all shall be well, and all shall be well, and all manner of things shall be well'. To find this, said Krishnamurti, 'You do not have to go anywhere. You are already there.' The effortlessness of

273

finding an inner truth and peace is contained in the Taoist concept of 'wu-wei', meaning not forcing, rolling with the punch, going with the grain, swimming with the current, stooping to conquer – the concept at the centre of the Zen arts and now the 'inner game' practised by those of us who want to win without trying. 'The Tao does nothing and yet nothing is left undone,' said Lao Tsu. For Robert Browning,

> Truth is within ourselves: it takes no rise
> From outward things, whate'er you may believe
> There is an inmost centre in us all
> Where truth abides in fullness, and around
> Wall upon wall, the grass flesh hems it in,
> This perfect, clear perception – which is truth.
>
> A baffling and perverting carnal mesh
> Binds it, and makes all error: and to know
> Rather consists of opening out a way
> Whence the imprisoned splendour may escape,
> Than in effecting entry for a light
> Supposed to be without.

The core of meaning shared by all these concepts of inner truth and security relates, too, to what Erik Erikson called 'basic trust', which is the essence of the belief that we are valuable because of what we *are* and not just because of what we *do*, that we do not have to justify our existence by good works. The child who fails to develop basic trust is then handicapped in his relationships with others and with himself until such time as he can have the experiences which repair and restore this basic trust. When I contemplate the evidence of the damage done to a person who has not had 'good enough' mothering to achieve satisfactory 'attachments' or 'bonding' in his early years, I sometimes wonder if I am foolish to believe that we each have available within us some inner truth or strength. Perhaps certain devastating events in childhood can destroy such a centre or prevent it from ever coming into being. Then I remind myself that this question is as vain and useless as the question of how many angels can stand on the point of a needle. If I act towards other people in the belief that they can find this inner strength, then I am not hindering and, indeed, I may even be helping them find it. But, if I act towards others as if they have no centre of truth and strength – if I treat them as lifelong schizophrenics, or irredeemable psychopaths, or incorrigible character disorders – then I am actively preventing them from summoning up sufficient trust in themselves to attempt the search for inner truth. And in any case, though I might have been brought up as a Presbyterian, I really do not like the doctrine of the elect. If there is a God, then surely He has given us all a chance of redemption?

Developmental studies can show a link between certain childhood experiences and the capacity to form relationships, but there are problems in applying a determinist model to the development of human relationships, since the essential emotion of a relationship is love in one or other of its many guises. We can be forced or we can force ourselves to go through the form of a relationship, but we know that we are only play-acting if we do not feel a measure of affection for the other person, and we cannot love on demand. As the recipient of love we want to feel that the love we receive is a gift freely given and not something coerced from the other person or come into being simply as the inevitable end-product of a chain of causes. Love has to do with freedom and choice. Construing a person as lovable and loving that person are really the same act.

Psychologists write very little about love, and have probably decided to leave it alone because it raises the dilemma of free will and determinism. So I sought out my friend Simon Phipps, the Bishop of Lincoln, to ask him about love and freedom, I also wanted to ask him about the unforgivable sin against the Holy Ghost, something which always seemed to me to detract from Jesus' message of love.

Simon began by talking about love and freedom. 'If you believe in God there cannot be anything outside God because the word God means everything that there is. I think that one of the things about the Christian belief in God, and I daresay other beliefs in God, is that His greatest gift to us is our freedom, or you could put it another way, He made us to love Him in response to His love, and love must be a free response. It can't be required, demanded, it must be a freely given thing. That way

275

you have to be free to do it. We are free to go against His will as well as to respond to it, hence the bad things and the good things. So I very much do believe in our responsibility, but there is a very fascinating, mysterious paradox about it, in that if it is so it means that I stand freely, as me, discrete, separate, free to make my own choices, but I can't be outside God. I sometimes think of this when praying. Here I am talking to God, as if He's somewhere else and I'm here, and yet you can't use the word God in a valid sense as if He's someone else, because He must be that in which we live and have our being. I think I find my way through that one by saying that although everything we are is in Him, nevertheless He has given us this gift, that part of our being in Him is to be able to be outside Him. It is a paradox, but I think it's a true one – in order to be able to be free and respond to that in which we are . . . I think that free choices can be very narrow – I mean, we are heavily conditioned. But I suppose growing up in the true sense enables our "usness" to grow into itself in some sort of independence. I would think that psychotherapy is enabling people to come to themselves in the midst of the things that have made them what they seem to be – by understanding their process of conditioning, so that they can – not exactly be free of it, but be free with it – make something of it instead of being made something by it. I think it's very easy to live as if something were the case. Say your parents have had a certain effect on you that makes you be whatever you are, and yet if you could see what had really happened, you could see that you could be free of that and be in fact what you really are. If you haven't got from the first one to the second one, you're living as if the first one was true, as if it is the case that what you've been conditioned to be is how you are . . . God in creating us must have created something that is good, but He's created us free in order that we may do the goodest thing, which is to love one another and Him, and that means that we are free, and because love is an alarming thing, and certainly faith is, we have the fundamental tendency to pull back in self-defence and self-interest, and that, I think, is what original sin is. There is a flaw in our nature which makes us erroneously pull back in self-defence instead of going forward in self-risk, towards self-realization. God's intention about us is obviously a good one, and our destiny is to discover that. I think the story of Jesus is about that which sets us free from ourselves to become ourselves. I would see His life and death and resurrection as being a message to us that He lived, not this self-interested life, but an open self-giving life, and, because that was so challenging to everybody, they killed Him for it. The resurrection was a public vindication of it all by God – God's way of saying to us that it is all right to live like that, however dangerous it looks. That is what the Church has claimed, and other people have tried it and found it to be true. In the end what Christianity says is a claim – you can't pin it down as historically true.'

I asked Simon what was meant by a sin against the Holy Ghost. He replied, 'I suppose it would mean absolutely basically turning your back consciously, deliberately on what you saw as what God stood for. There are lots of sins, lots of things which you might do which might be called sins, categories of ways in which we can do damaging things, but this sin against the Holy Ghost means not so much that you *do* something as you actually decide to *be* something which is totally over and against what you see God to be. I think the Holy Ghost, the Holy Spirit, is an attempt to put a name to the actual impinging upon our experience of God. Behind everything and within everything is this mystery which is personal, so that we can use personal categories about Him, but He is quite beyond our ken, infinite, and yet He impinges on our lives. It's God in action that's been called God's spirit. And if we say, yes, but I don't want anything of that, I'm just going to turn my back on that, that's something more fundamental, isn't it, than the more peccadillo things that go against it. It's a writing of God off completely.'

Simon's explanation of the sin against the Holy Ghost reminded me of one of the people in Robinson's *Living the Questions* – an elderly woman, trained in the scientific tradition, who said of her special experience (which could be called God impinging on her, or discovering her Ground of Being, or Atman, or her 'imprisoned splendour', or relying on her 'basic trust'), 'It was as if something said to me: "Don't ever allow yourself to question this". And I knew I mustn't; that to do that would be a great betrayal, the "sin against the Holy Spirit" for which there is no forgiveness. I had often wondered what that dreadful sin might be, and why it could not be forgiven. Now I saw: it would be this, because it would mean I had turned my back on the light and the truth. I should have made myself a hopeless case; I would have become a no-thing: there would have been nobody to forgive.'

There are many people who expect their particular set of beliefs (religious or non-religious) to provide them with absolute certainty. When I asked Simon about certainty and doubt he said, 'This is what happens to religious people, which is very different from people with faith. Faith means that you trust that God is there and is to be trusted, even though He's the invisible God. I believe that He's there and to be trusted, and I don't like that at all sometimes. Sometimes it seems to me that He's suggesting that what I have to trust Him about is very alarming. Therefore an awful lot of people who begin to get this uncomfortable glimpse of God opt for religion, opt for a sort of rules and regulations, institutional, all tied up, Sunday affair which absolves you of seeing God standing in life as it is, really is, and getting on with the strenuous business of trying to see what way it is you ought to go. I think religious people are particularly prone to this. A glimpse of God can be so difficult. I think that doubt is a necessary thing. I don't see how we can live without doubt. But I think it can be a good thing if it means that you are genuinely wrestling with the mystery, with the real truth which must be beyond us. For the word of God to mean anything it must mean something that infinitely transcends us, however close and caring of us it also is. Therefore there must be an element of doubt in that. I think that people who aren't genuinely, strenuously, wrestling with the mystery as such, as mystery, are sort of short-circuiting reality and building a God which is too small. There are lots of people who are quite content with a small, manageable God – much easier than an infinite one who involves us in – well, as the Psalmist says, we're fearfully and wonderfully made – both, fearful and wonderful. So I think I would want to encourage people when they find themselves in doubt, which I don't think is so much a matter of saying "I wonder if that's really true", though it can mean that, as saying "I can't see this clearly". But then faith means that's all right, because God is there and to be trusted, and so we want to keep on in the dark and find a way. There is a way and He'll show it to us.'

When we were small we were told that if we behaved in certain ways (were good) then things would go well for us. But as we got older we found that life was not that simple. Suffering has a lot to do with wanting things to remain the same. Accepting change without guarantees of results is a fearful enterprise; doubting and yet trusting those aspects of our experience that must forever lie beyond our understanding makes for dangerous living. It is no wonder that when the guns come to allow us 'the breakthrough to the warm, wide plain' some of us prefer to remain 'hemmed in a close cirque of one's own creating'.

Yet some people do manage to break out of the cirque. After he had returned to work, Peter told me how he no longer set himself such impossibly high standards. 'If I can just succeed in leaving a sort of pleasant feeling around as far as my family and the people I know closely are concerned, maybe for me this is the most I can do. I am back to functioning much more as I did some years ago – more placidly – a lot more of my humour has come back – a lot more of the fun. And what you call my mythology – I'm able to laugh at it, I'm able to diminish its importance. It's still there, but I'm able to take far less notice of it now. It doesn't have the importance, it doesn't have the threat. I'm openly able to recognize that it's a bit silly, it looks smaller and less real and more ephemeral. This is a change in the basics. The house is not so haunted. There's glass in the windows. When we first talked about structure – I can't remember whether we talked about it or whether it's just what happened in my mind – but I do remember I had an image of a house, and at the time, I remember it very clearly, almost too clearly for comfort, the house was sort of stone. It was big, it was forbidding, it was greenish, it was swathed in mist, the floors were all uneven, the stairs didn't exist, or if they did you couldn't find them, there was no glass in the windows, it was bloody cold. I had quite a clear physical picture and this structure remains, again quite clearly, but now it's got glass in the windows, it's got stairs, it's much smaller than it seemed, it's been polished up and painted, but the basic structure, in picture terms, is there still, but vastly altered both in appearance and in effect on me.'

Tony came to say farewell. Any more encounters between us, he said, would be as friends and not as client and therapist. He told me, 'I hadn't realized how much deception there was in myself, and I was worried about self-deception. So in a sense being worried about self-deception means that there was no self-deception – and that's not the case.'

'People usually go on and on about the virtue they have the most difficulty with,' I said.

'What did I go on and on about?'

'Generosity.'

'Only because you attacked me about it – oh, well, obviously, yes.' He beamed at me. 'Do you know something, Dorothy, everyone that I love loves me. Of course the old me keeps coming back to challenge, but it doesn't get very far because it's absurd now.'

I asked him how he saw God now.

'I think, I tend to think – I don't think too much – the more I look at God the more I find Him in human beings. I would rather let notions come and go than fall back on a set formula. In times past, when I have really got uptight, I've belted this God. My friend Harry said that God's basic nature is quite neutral. He neither loves you nor hates you but just is. The rain doesn't care whether it hits you or not. To a certain extent God is irrelevant. The notion of a God is quite irrelevant. Enlightenment – that sort of thing would appear to be God – except that I don't want to stick a label on it. God is a label and I really don't like labels. They're universally restricting, aren't they? So one thing, if you stick a label on Him you immediately diminish Him. If there is a God I'd prefer not to diminish Him by sticking a label on Him, even by calling Him God. That seems to me to narrow it down to the bit of universe you can see, and that is insane. The answer is that I don't think very much about God. When I'm happy I don't need to think about Him.'

9

Conclusions

Freedom and captivity coexist. We cannot escape from our structures; we are condemned to structuring our worlds since this is the form of life in which we exist. But although we are imprisoned, we are free to choose what form our prison should take. Our construct systems, like all systems, even the universe, have boundaries, and within these boundaries the system is, in Shotter's terms, coercive, reflexive and incorrigible. But we have a great deal of freedom to choose what we put in that system – what we choose to perceive and how we evaluate what we perceive. We can choose to make our system completely rigid and impenetrable or we can choose to make it flexible and permeable. We can choose to let nothing into our system which is not strictly controlled and defined or we can build into our system some principle of openness to change, some stochastic process which allows us to exist in a form of creative becoming instead of unalterable being. We can choose, too, a system which aims to maximize content or a system which aims to maximize suffering.

Birth and death limit our freedom to choose. We have no choice about when and where we awake into self-consciousness (although we can later choose to construe this awakening as the outcome of our karma or of God's will) and while we can choose to kill ourselves instead of letting death come in its own time, we cannot choose to live forever. The saying that nothing is certain except death and taxes recognizes that society makes demands on us which are hard to avoid or to see as construable in a wide variety of ways. But taxes we can avoid, even if it means going to prison or living on a desert island. Death we cannot avoid.

If we fear death then we have condemned ourselves to a life of misery. We have to find some way of living with death. There is no way of avoiding the knowledge of death. Maurer, in his study of the maturation of concepts of death, advised, 'tell the child the truth for he knows it in his bones anyway. Fortuitous acquisition of the information be what it may, the demand to know about death is as universal as the demand for information about origins. So earnest has been the search, so sharply attuned the senses to pick up stray clues and so deep the premonition that when the child is finally told, he recognises rather than learns.' The knowledge which the child recognizes Maurer sees as being begun to be acquired soon after birth, as the baby experiences the transition from sleep to waking, from non-being to being. The fascination which death exerts upon us is seen in the alternate terror and delight which the baby shows in the game of Peek-a-Boo, which, in Old English, means 'alive or dead'.

Not living in fear of death means coming to terms with it, accepting it however hard and unacceptable it may seem at first. We need to be able to die our own death, what Erik Erikson called 'die actively'. As Bernard said, 'Death is part of my life, after all, it does belong to me, as much as my body does, and I want to experience it fully, for what it is, not turn my face away because it looks ugly at a distance. Who knows what it will be like when it comes? No one does. No one. And I want it to be mine, whatever it's like.'

To die our own death we should, in D. H. Lawrence's words, 'build our ship of death':

> We are dying, we are dying, so all we can do
> is now to be willing to die, and to build the ship
> of death to carry the soul on the longest journey.
>
> A little ship, with oars and food
> and little dishes, and all accoutrements
> fitting and ready for the departing soul.
>
> Now launch the ship, now as the body dies
> and life departs, launch out, the fragile soul
> in the fragile ship of courage, the ark of faith
> with its store of food and little cooking pans
> and change of clothes
> upon the flood's black waste
> upon the waters of the end
> upon the sea of death, where still we sail
> darkly, for we cannot steer, and have no port.

*   *   *   *

Oh build your ship of death. Oh build it!
for you will need it.
For the voyage of oblivion awaits you.

How do we build our ship of death? No funeral barque or chariot or urn or coffin will make the journey. Our ship of death is made of the continuity we create in the face of death, the continuity which denies that death is the end and which carries us forward and over into another space which we may choose to call heaven or nirvana or re-birth or nature. We each have to build our ship, establish our continuity, and to do this we have to develop a set of beliefs which can be called metaphysical or religious. Such beliefs not only define our death, they define our life and the world we live in. 'The sacred,' wrote Mircea Eliade, 'reveals reality and at the same time makes orientation possible; hence it *founds the world* in the sense that it fixes the limits and establishes the order of the world.'

For the atheistic scientist perceptible reality is sacred. It establishes the order of the world and anything that is claimed to lie beyond it is profane. Unfortunately, many workers in the mental health field who regard themselves as atheistic (or at least agnostic) scientists behave towards people with religious beliefs much in the way that nineteenth century Europeans regarded the natives of the colonial empires as ignorant children and imbeciles. Such a view engendered the mistrust and misunderstanding which is at the root of much of the conflicts of this century. Taking pride in our atheism and scientific objectivity, we may forget that we *all* have metaphysical beliefs and that these metaphysical beliefs are *true*, not for one another but for oneself. If we forget this, we render ourselves unable to understand the other person. When I wrote, somewhat flippantly, to Gerald Priestland, the BBC Religious Affairs correspondent, about choosing one's religious beliefs, he replied in no uncertain terms, 'The experience of damnation can be as compelling as the experience of salvation. You must figure that out for yourself, but unless you understand it your work among depressives is in vain.'

In my world I had learned to see most problems as humanly made and therefore capable of a human solution. It came as a shock for me to realize that I was trying to help people for whom an evil God or the inevitable force of tragedy was as real as the chairs we sat in or the coffee that we drank. I was like those scholars of comparative religions described by Mircea Eliade who 'defend themselves against the messages with which their documents are filled. The caution is understandable. One does not live with impunity in intimacy with "foreign" religious forms, which are sometimes extravagant and often terrible. But many (scholars) end by no longer taking seriously the spiritual words they study; they fall back on their personal religious faith, or they take refuge in a materialism or behaviorism impervious to every religious shock.' I have had to accept the advice given by Robert Towler to sociologists who wish to study 'homo religiosus':

The sociological study of religion . . . forces a scholar to confront a view of the world which is foreign to him; it brings him into face-to-face contact with that which is entirely alien. In itself this is both dangerous and potentially rewarding, for it is a personal as well as an intellectual exercise . . . The sociologist's task, difficult and uncomfortable though it may be, is to take seriously the beliefs of those whom he studies and to seek to enter into the mentality which they bring to their ritual and to their everyday lives, even if in doing so he runs the risk of 'going native'. The task is comparatively easy for the field anthropologist studying peoples in far-off places but it is no less important for the sociologist of religion who studies less inaccessible peoples. Only thus will he be able to grasp the full significance of elements which constitute a radically alien world of meaning; only thus will a foreign symbolism retain its essential life while under study, and not be transformed into a sterile and inert specimen. Avowed methodological atheism is a fail-safe device which protects the sceptical researcher from taking the beliefs of others too seriously, and which protects also the religiously or ideologically committed researcher from allowing his beliefs from polluting his research . . . (but) it precludes the possibility of a serious confrontation with an alien set of beliefs, whereas that is in fact the first prerequisite of a worthwhile sociology of religion.

Labelling the possession of a religious belief as evidence of inadequacy or neurosis does nothing to advance one's understanding of another person and indeed actively prevents it. While it does seem that our early experiences have a great deal to do with the form our metaphysical beliefs take – whether we see God as benevolent or dangerous, or the universe as there for the understanding or dark with the mysterious forces of good and evil – it does not mean that our mature perception of life is necessarily inhibited by childish metaphors and images. The loving relationship of parents with a small child has a numinous quality which the fortunate child can carry with him and project upon his world in a way which can only enhance his life. Whether he calls his experience love of God or of humanity or of nature does not matter.

Religious belief has shown itself to be most resistant to the political propaganda of the various Communist regimes, and in non-Communist countries this fact is often taken as evidence not only of the sterling character and strength of mind of the believers, be they Christian or Moslem, but also of the certainty that one day the Communist regime will disappear. National surveys of religious belief in Britain and America show that a large percentage of the population report possessing some religious faith. Where the survey contains questions to do with mental health or general happiness it is found that believers, on the whole, do not regard themselves as especially neurotic or unhappy.

There is currently in the United States a considerable religious revival. David Henshaw, reporting for the BBC in 1980, said that:

Something is stirring in America – something that may well provide a mirror image to the momentous revival of Islam in the Middle East. In this year of the presidential elections, all three major candidates claim to be 'born again' Christians, and all of them expect that label to be a vote-winner. Electronic evangelism is on the march: America now has 1,300 radio stations devoted to religious broadcasting and 36 TV stations. One new Christian radio station opens every week, a TV station every month. Opinion polls show that while attendances at the conventional 'mainline' churches of America continue their slow decline, the evangelicals are gaining by leaps and bounds: one-third of all Americans now claim to be 'born again' Christians. Among their ranks are to be found a remarkable, if ill-assorted, list of the famous: astronauts, sportsmen, politicians (including several disgraced Nixon henchmen), and a welter of rock stars, including disco queen Donna Summer and, more significantly, Bob Dylan. Fifteen years ago, Dylan mocked the prime-time evangelists who sold 'flesh-coloured Christs that glow in the dark'; now he's joined them.

Eight years after this was written a television evangelist became a presidential candidate.

Evangelical Christianity offers hope and salvation to those in despair. Its message is in complete contrast to the attitudes expressed by Steven Weinberg, Higgins Professor of Physics at Harvard, in his book *The First Three Minutes*, where he describes current theory about the origins and the expansion and possible contraction of the universe. Whether the universe is expanding to the point of disintegration or whether it expands and contracts an infinite number of times – current theory cannot decide between these alternatives – our Earth would not survive the extremes. Weinberg concludes his book by saying:

> However all these problems may be resolved, and whichever cosmological model proves correct, there is not much comfort in any of this. It is almost irresistible for humans to believe that we have some special relation to the universe, that human life is not a more-or-less farcical outcome of a chain of accidents reaching back to the first three minutes, but that we were somehow built in from the beginning. As I write this I happen to be in an airplane at 30,000 feet, flying over Wyoming en route home from San Francisco to Boston. Below, the earth looks very soft and comfortable – fluffy clouds here and there, snow turning pink as the sun sets, roads stretching straight

across the country from one town to another. It is very hard to realise that all this is just a tiny part of an overwhelmingly hostile universe. It is harder to realise that this present condition has evolved from an unspeakably unfamiliar early condition, and faces a future extinction of endless cold or intolerable heat. The more the universe seems comprehensible, the more it also seems pointless. But if there is no solace in the fruits of our research, there is at least some consolation in the research itself. Men and women are not content to comfort themselves with tales of gods and giants, or to confine their thoughts to the daily affairs of life; they also build telescopes and satellites and accelerators, and sit at desks for endless hours working out the meaning of the data they gather. The effort to understand the universe is one of the very few things that lifts human life a little above the level of farce, and gives it some of the grace of tragedy.

There was a time, earlier this century, when it was possible to believe that a combination of scientific knowledge and general goodwill and commonsense would ensure a peaceful and happy life, if not for us, at least for our children. Now it is no longer possible to be certain of a continuing human life on this planet, much less a happy one. It is not surprising that many people, feeling betrayed and fearful, turn to a belief that takes them beyond the confines of this immediate reality. It was not until he was no longer angry and frightened that Tony could say, 'I don't think very much about God. When I'm happy I don't need to think about Him.'

To establish our continuity in the face of death we have to step outside the space of immediate reality. There is more in this than just deciding to pray to God or to be saved at a revivalist meeting. It is that one in some way *knows* of the mystery beyond the immediately perceptible world, whether we call this knowledge of the sub-atomic world or of nature or of a transcendent God. For some of us such knowledge is felt simply in the certainty of belief; for others it resides also in the memory of a strange and wonderful experience. It is difficult to determine just how many people have had such experiences, since those who do are usually reluctant to talk about them. Hay found that more than two-thirds of the people who reported having such experiences also said that this was the first time they had told anyone about them. The reasons they gave for this were that they feared they would be ridiculed or declared mad. Not even the clergy were credited with understanding.

However, in no way did Hay's 'experiencers' accept that they were stupid or crazy. Rather, they showed contempt for 'non-experiencers'. Hay asked everyone what sort of person would not have had these experiences and was surprised by the vehemence of the answers given by the 'experiencers', whose chosen terms to describe the 'non-experiencers' Hay listed as 'apathetic, bitter, conformists, cowards, dull, emotionless, hard, ignorant, insecure, insensitive, know-alls, lacking capacity, liars, materialists, mean, miserable, morally lax, narrow-minded, over-controlled, sceptics, self-centred, sneerers, superficial, too busy, unaware, unimaginative, unintelligent, unpleasant, and weak.'

Hay's discovery of the attitude of 'experiencers' to 'non-experiencers' is of particular relevance in the mental health services where so many patients report that they 'cannot talk to' the staff who are there to help them. It seems that it is not simply that the patient fears being hurt by being rejected by the member of staff who sees his reporting of religious experience or simply of his faith as evidence of neurosis or psychosis. It is also that the patient rejects the member of staff for his lack of experience or belief. Several of my clients who felt that they knew me well enough to criticize me have told me that, knowing that I did not share their faith, they would not discuss their religious beliefs with me in case I used my power as a therapist to eradicate the beliefs which to them were the source and reason for their being. They did not know that firmly held metaphysical beliefs are as impervious to magic as they are to reason, but they did know how cruel and insensitive a non-believer could be.

But even non-experiencers and non-believers know, though they may not admit it, that there is some kind of wonderful and fearful reality beyond our immediate perception; and they know, too, that to experience our world as 'value free' is an intellectual exercise. Our world comes to us in the guise of good and bad. (Of course, for some of us 'value free' perceptions are classed as good, and for others of us 'value free' perceptions are classed as bad.) This transcendent reality and the 'goodness' and 'badness' can be conceptualized in an infinite number of ways, and each way brings forth a different form of action. Any theory which sets out to explain why human beings behave as they do must, to be adequate, take account of this aspect of human experience which can be called our metaphysical beliefs.

There is no set of metaphysical beliefs which does not contain problems and paradoxes. One of the greatest problems is that of the ease of *knowing* and the difficulty of *saying*. William James considered that the outstanding characteristic of religious experience was its 'ineffability'. Neither the rolling sonorities of churchmen, nor the stumbling 'y'knows' of the simple faithful, nor the pulpit-banging statements of the revivalists can convey the meaning of the experience. Only occasionally does a poet capture and convey it, and then not to all his readers. What words are available for us to use in describing our metaphysical beliefs are so loaded with religious, philosophical, and psychological connotations that we cannot use them without running the risk of being misunderstood. The way in which Indo-European languages convert so much of experience into nouns rather than verbs, thus producing 'labels' which turn living experience into stone, gives to any statement of belief a fixity and solidity which the belief as experienced does not have. Rather than be misunderstood we remain silent. How much better it would be if we, as listeners, could give to statements about such fearfully wonderful experience the same acceptance and concern that we give to statements, equally unprovable, like 'I have a pain in my stomach'.

The paradoxes of a particular belief are often more noticeable to the non-believer than to the believer. When I was taking a seminar on depression with twenty psychologists, all working as psychotherapists and counsellors, I asked how many of them believed in a life after death. Only two did; the rest believed that their identity ended in death. Later I asked them whether they would prefer, when dead, to be buried or cremated. A lively discussion followed, with each person giving vivid accounts of how he wished to see his body disposed of. I then pointed out the discrepancy in the belief that their identity ended in death and their way of imagining their death and funeral as if they would be there to see it and, if it were carried out in accordance with their wishes, even enjoy it. This did not appear to be an argument which threatened their belief that life ended in death. They were simply amused at the paradox. Yet to one who did believe in a life after death this paradox would be seen as evidence against the belief of life ending in death.

The discrepancy between religious precept and practice, though of great concern to some churchmen, is often more of a problem and a paradox for non-believers than believers. Terrible crimes are committed in the name of Christ who has been claimed as supporting all kinds of nefarious practices and beliefs. To the believer events like these are deplorable but irrelevant to belief. The non-believer may agree with Stevie Smith that we should

> learn to teach children
> To be good without enchantment, without the help
> Of beautiful painted fairy stories pretending to be true,

but for the believer the protective figure of Jesus exists within the harsh reality of life.

The essence of God in Christian belief is that He is personal. It may be comforting to think of God as someone who takes an interest in us, like a kindly father, but once we make our God personal He becomes capricious and cruel, and even more so if He is seen as infinite. God, it seems, cannot be contained within the restraints of logic. John Mackie described the problem in its simplest form thus: 'God is omnipotent, God is wholly good, and yet evil exists. There seems to be some contradiction between these three propositions, so that if any two of them were true the third would be false. But at the same time all three are essential parts of most theological positions: the theologian, it seems, at once *must* adhere and *cannot consistently* adhere to all three.' Luther had given his solution to this problem in his *De Servo Arbitrio*. 'This is the acme of faith, to believe that God who saves so few and condemns so many, is merciful; that He is just who, at his own pleasure, has made us necessarily doomed to damnation, so that He seems to delight in the torture of the wretched and to be more deserving of hate than of love. If by any effort of mine I could conceive how God, who shows so much anger and harshness, could be merciful and just, there would be no need of faith.'

People who lack such faith may sneer at those who choose to live with such a paradox, but those whose faith lies in the determinist model of science still, paradoxically, experience themselves as making choices and acting freely. 'Free will' as a motive force and the 'volition' which old-fashioned psychiatric textbooks described schizophrenics as lacking may not feature in current scientific psychology, but 'decision-making' does. And all of us, religious or not, have to live with the paradox that as much as we wish to merge ourselves with others, with nature or with God, we just as much wish to stand alone and unique.

Since it is the nature of human thought that when we know one thing we necessarily know its opposite, we cannot help but find that life presents us with paradoxes. Our metaphysical beliefs, whatever they may be, are an attempt to encompass these paradoxes and perhaps resolve them to our benefit. But no system of belief offers complete comfort. Oblivion can be an insult, Judgement Day an injustice, and re-birth boredom.

Since we want security we may do all we can to be unaware of the uncomfortable parts of the paradoxes of our beliefs. We might try to remain as children who see the world divided into goodies and baddies, with justice, in the end, triumphant. (Part of the fascination with the prospect of a Third World War is the remembrance of the certainties of the Second World War, when you knew who your enemies were and why you were fighting. Life has never been so clear-cut since.) On the other hand, facing up to the harshest of life's reality can strengthen and secure a faith. Georgi Vins, the Soviet Baptist leader said on his expulsion from the Soviet Union, 'My experiences in concentration camps over the past five years have brought me closer still to my God. Christ has become closer and dearer . . . I have no doubts. For me, Jesus Christ is a real person, as real as you and I talking together here. I have just such a constant spiritual communication with Jesus Christ. That is how it was in the most difficult years and I think that is how it will continue to be in my new circumstances.' If Christ is not available, some other figure can be found to give a sense of security and comfort – a political leader or a pop star like Elvis Presley.

If unquestioning faith in a religion or a cause eludes us we may try to find security by the use of our intellect. Over recent years there has been a great upsurge of interest in the phenomenon of death. Colleges run courses on death and dying, assisted by journals like *Death Education*, while seminars and workshops on counselling the bereaved and the dying are commonplace. Helpful though these activities undoubtedly are, no amount of study and discussion will abolish or control the real immediacy of one's own death when it comes. Any woman who has carefully prepared for her baby's birth with all the proper exercises and breathing routines will later report how in the event the process of birth took control and showed itself to have far greater powers than those of the diligent student. Death must be the same.

We can attempt to find our security by insisting that our construction of our world is the only correct one and that everyone else must agree with us. Conflicts between people are always over who should have the right to decide on the construct to be used – whether it is a mother telling her child that he is not hungry but tired and must go to bed, or the psychiatrist telling the patient who claims that he is exhausted and fed-up that he is suffering from the illness of depression, or the politician who says that unpopular government measures are for the people's own good. If we try to coerce others by domestic or political tyranny to accept our constructions, we cause suffering, for it is painful trying to live with constructions which are not our own. Cruelty is at its greatest when we try to impose our metaphysical beliefs on others, as religious persecution down the ages and the concentration camps of the totalitarian regimes have shown. If we fail to coerce or persuade others to accept our constructions, we may indulge in bitterness and envy and so increase our own suffering.

When we fail to convince others of our point of view we run the risk of discovering just how many different points of view are possible. We can quickly retreat into the belief that those who disagree with us are mad or bad, for to do otherwise is to risk falling into what Douglas Adams called the worst possible fate in the universe – the Total Perspective Vortex. He observed that as the universe is such a large place, most people move to somewhere smaller of their own devising.

For instance, in one corner of the Eastern Galactic Arm lies the large forest planet Oglaroon, the entire 'intelligent' population of which lives permanently in one fairly small and crowded nut tree. In which tree they are born, live, fall in love, carve tiny speculative articles in the bark on the meaning of life, the futility of death and the importance of birth control, fight a few extremely minor wars, and eventually die strapped to the underside of some of the less accessible outer branches.

In fact the only Oglaroon who ever leave their tree are those who are hurled out of it for the heinous crime of wondering whether any of the other trees might be capable of supporting life at all, or indeed whether the other trees are anything but illusions brought on by eating too many Oglanuts.

Exotic though this behaviour may seem, there is no life in the galaxy which is not in some way guilty of the same thing, which is why the Total Perspective Vortex is as horrifying as it is.

For when you are put into the Vortex you are given just one momentary glimpse of the entire unimaginable infinity of creation, and somewhere in it a tiny little marker, a microscopic dot, which says, 'You are here'.

Trin Tragula, who invented the Total Perspective Vortex, 'realized that he had proved conclusively that if life is going to exist in a Universe of this size, then the one thing it cannot afford to have is a sense of proportion'.

(Awesome though the Total Perspective Vortex may be, I often wish I had such a machine in my office so I could pop my rigid, unchanging clients into it, just for a second, and let them discover that their world does not have to be what they have made it and that other people have valid points of view.)

The 'unimaginable infinity of creation' appears to us as chaos, and this we find terrifying. Fearing chaos, we do not want to test out our beliefs or to doubt, and in doing so we may blind ourselves to the necessity of uncertainty. Uncertainty is present in our physical world, as physicists have been telling us for many years. Nor can such uncertainty be contained within the strictures of mathematics. Morris Kline, in his book *The Loss of Certainty* writes, 'the attempt to establish a universally accept-able, logically sound body of mathematics has failed . . . Any formal, logical account is pseudo-mathematics, a fiction, even a legend.' From cybernetics we learn that no system can produce anything new unless that system contains some source of the random. To survive, we have to be creative, even if it is only in devising new ways of getting to work when petrol prices increase, and so it seems that we must allow in our construct system some source of the random. Of course, creative systems are divergent, and so can lead to all sorts of unknowns. Hitching a ride to work is full of possibilities!

The random element in our construct system can be the decision to let things take their course, to see what turns up. It can also be the recognition of the mystery, the unknown, and the decision to open oneself to the possibility of contact with it. Contact, not control. Control of the mystery is magic, the attempt to bring the mystery within the narrow confines of our imagination. Magic tries to determine the outcome (and praying to God for gifts in return for good behaviour is a form of magic); mystery inspires the wonder and terror of the unknown and the unknowable.

Contact with the mystery is not just some great and rare experience. It is present when we feel ourselves most alive, when we are suffused with wonder, curiosity, surprise, or laughter. When we are most alive we are hopeful, and hope is only possible when there is uncertainty. To be certain is to be hopeless.

For some people the realization that we live within our own constructed world makes all too clear the essential loneliness of every human being. But accepting this aloneness makes it possible to overcome the terrible loneliness of the person who, by making himself the absolute centre of his world, relates everything he perceives to himself and denies the validity of any other person's point of view. Such an attitude always leaves the person feeling lonely and uncared for, since most people are busy inside their own worlds and nature does not care whether we live or die. It is only when we start to look at people and things as they are in themselves, without asking how these objects can enhance our personal vanity, that we start to realize how much there is to be experienced in such an infinite variety that we cannot ever be lonely or bored.

It takes courage to accept and to exist in the knowledge that we live in a world which we have made. It means accepting not only uncertainty but also responsibility. It means accepting what Kierkegaard called 'the anguish of Abraham'. Abraham obeyed the voice of the angel who bade him sacrifice his son Isaac. But even in the act of such obedience, it was Abraham who made the decision to construe the voice he heard as that of an angel from God, and not as a tempting devil or as a febrile hallucination. Abraham was responsible for the act of sacrificing his son – and for saving him as well.

It takes courage to live with uncertainty and responsibility, but the alternatives are hardly attractive. If we insist that our construction of reality is the true and only one, we condemn ourselves to suffering. If we try to force other people to accept our one and only construction of reality, then we condemn both them and us to suffering. If we accept that our constructions are structures and not reality itself, and that each person has his own construction of reality, then we have to live with uncertainty. But we can choose to define that uncertainty as either prison or freedom. I prefer freedom.

REFERENCES

Adams, D. (1979). *The Hitch-Hiker's Guide to the Galaxy*, Pan, London.

Adams, D. (1980). *The Restaurant at the End of the Universe*, Pan, London.

Aldrin, 'Buzz' (1980). 'His long journey from the moon down to Earth', *The Listener*, 6th March.

Allport, G. (1951). *The Individual and His Religion*, Constable, London.

Anthony, S. (1973). *The Discovery of Death in Childhood and After*, Penguin, Harmondsworth.

Argyle, M., and Beit-Hallahmi, B. (1975). *The Social Psychology of Religion*, Routledge, London.

Aries, P. (1962). *Centuries of Childhood*, Jonathan Cape, London.

Aries, P. (1976). *Western Attitudes to Death from the Middle Ages to the Present*, Marion Boyars, London.

Bakan, D. (1971). *Disease, Pain and Suffering*, Beacon Press, Boston.

Barrett, W. (1972). *Irrational Man*, Heinemann, London.

Bateson, G. (1979). *Mind and Nature*, Wildwood, London.

Beauvoir, S. de (1959). *Memoirs of a Dutiful Daughter* (trans. James Kirkup), André Deutsch, London.

Beauvoir, S. de (1966). *A Very Easy Death*, André Deutsch, London.

Beauvoir, S. de (1972). *Old Age*, André Deutsch, London.

Beck, A. (1980). *Cognitive Therapy of Depression*, Wiley, New York and Chichester.

Becker, E. (1973). *The Denial of Death*, The Free Press, Glencoe.

Bellow, S. (1972). *Hertzog*, Weidenfeld and Nicolson, London.

Bellow, S. (1977). *Dangling Man*, Weidenfeld and Nicolson, London.

Benn, A. (1980). 'My Mother', *The Guardian*, 22nd April.

Berlin, I. (1976). *Vico and Herder*, Hogarth, London.

Brown, G., and Harris, T. (1978). *Social Origins of Depression: A Study of Psychiatric Disorder in Women*, Tavistock, London.

Brown, L. B. (1962). 'A study of religious belief', *British Journal of Psychology*, 53, 259–272.

Camus, A. (1975). *The Fall*, Penguin, Harmondsworth.

Camus, A. (1976). *The Myth of Sisyphus*, Penguin, Harmondsworth.

Carpenter, E. (1976). *Oh, What a Blow the Phantom Gave Me*, Paladin, London.

Carse, J. P. (1980). *Death and Existence*, Wiley, New York.

Cassirer, E. (1945). *Essay on Man*, Yale University Press, New Haven.

Cassirer, E. (1946). *The Myth of the State*, Yale University Press, New Haven.

Cassirer, E. (1953a). *The Philosophy of Symbolic Forms*, Yale University Press, New Haven.

Cassirer, E. (1953b). *Language and Myth* (trans. Suzanne K. Langer), Dover Publications, New York.

Cavafy, C. P. (1966). *Expecting the Barbarians*, in *Complete Poems*, Hogarth, London.

Choron, J. (1978). *Death and Western Thought*, Collier Books, New York.

Conquest, R. (1979). *1944 and after*, in *Forays*, Chatto and Windus, London.

Danto, A. C. (1976). *Mysticism and Morality*, Penguin, Harmondsworth.

Davy, J. (1979). 'Life after life', *The Observer*, **8**, 15th April.

Dods, M. (trans.) (1871). *The City of God* by St Augustine, T. and T. Clark, Edinburgh.

Douglas, M. (1974). *Natural Symbols*, Penguin, Harmondsworth.

Eliade, M. (1959). *The Sacred and the Profane*, Harcourt Brace Jovanovich, New York.

Eliade, M. (1969). *The Quest: History and Meaning in Religion*, University of Chicago Press, Chicago and London.

Eliot, G. (1967). *Middlemarch*, Oxford University Press, Oxford.

Erikson, E. (1964). *Insight and Responsibility*, W. W. Norton, New York.

Eyre, R. (1979). *On the Long Search*, Collins, London.

Fanthorpe, U. A. (1980). *Inside*, Peterloo Poets, Cornwall.

Feinstein, E. (1979). 'Melancholia', *The Listener*, 1st February.

French, P. (1978). *The Listener*, 21st November.

Freud, S. (1907). *Obsessional Actions and Religious Practices* (trans. J. Strachey), Collected Works, Vol. 9, Hogarth, London.

Freud, S. (1913). *Totem and Taboo*, Hogarth, London.

Freud, S. (1927). *The Future of an Illusion* (trans. W. D. Robinson-Scott), Hogarth, London.

Freud, S. (1953). *Thoughts for the Time on War and Death* (Ed. James Strachey), Standard Works, Vol. xiv, p. 289, Hogarth, London.

Fromm, E. (1978). *The Anatomy of Human Destructiveness*, Penguin, Harmondsworth.

Gillott, J. (1976). 'Depression', *Cosmopolitan*, May.

Gorer, G. (1965). *Death, Grief and Mourning in Contemporary Britain*, The Cresset Press, London.

Gordon, M. (1978). *Final Payments*, Hamish Hamilton, London.

Graham, B. (1980). Talking on '*Jaywalking*', Independent Television, London, 18th May.

Greene, G. (1974). *The End of the Affair*, Heinemann, London.

Guardian, The (1980). 'Mayors refuse to be intimidated', and 'West Bank attack makes new martyrs', 4th June.

Happold, F. C. (1977). *Mysticism*, Penguin, Harmondsworth.

Hardy, A. (1977). In *The Original Vision* (Ed. E. Robinson), The Religious Experience Research Unit, Manchester College, Oxford.

Hardy, A. (1979). *The Spiritual Nature of Man*, Oxford University Press, Oxford.

Hay, D. (1981). *Exploring Inner Space. Scientists and Religious Experience*, Penguin, Harmondsworth.

Heisenberg, W. (1971). *Physics and Philosophy*, George Allen & Unwin, London.

Henshaw, D. (1980). 'Prime-time evangelism: selling Christ across the airwaves', *The Listener*, 25th September.

Hesse, H. (1966). In *C. G. Jung and Herman Hesse* (Ed. Miguel Serrano).

Howarth, C. I. (1980). In *Models of Man* (Eds A. J. Chapman and D. M. Jones), British Psychological Society, Leicester.

Humboldt, W. von (1953). In Ernst Cassirer's *The Philosophy of Symbolic Forms*, Yale University Press, New Haven.

Jahoda, M. (1980). In *Models of Man* (Eds. A. J. Chapman and D. M. Jones), British Psychological Society, Leicester.

James, C. (1980). *Unreliable Memoirs*, Jonathan Cape, London.

James, H. (1972). *What Maisie Knew*, Bodley Head, London.

James, W. (1897). *The Will to Believe*, Longmans, London.

James, W. (1977). *The Varieties of Religious Experience*, Collins, London.

Jhabvala, R. P. (1971). *An Experience of India*, John Murray, London.

Jones, E. (1974). 'The psychology of religion', in *Psycho-Myth, Psycho-History*, Vol. 1, Hillstone, London.

Jung, C. G. (1960).*The Soul and Death* (trans. R. F. C. Hull), Collected Works, Vol. 8, Routledge, London.

Jung, C. G. (1971). *Memories, Dreams, Reflections*, Collins, London.

Jung, C. G. (1978). Quoted in Laurens Van der Post's *Jung and the Story of Our Time*, Penguin, Harmondsworth.

Keegan, J. (1976). *The Face of Battle*, p. 24, Jonathan Cape, London.

Kennaway, J. (1969). *The Cost of Living Like This*, Longmans, London.

Kline, M. (1980). *The Loss of Certainty*, Oxford University Press, Oxford.

Koestenbaum, P. (1978). *The New Image of the Person*, Greenwood Press, Connecticut.

Koestler, A. (1952). *Arrow in the Blue*, Collins, London.

Koestler, A. (1954). *The Invisible Writing*, Collins, London.

Koestler, A. (1966). *Dialogue with Death*, Hutchinson, London.

Kubler-Ross, E. (1978). *On Death and Dying*, Tavistock, London.

Lao Tsu (1973). *Tao Te Ching* (trans. Gia-Fu Feng and Jane English), Wildwood Press, London.

Larkin, P. (1955). *'Next Please'*, in *The Less Deceived*, The Marvell Press, Hessle, Yorks.

Lawrence, D. H. (1952). 'The Hands of God', in *The Ship of Death and Other Poems*, Faber and Faber, London.

Lee, D. (1950). 'Codifications of reality; lineal and nonlineal', *Psychosomatic Medicine*, **12**, No. 2, 89–97.

Lewis, C. S. (1961). *A Grief Observed*, Faber, London.

Lifton, R. J. (1973). *Home from the War*, Simon and Schuster, New York.

Lifton, R. J. (1976). *The Life of the Self*, Simon and Schuster, New York.

Mackie, J. L. (1978). 'Evil and omnipotence', in *The Philosophy of Religion* (Ed. B. Mitchell), Oxford University Press, Oxford.

MacLeod, S. (1981). *The Art of Starvation*, Virago, London.

MacManus, J. (1977). *The Guardian*, 25th March.

McTaggart, J. M. E. (1906). *Some Dogmas of Religion*, Cambridge University Press, Cambridge.

Malinowski, B. (1954). *Magic, Science and Religion*, Anchor Books, New York.

Mann, T. (1956). *Stories of Three Decades*, Secker and Warburg, London.

Marston, M. (1978). Letter to *The Guardian*, 23rd January.

Marvell, A. (1978). *A Dialogue Between the Soul and the Body*, in *Complete Poems*, Penguin, Harmondsworth.

Maurer, A. (1966). 'Maturation of the concepts of death', *British Journal of Medical Psychology*, **39**, 35.

Mendelson, M. (1974). *Psychoanalytic Concepts of Depression*, Wiley, New York.

Miller, A. (1980). 'People invest a whole lifetime in falsehood', *The Listener*, 13th November.

Moody, R. (1976). *Life after Life*, Bantam Books, New York.

Moody, R. (1978). *Reflections on Life after Life*, Bantam Books, New York.

Munch, E. (1980). Quoted in Robert Hughes' *The Shock of the New*, BBC Publications, London.

Needham, J. (1956). *Science and Civilization in China*, Vol. 2, Cambridge University Press, Cambridge.

Oakeshott, M. (1975). *On Human Conduct*, Clarendon Press, Oxford.

O'Brien, C. C. (1979). 'Long day's journey into prayer', *The Observer*, 4th February.

O'Shaughnessy, T. S. J. (1969). *Muhammad's Thoughts on Death. A Thematic Study of Qur'anic Data*, E. J. Brill, Leiden.

Pagels, E. (1979). 'Who was the real Jesus', *The Observer*, 23rd December.

Paisley, I. (1980). In Jack Pizzey's 'The Madonna and the drum', *The Listener*, 24th April.

Piaget, J. (1959). *Language and Thought of the Child*, Routledge and Kegan Paul, London.

Phillips, L. (1978). In *The Australian*, 4th October, p. 7.

Plath, A. S. (1975). *Sylvia Plath, Letters Home*, Faber, London.

Pollard, S. (1971). *The Idea of Progress*, Penguin, Harmondsworth.

Priestland, G. (1980). Personal communication.

Rank, O. (1973). Quoted in E. Becker's *The Denial of Death*, The Free Press, Glencoe.

Rilke, R. M. (1946). *Selected Letters of Rainer Maria Rilke, 1902–1926* (trans. R. F. C. Hull), Macmillan, London.

Robinson, E. A. (1976). 'Experience and authority in religious education', *Religious Education*, **74**, 451–463.

Robinson, E. A. (1977). *The Original Vision*, Religious Experience Research Unit, Manchester College, Oxford.

Robinson, E. A. (1978). *Living the Questions*, Religious Experience Research Unit, Oxford.

Rowe, D. (1978). *The Experience of Depression*, Wiley, Chichester and New York, re-issued as *Choosing Not Losing*, Fontana, London, 1988.

Rowe, D. (1983). *Depression: the Way Out of Your Prison*, Routledge, London.

Rowe, D. (1984). *Living with the Bomb: Can We Live Without Enemies?*, Routledge, London.

Rowe, D. (1987). *Beyond Fear*, Fontana, London.

Rowe, D. (1989). *The Successful Self*, Fontana, London.

Russell, B. (1946). *History of Western Philosophy*, George Allen & Unwin, London.

Russell, B. (1957). *Why I am not a Christian*, George Allen & Unwin, London.

Russell, J. B. (1977). *The Devil: Perceptions of Evil from Antiquity to Primitive Christianity*, Cornell University Press, Ithaca.

Russell, J. B. (1981). *Satan: the Early Christian Tradition*, Cornell University Press, Ithaca and London.

Russell, J. B. (1984). *Lucifer: the Devil in the Middle Ages*, Cornell University Press, Ithaca and London.

Russell, J. B. (1986). *Mephistopheles: the Devil in the Modern World*, Cornell University Press, Ithaca and London.

Ruysbroeck, The Blessed John (1973). 'The active, inward and superessential lives', in *Mysticism* (Ed. F. C. Happold), Penguin, Harmondsworth

Sartre, J-P. (1964). *Words*, Hamish Hamilton, London.

Scargill, A. (1979). 'I don't like losing', *The Listener*, 9th August.

Schulkind, Jeanne (Ed.) (1976). *Moments of Being*, unpublished auto-biographical writings of V. Woolf, Sussex University Press.

Scott, P. (1975). *A Division of the Spoils*, Heinemann, London.

Shaver, P., Lenauer, M. A., and Sadd, S. (1980). 'Religiousness, conversion and subjective well-being: the "healthy-minded" religion of modern American women', *American Journal of Psychiatry*, **137**, No. 12, 1563–1568.

Shotter, J. (1979). 'Vico, moral worlds, accountability and personhood', in *Indigenous Psychologies: Implicit View of Mind and Human Nature* (Eds P. Heelas and A. Lock), Academic Press, London.

Slater, E., and Roth, M. (1979). *Clinical Psychiatry*, Bailliere, Tindall and Cassell, London.

Smart, N. (1958). *Reasons and Faiths*, Routledge and Kegan Paul, London.

Smith, S. (1972). *Scorpion and Other Poems*, Longmans, London.

Solzhenitsyn, A. (1968). *The First Circle*, Collins, London.

Steiner, G. (1972). *Extraterritorial*, Penguin, Harmondsworth.

Steiner, G. (1974). *The Death of Tragedy*, Faber, London.

Stevenson, M. (1979). Interviews in *The Listener*, 12th July.

Strindberg, A. (1913). *The Son of a Servant*, Rider, London.

Taylor, D. (1980). *In Hiding*, BBC TV.

Thouless, R. H. (1935). 'The tendency to certainty in religious beliefs', *British Journal of Psychology*, **26**, 16–31.

Tillyard, E. M. W. (1943). *The Elizabethan World Picture*, Chatto and Windus, London.

Tolstoy, L. (1973). *The Devil* (trans. Aylmer Maude), Oxford University Press, Oxford.

Tolstoy, L. (1977). Quoted in H. Boll's *Missing Persons*, Secker and Warburg, London.

Towler, R. (1974). *Homo Religiosus*, Constable, London.

Toynbee, A. (1968). *Man's Concern with Death*, Hodder and Stoughton, London.

Twain, M. (1963). *Reflections on Religion*, Harper and Row, New York.

Viney, L. (1980). *Transitions*, Cassell, Australia.

Vins, G. (1979). 'On his faith, his imprisonment and his exile', *The Listener*, 17th May.

Warner, M. (1978). *Alone of All Her Sex*, Quartet Books, London.

Waugh, E. (1980). *The Letters of Evelyn Waugh*, Weidenfeld and Nicolson, London.

Weakley, B. S. (1979). 'Riches of the brain', letter to *The Observer*, 22nd October.

Weinberg, S. (1977). *The First Three Minutes. A Modern View of the Origin of the Universe*, The Scientific Book Club, London.

Wheatley, D. (1973). *The Devil and All His Works*, Arrow Books, London.

Wilson, C. (1977). *Men of Mystery*, W. H. Allen, London.

Woodward, F. L. (trans.) (1939). *Some Sayings of Buddha*, Oxford University Press, Oxford.

Wordsworth, W. (1947). 'Intimations of Immortality', in *The Albatross Book of Living Verse*, Collins, London.

Wordsworth, W. (1973). Quoted in Michael Pafford's *Inglorious Wordsworth*, Hodder and Stoughton, London.

INDEX

301